Natural Gas in India

This book provides a detailed discussion on India's energy mix including descriptive use of the Shannon Wiener diversity index for numerically comparing India's diversity in energy supply with other leading energy-consuming countries. The likely supply scenarios of both domestic and imported gas, and price competitiveness with competing fuels in differing consuming sectors, have also been presented. Overall, it covers energy systems, a comparison of the Indian natural gas economy with other countries and a scenario-based analysis of gas demand in India in 2030.

Features:

- Presents a well-structured and robust thesis on the challenges and opportunities for natural gas in India's energy future.
- Draws upon key insights, lessons and ways forward from the gas sector reform process.
- Addresses the energy transition scenario towards net zero.
- Includes comparative analysis of India's diversity of commercial primary energy supply.
- Uses granular data and visual representations of the same to convey the key arguments.

This book is aimed at oil and gas industry stakeholders including professionals, business executives, techno-managerial personnel and students in chemical engineering.

Natural Gas in India
Challenges and Opportunities

Anil Kumar Jain

CRC Press
Taylor & Francis Group
Boca Raton London New York

CRC Press is an imprint of the
Taylor & Francis Group, an **informa** business

First edition published 2023
by CRC Press
6000 Broken Sound Parkway NW, Suite 300, Boca Raton, FL 33487-2742

and by CRC Press
4 Park Square, Milton Park, Abingdon, Oxon, OX14 4RN

CRC Press is an imprint of Taylor & Francis Group, LLC

© 2023 Anil Kumar Jain

Library of Congress Cataloging-in-Publication Data
A catalog record has been requested for this book

ISBN: 978-1-032-30985-9 (hbk)
ISBN: 978-1-032-31027-5 (pbk)
ISBN: 978-1-003-30769-3 (ebk)

DOI: 10.1201/9781003307693

Typeset in Times
by codeMantra

Contents

List of Figures

List of Tables

Preface

This book is focused on the challenges and opportunities that natural gas presents for India's dynamic energy sector. Understandably, it is difficult to focus on one fuel within a nation's energy basket and project its future role without considering an inter-fuel substitution. The factors that underpin the demand and supply of different fuels naturally pass on their respective influence(s) to the fuel chosen for study. Nevertheless, with heightened environmental concerns coupled with a pressing need to 'phase-down' coal over time, natural gas assumes significance for the Indian economy. Additionally, natural gas has been accorded a high enough priority by the Government of India with sizeable 'targets' for its share in the commercial primary energy supply. This makes it still more relevant to limit the scope of this study to one fuel, that is natural gas, and analyse the extent to which it might substitute other sources of energy.

India's energy basket presents a complex picture. While 'mature' fuels, namely, biomass, coal and oil are understood better, a 'new' fuel like natural gas poses several questions, for which there is only a limited experience to lead us to some convincing answers. Simultaneously though, this study delves into a number of uncertainties around the future role of this 'new' fuel.

What might be the total energy demand in India in 2030, is the first major question. Without a near-accurate estimation, the scope of one fuel within the total energy scenario cannot be appreciated with confidence. The answer to this question is also dependent on the likely growth in India's per capita energy consumption from the present levels of a lowly one-third of the global average. While the developed countries display a much higher per capita energy demand, many experts are of the view that India may not go the same way and instead expeditiously tread forward on the energy-efficiency pathways by deploying energy-efficient technologies and adopting energy-conservation measures in a significant manner. India's rapid transition to LED bulbs for lighting has surprised one and all. This will certainly help India in meeting its energy requirements even with a lower magnitude of per capita energy consumption. These developments in the energy sector would invariably impact the demand for natural gas, and this aspect has been adequately addressed in this book by undertaking 'bottom-up' demand estimations. There is a discussion around the 'energy service' requirements to be fulfilled by natural gas in 2030, and the likely scenarios have been generated, bringing an expected realism to the analysis. This book draws such inferences from the thesis work to project the demand and role of natural gas in India in 2030

This book offers a big picture as important aspects like changing the consumer behaviour such as preference for electric vehicles and shared mobility together with technological and cost breakthroughs in battery storage, timelines of global consensus on phasing down fossil fuels, etc., are factors that cannot be readily anticipated with certainty.

Importantly, the price of fuel plays a quintessential role in determining consumer choices, more so for an imported commodity like natural gas, whose prices conform to the global markets. Domestic natural gas is priced administratively in India, whereas liquefied natural gas (LNG) is sold at market price. This obviously leads to a situation, where the supply coming from two different sources becomes almost different fuels. While addressing this grim reality as lower-priced domestic gas produced by National Oil Companies is expected to continue for a while, this book also offers a detailed comparative price analysis of all the fuels relevant to various demand sectors. While no future projection of prices has been presented in the book, the present competitive distance between the gas and other fuels has been brought out.

In India, an overriding role of 'planning' over the 'markets' is still manifested. However, selective few markets are now emerging strongly, especially with the renewable power capacity coming mostly from the private sector. Whether the markets will endorse natural gas or not has so far not been studied in much detail. It is pertinent that in the two major natural gas-consuming sectors, namely power generation and fertilisers manufacturing, government subsidy still impacts the fuel/feedstock availability choices. This marks the due importance of 'planning'. Tweaks in the subsidy and pricing policies may result in 'planning' even overriding 'markets'

Yet another important consideration for India relates to an uncertain policy mandate on clean energy. This is an important consideration as natural gas might have received an impetus over other fossil fuels such as coal and oil, due to its lesser emission capability. However, there is no clear policy recommendation in India for this fuel which prioritises its use over the polluting fuels. There is a recent announcement at COP26 at Glasgow towards achieving a 50% share in the power generation capacity from the non-fossil fuels by 2030 by way of a 500 GW target for renewable sources and a reduction in emission intensity by 40% over 2005 figures by 2030. India's announcement at COP26 may trigger such developments as were not so clearly anticipated in the Indian energy sector earlier on. Importantly, commitments toward an increasingly clean energy utilisation may trigger the markets to drive investments for achieving net-zero emissions status by 2070. This is likely to impact the fuel choices including natural gas, which is the fuel of our immediate interest.

Over time other policy announcements have also been made that do not relate directly to fuels but will have some impact on their demand. For example, the government has mandated adherence to tight emission standards for fuels in different sectors (vehicular emission/thermal power plants). While there is no overt carbon tax, India does tax its fossil fuels very highly. Thus, while there is a major policy push for the use of natural gas in urban transport besides cooking and industrial use, there is complete freedom for consumers for converting to PNG/CNG or even stay with liquid (and solid) fuels. In the light of the above, the principal advantage enjoyed by natural gas of being a cleaner fuel over coal and oil does not translate into a meaningful demand for it. A policy announcement on stringent 'carbon cap and trade' in the country may suddenly change the outlook on the utilisation of different fuels. This is now likely after India's commitment to 'net-zero' emissions by 2070. The book advocates a need to have a clear policy on clean energy which embodies natural gas in its rightful place and recognises that this singular announcement by Prime Minister Narendra Modi may be a shot in the arm for natural gas and other such clean fuels.

After the Glasgow Conference, this is presumably the first book on India's energy mix and the pathway that natural gas might take from now to 2030. The debates arising out of this book are expected to spring forth and discuss the Indian energy scenarios to 2030/2070.

To conclude, this book while navigating through a complex scenario does unravel several significant energy sector-specific questions through free-flowing discussions on natural gas. A number of policy recommendations emerge from the above and have been put across in the last chapter. Expectedly, the book will stimulate a purposeful debate amongst the energy sector stakeholders and ultimately help India to fuel its economic growth in a sustainable, competitive and secure manner.

Atul Kumar
Professor & Director, Energy Studies programme
School of International Studies
Jawaharlal Nehru University
New Delhi

Acknowledgements

The fact that this discussion on the Indian gas sector is appearing as a book is largely due to Dr Atul Kumar, Professor at the Jawaharlal Nehru University, New Delhi. In his previous stint at TERI School of Advanced Studies, he was a great help in undertaking my PhD. After my doctoral research was over, he encouraged me to go on to publish this work as a book. I owe a big debt of gratitude to him. I am also grateful to Dr Ritu Mathur, who directly oversaw my doctoral research, which has now been updated in this publication.

My research and then the efforts that went into this book took place during the same time when I was serving in different postings in the Government of India. I was a part-time scholar and did not take a sabbatical. A large number of colleagues at the workplace in NITI Aayog, the think-tank of the Government, the Ministry of Environment, Forest & Climate Change and now the Ministry of Coal, have helped in my research work. If they had not shared information and insights, this book would not have been possible. This is an outcome of a collaborative exercise, and the common intention has been to put together ideas that might help India achieve a higher degree of energy security. I am extremely grateful to all my colleagues who have shared their valuable insights in the numerous discussions we had on various aspects of India's energy policy.

I want to thank Anoop Variyambath, Secretary at the (The Energy and Resources Institute) TERI, New Delhi for typing the text of this book. Ripunjaya Bansal, Consultant at the Coal Ministry has been of great help in data collection. I also want to thank Francis & Taylor, Publishers, for this collaboration and their hand-holding me in bringing this book into its present shape. A number of colleagues of the former have helped make this book possible.

Lastly, but in a large measure, I want to thank my family. My wife, Anuradha, a writer herself, took the time to read and understand this technical manuscript and correct it. My children, Bahaar and Maahi, complained all along that the little time I spent at home after the huge demands of the workplace on me, was all consumed first in the thesis writing, and then this book. But, they acknowledged my passion for academic work, and have waited for years for me to finish this project. I do hope I can now retrieve some of the lost family time before they leave home to follow their dreams.

The views expressed in this book are my personal views based on an academic enquiry into the subject and do not in any way represent the views of the Government of India.

Anil K. Jain
New Delhi, June 2022

About the Author

Anil Kumar Jain is a member of the Indian Administrative Service, who is presently posted as Secretary in India's Coal Ministry. Over the past 35 years, he has worked in multiple sectors of the Government, with a particular focus on energy and the environment. He has the rare distinction for a bureaucrat to have specialised across the varied energy domain including fossil fuels, renewables, environment and energy policy. He was head of the upstream vertical in the Petroleum Ministry and oversaw the opening up of the exploration and production regime during the period 2003–08. Thereafter, he headed the Energy Division at the Indian Government policy think tank, the NITI Aayog, where he spent five years overseeing the preparation of the energy demand and emission calculating tool, IESS, 2047, and also wrote the draft National Energy Policy. He led Indian delegations to the energy- and climate-related working groups of G20 under various Presidencies between 2013 and 2017. He has also had a two year stint at the Environment Ministry handling multiple subjects related to the environment and biodiversity. Since September 2019 he heads the Coal Ministry. While working towards reforming the coal sector with a view to dismantling the monopoly of the Government Undertaking, Coal India Ltd, he has founded the Sustainable Development Cell in the Ministry and coal companies to address energy transition concerns.

He was associated as a Visiting Senior Research Fellow with Oxford Institute for Energy Studies, through which he published his book *Natural Gas in India: Liberalisation and Policy* in 2011. He holds a BA (Hons) in Economics, an MBA, a Diploma in International Trade and a PhD on prospects and challenges faced by the Indian natural gas sector.

Abbreviations

ADB	Asian Development Bank
APM	administered pricing mechanism
ASEAN	Association of Southeast Asian Nations
BAU	business-as-usual
BCM	billion cubic metres
BP	British petroleum
BRICS	Brazil, Russia, India, China and South Africa
BU	billion units
CAGR	compound average growth rate
CEA	Central Electricity Authority of India
CGD	city gas distribution
CIF	cost insurance freight
CII	Confederation of Indian Industry
CIL	Coal India Ltd.
CNG	compressed natural gas
COP	conference of parties
CPCB	Central Pollution Control Board
CSE	Centre for Science and Environment
CSTEP	Center for Study of Science, Technology and Policy
DECC	Department of Energy & Climate Change (UK)
DGH	Directorate General of Hydrocarbons
DI	diversity index
DOE	Department of Energy
DTI	Department of Trade & Industry (UK)
E&P	exploration and production
EPS	electricity power survey
ET	economic Times
EU	European Union
EV	Electric vehicle
FAI	The Fertiliser Association of India
FO	furnace oil
GA	geographical area
GAIL	Gas Authority of India Ltd
GDP	gross domestic product
GHG	greenhouse gas
GOI	Government of India
GPCA	Gulf Petrochemicals and Chemicals Association
GSPA	gas supply and purchase agreement
GSPC	Gujarat State Petroleum Corporation
GST	goods and services tax
GW	giga watts

HDS	high demand scenario
HH	household
HT	Hindustan Times
HVJ	Hazira-Vijaipur-Jagdishpur
IEA	International Energy Agency
IGU	International Gas Union
IHV	India Hydrocarbon Vision
INR	Indian rupee
IOC	international oil companies
IPCC	Inter-Governmental Panel on Climate Change
IPI	Iran Pakistan India gas pipeline
IRENA	International Renewable Energy Agency
KERC	Karnataka Electricity Regulatory Commission
KG Basin	Krishna Godavari basin
kgoe	kilograms of oil equivalent
kwh	kilowatt hour
LCOE	levelised cost of electricity
LDO	light diesel oil
LDS	low demand scenario
LNG	liquefied natural gas
LPG	liquefied petroleum gas
MMBTU	million British thermal unit
MMSCMD	million standard cubic metres per day
MMT	million metric tons
MMTPA	million metric ton per annum
MNRE	Ministry of New and Renewable Energy
MoEFCC	Ministry of Environment, Forest & Climate Change
MoPNG	Ministry of Petroleum and Natural Gas
MOSPI	Ministry of Statistics and Programme Implementation
MS	motor spirit
MT	metric ton
Mtoe	million tonnes of oil equivalent
MTPA	million tons per annum
MW	megawatt
MWh	megawatt hour
N, P, K	nitrogen, phosphorus and potash
NA	not available
NCAP	National Clean Air Programme
NCR	national capital region
NDC	nationally determined contributions
NELP	New Exploration Licensing Policy
NEP	National Electricity Plan
NFL	National Fertilizers Limited
NGT	National Green Tribunal
NITI Aayog	National Institution for Transforming India Aayog

NTPC	National Thermal Power Corporation Ltd
OECD	Organisation for Economic Co-operation and Development
OIES	Oxford Institute for Energy Studies
OIL	Oil India Limited
OMC	Oil Marketing Company
ONGC	Oil and Natural Gas Corporation Ltd
PES	primary energy supply
PIB	Press Information Bureau
PLF	plant load factor
PLL	Petronet LNG Ltd
PNG	piped natural gas
PNGRB	Petroleum and Natural Gas Regulatory Board
POSOCO	Power System Operation Corporation Limited
PPA	power purchase agreement
PPAC	petroleum planning & analysis cell
PSC	production sharing contracts
PSU	public sector undertaking
RBI	Reserve Bank of India
RE	renewable energy
RIL	Reliance Industries Ltd
R-LNG	regasified liquefied natural gas
RPO	renewable purchase obligation
RQ	research questions
SAUBHAGYA	Pradhan Mantri Sahaj Bijli Har Ghar Yojana
SCM	standard cubic metre
SEC	specific energy consumption
SECI	Solar Energy Corporation of India Ltd
TAPI	Turkmenistan Afghanistan Pakistan India gas pipeline
TCM	trillion cubic metres
TMT	thousand metric tonnes
TOI	Times of India
TPP	thermal power plant
UAE	United Arab Emirates
UJWALA	pradhan mantri ujjwala yojana
UK	United Kingdom
UNCTAD	United Nations conference on trade and development
UNFCCC	United Nations framework convention on climate change
UP	Uttar Pradesh
USA	United States of America
USAID	United States Agency for International Development
USSR	Union of Soviet Socialist Republics
VAT	value added tax
WEO	World Economic Outlook

1 Introduction

1.1 INDIA'S ENERGY CHALLENGES

India is the world's third-largest energy consumer and its demand for energy is expected to keep growing in the foreseeable future. As per International Energy Agency (IEA), India's energy demand growth may even outstrip China's increments (IEA, 2018a, b). From a climate change perspective, India was the world's third-largest greenhouse gases (GHG) emitter nation (after China and USA, and fourth if EU is considered as a single entity) in 2019. This has attracted global attention on India's energy pathways like—the role of coal, might renewables replace the fossil fuels, future of electric mobility—and other such questions as have a direct bearing on India's energy-related emissions. Energy is a key input to economic growth (Bayramov & Marusyk, 2019) and therefore its availability in a sufficient quantity and required form—liquid/solid/gaseous, and both in its original form as well as transformed shape as electricity—is a must for fuelling a nation's GDP. Indeed, national energy policies in India have so far aimed to provide the required quantity of energy at all times, at the right price and throughout the expanse of the jurisdiction (Planning Commission, 2006). This aim has been pivotal to Indian energy policies under the successive governments. India has historically faced a number of domestic energy challenges. Its annual per capita energy consumption in 2019 at 580 kgoe is one-third of global average and calls for a massive increase in energy infrastructure (BP Statistics, 2020). This is reinforced by the fact that despite a nearly eight times increase in the commercial energy supply over three decades (1985–2019), India still continues to report low per capita energy consumption numbers (BP Statistics, 2020).

One startling study that evaluated an overall energy security performance of Brazil, Russia, India, China and South Africa (BRICS countries) over a quarter century (1990–2015) by taking four core dimensions—availability, affordability, energy efficiency and environmental stewardship—has found India's energy security performance index to have worsened over the years (Bogoviz et al., 2019). The lack of modern energy sources such as electricity and liquefied petroleum gas or LPG (predominant cooking fuel in India's urban areas) in the rural areas has largely been addressed recently through launch of ambitious national schemes like SAUBHAGYA and UJWALA aimed at a universal coverage. Other critical challenges include the need to liberalise energy markets, and free energy sector from the control of government companies. With a greater recognition of climate change concerns, recent Indian energy policies have adopted renewables and energy efficiency as key ingredients of the national energy agenda. This stands reflected in India's commitment to achieving 175 GW of renewable power capacity by 2022, and even beyond to 500 GW in the subsequent years. India's energy

DOI: 10.1201/9781003307693-1

mix has a high fossil share at present, which has been harnessed in addressing the challenges of making the desired provision of modern energy services. The coal-based power and LPG have addressed a universal coverage of electricity and clean cooking fuel in India. The global climate change concern has emerged as an energy transition challenge, which India has to quickly internalise in its energy agenda.

1.2   KEY FACTORS AFFECTING ENERGY TRANSITION

Government and markets of the day have played key roles in delivering energy to the consumers including adapting to emerging technologies, and thus attracting investment in laying down the much-needed infrastructure. Even in the energy transition agenda, there will be a collaborative role for the above change agents. Markets are often hailed as being a good allocator of resources, and pursuit of economic rewards is often expected to ensure a timely realisation of the goals of availability, price, etc. Nonetheless, there is a considerable agreement amidst the academics that due to its strategic nature, the energy-related objectives cannot be left to the market choices alone, and the role of national policies remains vital (IEA, 2018a; Jain, 2011; UNCTAD, 2018). There are many examples of adoption of non-market interventions by the respective governments. For example, China targets a substantial increase in the share of natural gas within its primary energy supply (PES), and in the absence of a complete market, it has instead sought to reform its natural gas pricing through phased interventions (Dong et al., 2019). Global climate change concerns now override the markets, and especially after nationally determined commitments (NDCs) made by the nations at Conference of Parties (COP 21) held at Paris in November–December 2015 under the aegis of United Nations Framework Convention on Climate Change (UNFCCC, n.d.), governments are increasingly using various policy frameworks to promote the use of clean energy (IRENA, 2018). Further, national energy policies do not only supplement the existing markets, they also support them by assuring investors of adequate returns. This has resulted in an enriched blend of energy policies and markets in many countries, which are working towards an attainment of energy-related objectives (Atalla et al., 2017). Markets and policy may even need a more streamlining of sorts, but they are argued to be necessary for meeting the targeted energy objectives (New Indian Express, 2017).

What are the commonly enunciated key objectives of national energy policies? Energy security, that lends itself to multiple definitions, has been a significant objective, with many countries adopting availability, affordability and environmental sustainability as essential ingredients of achieving the much needed energy security (IEA, 2019; Ranjan & Hughes, 2014a). Yergin (2006) defined energy security as 'the security and integrity of the world supply chain and infrastructure, from production to consumer'. IEA defines it as 'the uninterrupted availability of energy sources at an affordable price' (IEA, 2019). The disruption caused by natural calamities in energy supply systems as that happened in the wake of Katrina cyclone in 2005 in the USA, highlighted the need for supply assurance at all times being included in the energy security agenda (Chow & Elkind, 2005). The EU is discussing a net-zero greenhouse gas emissions target by 2050 by adoption of a comprehensive strategy at the heart of which lies a transition to renewable energy (European Commission, 2018). Reducing import dependence to meet energy demand of a jurisdiction is a common energy policy objective across various countries including India (Planning Commission, 2006). The role of specific fuels in promoting sustainability of the energy system is yet another common theme. Skea et al. (2012) have studied the role of natural gas in UK's energy system. The balanced pursuit of clean energy and renewables is underpinned by supply concerns normally associated with the conventional sources of energy, as the former are by definition assumed to be devoid of any supply risks. Cooke et al. (2013) have advocated the pursuit of 'diversity' to address concerns relating to energy security as well as the price risks, ecological integrity and as a means to catalysing innovation. Some researchers have focused on the threats underlying energy security and have identified improvement of energy security in the face of challenges present from both the external and internal events (Ranjan & Hughes, 2014). From the above, it is clear that energy security is a vital part of the energy policy agenda of most countries, and it also lends itself to a number of interpretations varying from one country to another.

The impact of energy security related policies either on reduction or an increase in share of individual fuels in an energy mix is quite visible. On a global basis, the share of fossil fuels as a group in commercial energy supply has fallen from 92% in 1980 to 84% in 2019 (BP Statistics, 2020). The rise in share of wind/solar in global energy production from virtually nil in 1980 to 3.25% in 2019 is quite marked (BP Statistics, 2020). Most of the countries have seen transformations in their energy mix, both under fossil fuel and clean energy categories, including growth in many cases of natural gas and new renewables (wind, solar and small hydro), accompanied by simultaneous decline in oil and coal. Many researchers have broadly called changes in an energy mix as 'energy transition'. Different reasons have been responsible for this state of affairs. Atalla et al. (2017) found that drivers that triggered changes in fuel mix of USA, Germany and UK, during the period 1991–2002 were different across the three countries. Lauber and Mez (2004) have found that German clean energy policy was responsible towards the turn of the 20th century for a higher uptake of natural gas. In contrast, while natural gas rose in PES within the UK during the same period, but for an altogether different reason. Green (1991) argues that the above development was due to institutional changes in the way electricity was produced and sold. Climate change concerns have particularly triggered the need for a global energy transition and the UNFCCC has consistently stressed the need for the countries to migrate to cleaner fuels. The Paris COP for the first time acknowledged a concerted global action to combat climate change backed up effectively by the technical and scientific findings of the Inter-Governmental Panel on Climate Change (IPCC) in its reports since 1990. Thereafter, a global energy transition has followed thus leading to the advent of 'new renewables' that include various energy sources such as solar, wind and small hydro. The NDCs of countries submitted at the COP 21 are acknowledged as a major strategy towards an energy transition. As per IRENA, 105 out of 140 country specific submissions of NDCs as in 2020 include quantified renewable electricity targets. With the coming into office of Biden Administration, there is a new found impetus for the transition, and many countries have come forward to declare the year in which they might possibly achieve 'net zero' emission status.

This does not mean there was no energy transition at work prior to the above climate related developments. Markets were already driving the fuel demand by type for multiple reasons, much before the climate talks assumed a centre-stage. The rise in share of natural gas from a global share of 19% in 1980 to 22% in 2005, and fall of oil from 46% in 1980 to 37% in 2005 need to be seen in the light of other factors that are continuously at work on energy mix (BP, 2019). Similarly, the Fukushima incident in 2011 in Japan has led to second thoughts about continuing utilisation of nuclear energy in many countries including France and Germany. It is notable that an energy transition—planned in many cases such as 'Energiewende' in Germany, and yet unplanned in others—is underway in most of the large economies (Gillessen et al., 2019). Even as early as 1973, the oil embargo had given a supply shock to many oil import-dependent countries, who not only set about diversifying their oil import sources but also diversified their energy baskets (Yergin, 2006). Japan's energy mix had 73% share of oil in 1973, which has sharply come down to 40% in 2019.

1.3   INDIA'S ENERGY SECURITY CONCERNS

For the developing countries, 'energy security' is inalienably linked with a provision of an adequate supply of energy to all its citizens. In 2005, Abdul Kalam, the then President of India defined energy security as 'ensuring that our country can supply lifeline energy to all its citizens, at affordable costs at all times'. A truly balanced approach would require that growth is also kept in mind, while fulfilling the citizen-centric agenda. Economic development of a country demands a steady and secure energy supply, which is affordable in nature and reliable in character. Security of energy supply can be defined as a system's ability to provide a constant flow of energy to meet a growing demand within an economy in a manner and price that does not disrupt the economy (Lo, 2011). There is an ample evidence that necessary economic growth and development is linked to a country's stable and reliable energy system. However, it is also true that reliable energy systems need diversity in the supply portfolio, which provides an adequate security and stability.

As stated earlier, India's domestic energy outlook has led to energy security concerns being viewed largely from an import dependence perspective. Domestic production of oil and natural gas only meets a small part of demand and India's import dependence for oil and natural gas is high at 83% and 54% in 2020, respectively (PPAC). On an overall basis, in 2017–18, India imported over 50% of its commercial PES that has alarmingly grown in a short span of time from the level of 38% in 2011–12 (Energy Statistics, 2021; Jain, 2017). India's imports have a high share in global trade of many fuels—9.7% in crude oil accompanied by 7.3% in liquefied natural gas (LNG) and 13.3% in coal—all figures pertain to 2020 (BP, 2021). Even within the imports, the oil import dependence on the Gulf region in 2018–19 was above 50% resulting in a high risk of supply disruption (The Hindu, 2019b). This has been a constant cause of worry because of a fragile geopolitical situation in the region. Additionally, large import dependency brings into the fold different market risks through higher and more volatile prices (Steven et al., 2013).

A review of available literature suggests that energy security is increasingly being analysed in terms of its diversity in energy supply based on three key indicators, namely, variety of energy sources, balance in their inter-se shares and disparity between them (Lo, 2011). The UK Government has been measuring diversity in electricity generation and energy mix since 2006 on an annual basis through a statistical tool, i.e. the diversity index (DI) (DTI, 2006). It has recognised that an investment in diversity is key to the UK's energy security (DECC, 2011). A study of DI undertaken for this study reveals that the desired shifts in an energy mix have been more prevalent for some countries incidentally vis-à-vis India. While it is not as if, a change in energy mix is a necessary policy objective, a country's energy system must be able to avail of the available opportunities that technological advancements, price movements, enhanced availability and environmental superiority of certain fuels over others, present from time to time (Jansen et al., 2004).

From a purely 'diversity' angle, India's energy mix offers a unique case of 'stickiness' or inflexibility over the last few decades. Fossil fuels are firmly entrenched by now and as a group have remained high—87% in 1980 and 91% in 2019. Only two sources of energy have seen considerable changes—as a case specific example, share of hydropower has fallen from 12% in 1980 to a low of 4% in 2019, while natural gas has increased from a mere 1% to 6% in the same period. Likewise the respective shares of coal and oil have been nearly static at 55% and 30%, respectively. Contrasted with above, as discussed later in this book, all other leading energy consumers (excepting the USA) have seen large shifts, with a decline in energy share by even 9% or more in a single fuel (mostly oil) over time. Coal has registered a decline in all the major energy-consuming countries (except Japan, and static in India), and fossil fuels as a group entity has also declined. India is unique in registering an increase in the fossil fuel share during 1980–2019. Even China, which is a large coal consumer like India, has reduced its coal utilisation by 15% (2019 over 1980) and has set targets for achieving a high share of natural gas in its PES—rising from 6.4% in 2016 to 15% by 2030 (Rioux et al., 2019). Some trends are universal, such as oil that has registered a decline, and new renewables (wind and solar) that have grown, across all the major economies. In the light of both common and differing trends from within the major energy consuming countries, it becomes difficult to conclude as to 'which' countries have really registered a 'greater' shift in their energy mix, and whether this is a matter of significance from an 'energy transition' specific agenda viewpoint

DI can be used to measure the 'mobility' in an energy mix for a set of countries. Higher the index, more diverse is the energy supply position. While a number of academic papers exist on DI of developed countries, such studies are not so much seen for the developing countries scenario. No study exists as yet on the evolution of energy mix of India that might report on a relative comparison with other large energy category consumers. A close look at an energy mix of two different years with a sufficient lag that might allow an energy transition to take place does indicate that India's energy mix has not changed much over the years. This exercise has been undertaken in this book in Chapter 3.

1.4   PROSPECTS FOR NATURAL GAS IN INDIA

Natural gas has been playing a major role in global energy mix for several decades now. It is the fastest growing (2.7%–3% per year) conventional primary energy form worldwide. Even the energy transition in favour of clean energy has a place for natural gas (Gillessen et al., 2019). Stern (2012) further argued that until 1970s, natural gas consumption took place largely within natural gas producing countries. Gradually pipelines were set up and natural gas trade grew in the neighbourhood of such countries. In 1970, trade through pipelines reported for 43 BCM, while LNG was a mere 2.7 BCM (Stern, 2012). The same has grown to 2400 BCM and 750 BCM (IGU, 2019), respectively. As per BP Statistics, global natural gas share in the energy mix increased from around 14% in 1960s to above 20% during 1980s and further to 26% by 2019 (BP, 2020) A number of Reports have offered compelling reasons for India to promote natural gas. They also highlight the challenge of poor domestic production outlook (IEA, 2015). Bhattacharya and Bhattacharya (2014) have underlined the findings of multiple agencies as to why imported gas (LNG) could play a crucial role for India indeed. Given India's poor geological reserves of natural gas, LNG import is essential. Their study showed as to how regional cooperation between India and the South East Asian region can help India to procure LNG at a cost competitive price, particularly as individual initiatives turn out to be expensive in LNG import. The paper also suggested that in India, there is a lack of studies in terms of price rationalisation of natural gas. Corbeau et al. (2018) further argued that infrastructural, pricing and regulatory issues were the main reasons for natural gas not being able to take up a major share in India thus far. Amongst several other reasons, the following few are major ones: lower domestic gas production, higher LNG price, low coverage of natural gas pipelines and other necessary infrastructure to extract and transport it within the country. The outlook on demand for natural gas in India presents a complex situation of sorts as different issues impinge across multiple end-use consumption sectors.

India being majorly an agricultural economy, production and consumption of urea has a direct correlation to economic development, food security and enhancing farmers' income. Natural gas is one of the major feedstocks for urea production. Parikh et al. (2009) estimated natural gas demand for India in the context of future demand of urea. They have found that under the Administrative Pricing Mechanism (APM) scheme of natural gas availability and with different urea prices, natural gas demand for urea production could vary between 20 and 35 BCM in 2025. This study indicates that the demand variability is correlated to the urea price amongst other reasons. Corbeau et al. (2018) in his paper on Challenges and

Perspectives for the Indian Gas Market discussed the future natural gas demand across various industrial sectors in India. The author argued that the main issues of natural gas demand in fertilizers sector would be the future price of imported urea, the price of natural gas used to produce urea and also the fertilizer policies. He further argued that industrial gas demand which is closely around one-third of the total natural gas demand in the country is facing challenge in accessing cheap domestic gas priced as per Administered Pricing Mechanism (APM) on the lines of urea plants. Industrial demand for natural gas has a potential to grow at the rate of 10% per annum in the coming years.

Domestic pricing is a complex subject in India even after initiating reforms in natural gas pricing policy. State level taxing system clubbed with central taxes including GST mechanism, has made the market price of natural gas extremely complex to understand. Paliwal (2017) discussed the matter of natural gas pricing in India elaborately in a chapter in the book titled *Natural Gas Markets in India: Opportunities and Challenges.* He argued that in India there are three different types of pricing mechanisms in natural gas: APM, International Market Determined, and Gas Hub pricing. APM is used mainly for pricing natural gas produced by Government companies, while international pricing is applied to imported LNG. Domestic natural gas is further priced at Gas Hub level. Therefore, a synergy is required in natural gas pricing. It is also shown that natural gas demand in the country is highly elastic to its price. Kar and Gupta (2017) have described the natural gas pricing policy reform in India after 2015 as a good move by the Government wherein, they have decided to divert natural gas from non-priority sector to the high demand sectors like city gas distribution (CGD). They have argued that CNG supply is envisaged to grow under this new policy as there will be more natural gas available at a lower price than that of liquid fuel. CNG is thus expected to assume an important fuel share within the transport sector in India. They have also stated that with the revised natural gas pricing mechanism, though the APM gas producers gas producers are not very enthusiastic, but the natural gas distribution companies are happy with increased profit margins. It is thus expected that CGD infrastructure will be encouraged in the country soon. With recent policy moves, there has been some harmonisation in prices of gas which was earlier selling at different prices, and the same has been discussed in this book.

Batra (2009) in his article 'India's Move To Cleaner Fuels' argued that it is important that the government promotes the use of natural gas and other petroleum fuels for cooking in the rural areas as much as possible for attaining better social, environmental and economic lifestyles. Paul and Bhattacharya (2004) further argued that natural gas is going to be the preferred source of energy in India in the 21st century and its demand is expected to increase locally due to increasing urbanisation, growing income level and improving standard of life. LNG is also going to play an important role. Jatinder Cheema et al. (2019) in their discussion on 'CGD: Creating Demand For India's Energy Future', mentioned that the CGD bidding rounds being held by the Government is an important move in terms of promoting natural gas demand at the consumer level. The Government aims to connect around 10 million households with piped gas supply by 2020 and it was argued to be in line with increasing the share of natural gas in the primary energy basket from 6% to 15% in a phased manner, over the next few rounds of bidding. The tenth CGD bidding round covered 50 geographical areas (GA) spread over 14 states and 124 districts. They further argued that the success of the CGD network is contingent on domestic demand, which is still resistant to the use of natural gas. In order to support the large investment that had already been made in the sector, local administrative authorities have come up with gas-friendly legislation pursuant to orders of the court in M.C. Mehta vs. Union of India and Ors7 to facilitate smooth transition to CNG fuelled vehicles, alongside other initiatives. These mainly include aiding public transport and the implementation of the 'odd-even' car rationing scheme, which exempts CNG run vehicles from the implementation of such scheme.

Stern (2017) has argued that China and India provide an interesting contrast in relation to both affordability and price reform. Both of these countries have population in excess of 1.3 billion, where natural gas is significantly less than 10% of their primary energy demand. As per IEA's World Energy Outlook (2017) projections of Chinese natural gas demand show that this could increase by 270–290 BCM by 2030 and to 400–450 BCM by 2040, as compared with 210 BCM in 2016. India's natural gas demand was projected to increase by 70–100 BCM in 2030 and 128–175 BCM in 2040, i.e. from 55 BCM in 2016. While these increases for India are significantly less than those for Chinese projections, they are very substantial and thus certainly important for natural gas marketers.

1.5   ISSUES ADDRESSED IN THIS BOOK

This book attempts to assess the likely role of natural gas in India's energy mix. It is acknowledged that natural gas has environmental (lower carbon intensity), economic (cheaper than oil) and technical (balancing of variable electricity) advantages over several other fuels. The Indian policymakers might benefit from an incisive study on what has largely been missing in the policy framework so far. The main objectives of this study follow from above:

- to examine the role of different factors in determining the demand for natural gas
- to evaluate the natural gas demand potential in the medium term (2030)
- to make specific recommendations as to what policy measures need to be taken to realise the above potential.

Apart from examining the factors influencing the role of natural gas and analysing the scope at sectoral levels, the range of natural gas demand in High and Low demand scenarios in 2030 has been estimated via historical growth rates and application of a number of levers, too. In light of the fact that despite an ambition to encourage natural gas penetration, this fuel has been unable to achieve appreciable growth in India. This book goes into both the structural and fuel-specific factors related to India's energy mix as a whole, and natural gas, as well. A detailed investigation has been made to analyse the growth trends in natural gas within other large energy consuming countries over a 39-year period (1980–2019). The common and unique trends in different countries have been identified, and the same were then applied to India. On the basis of several factors related to structural and fuel-specific drivers, on which the likely growth of natural gas has been anticipated. Inter alia, the interplay between three pillars (discussed below) on which demand may depend have been discussed in separate chapters.

- The first pillar is an analysis of energy mix of India and six other large energy consuming countries via the Shannon Wiener DI. This revealed that while the energy mix of all countries underwent significant evolution, Indian energy mix has been rather 'inflexible'. Not only did natural gas share not grow here appreciably, even other fuels registered only minor changes, indicating that Indian energy system has been rather 'rigid'.
- The second pillar is a study of supply and demand side factors that impinged on growth of natural gas. For this, the same set of major energy consuming countries for an equivalent period was taken as that for the study of energy mix. It was examined that whether the conditions that led to high gas share in countries of study existed in India too or not. Interestingly on the supply side, India's case was consistent with the analysis. Local availability of natural gas was found to be essential for this fuel to play an important role and in countries including India with poor access to natural gas, this fuel did not grow appreciably. Nonetheless the impact of demand side factors had different outcomes for natural gas in India. While India does have a supportive environment for natural gas demand, but this did not help this fuel to grow (unlike in other countries).
- The third and final pillar is a detailed demand analysis for natural gas in the four main consuming sectors—CGD, power generation, urea manufacture and industries/others.

This book makes a true departure from similar earlier studies by looking much beyond the natural gas sector, and contextualising it within the overall energy sector. It has been found that India's energy mix has sustained the other two fossil fuels (coal and oil), and it is only recently, that 'new renewables' such as solar and wind have started growing in a significant manner. With rising energy demand especially for transportation fuels (until Electric Vehicles or EV assumes pole position), and need for transitioning towards clean sources of energy, natural gas seems to be a good option for India. The analysis in various chapters has been duly supported by a discussion with experts from upstream and downstream sectors as well with academicians. Their views have been presented at relevant places, also in a tabular manner where they had been offered multiple choices. This book thus hopes to enhance understanding of why natural gas still continues to fall short of expectations, and also offers a strategic approach for it to play a bigger role in the future.

1.6 ORGANISATION OF CHAPTERS

The book comprises of eight chapters and is organised in the following manner. The Introduction chapter is followed by Chapter 2 on a detailed backgrounder on status and prospects of natural gas in India. The rationale for this study has been brought out.

Chapters 3 and 4 are analytical in their treatment and compare India with other large energy consuming countries on various parameters. In Chapter 3, there is a discussion on the concept of 'diversity index', a tool applied to measure rigidities in the Indian energy system. A comparative analysis between India and six other large energy consuming nations on a diversity of energy mix has also been undertaken. It examines flexibility in the Indian energy system to be able to respond to such opportunities that new fuels presented at different points of time, including reduction in the respective market shares of dominant fuels that may be causing an imbalance in the energy mix. Chapter 4 includes a comparison between the growth story of natural gas in India and other leading energy consumers of the world. It thus examines both supply and demand side triggers.

From key learnings of the above two chapters, the next three chapters are a deep dive into the Indian natural gas scene, by way of examining the supply side along with competitiveness of natural gas on price parameter, and then what might be the likely demand scenarios in 2030. Chapter 5 discusses the emerging supply situation, both from domestic and imported sources. The discussion includes the present supply options as well as the emerging ones such as those from gasification of coal and even transnational pipelines.

Chapter 6 includes a discussion on pricing wherein, the arbitrage between natural gas and competing fuels across the four main natural gas consuming sectors—CGD, Power, Urea manufacture and Industries—has been discussed.

Chapter 7 contains sector-wise scenarios of natural gas demand in 2030. It contains a full discussion on India's emerging natural gas scenarios—likely natural gas demand in main consuming sectors. The messages from preceding chapters on evolution of India's energy mix, and comparison of the Indian situation with others on natural gas growth triggers, respectively, figure in this chapter. The supply side and price competitiveness have also been brought together in this chapter.

Chapter 8 is the concluding chapter of the book and summarises the research findings, and policy recommendations.

BOX 1.1 INDIA AT GLASGOW CLIMATE CHANGE CONFERENCE

Prime Minister Narendra Modi took the world by surprise when he announced at the 26th session of the Conference of the Parties (COP 26) to the UNFCCC in Glasgow in November, 2021 that India pledges to achieve net-zero GHGs emissions by 2070. The 26th session was important as nations were expected to go beyond their climate action pledges for 2030 submitted earlier at COP 21 held in Paris. So far India had been insisting that it was not yet ready to make any commitments on its emission trajectory. While world's top energy consumers like USA and China had already announced their target years, India's announcement came only at Glasgow. India chose to join the ranks of the former and this was hailed by nations as a major achievement for the COP 26. Furthermore, Hon'ble Prime Minister Modi went on to make more commitments for 2030:

- Non-fossil capacity to be 50% of total power generation capacity (the announcement was that India will meet 50% of its energy requirement from renewable energy, but India's Minister for Environment has later clarified that this announcement refers to power generation capacity and not overall energy supply)
- GHG emission intensity to decline by 45% by 2030 over 2005
- Non-fossil power generation capacity to reach 500 GW
- Cutting absolute emissions by 1 billion tonnes.

A major element of the COP 26 outcomes of great significance to India (and the world) has been the substitution of the term 'phase-out' of coal with 'phase-down' in the communique. Post-COP 26, this new phraseology has attracted much attention of the world, and has pitted the developed world against both India and China for watering down a global consensus on burying coal sooner than later. Be that as it may, the Indian announcements have major implications on the messages of this first chapter of the book. The same has been briefly stated below.

In this introductory chapter, a brief description of India's energy challenges, key factors affecting energy transition coupled with India's energy security concerns, and the prospects of natural gas in India in the light of the above have been discussed. It is against this setting that the book goes on to offer some novel perspectives on India's energy pathway, with particular reference to natural gas. As is obvious, with the announcements at Glasgow, India's energy outlook would now be evaluated on its consistency or otherwise with the announcements made. For example, any new thermal power capacity would need to factor in the net-zero deadline of 2070. While 'net-zero' does not mean no emission, but every new emission will have to be matched with an equal carbon offset measure. As we go forward, India would have to report on measurement, reporting and verification (MRV) regime of its climate change actions. Implying thereby that investors would be wary of getting into fossil fuel related business and hence, fiscal policies would need to catalyse actions towards a particular direction. Additionally even local governments may conform to India's external commitments regardless of their political hue in the vibrant, democratic set-up of India.

India's energy challenges have now got expanded with the need for sustainability and impetus to clean energy deployment becoming important goals to achieve. While meeting the energy aspirations of the people, it may not be business-as-usual, and an energy transition agenda may need to be drawn out early. It is not that the above scenario will result in abandonment of current projects and plans, but there will be a cloud over future fossil capacity related investments. Amongst the Indian energy security concerns, adoption of low carbon strategy and the challenges that it brings (investment, appropriate technology, capacity in think tanks and bureaucracy to herald this transition), will get added. The last point addressed in this chapter—a glimpse of natural gas prospects in India—now looks brighter. In the succeeding chapters, there will be a sharper focus on as to how natural gas might bridge the present 'coal intensive' energy scenario to a clean energy future. The Indian announcements at Glasgow are a real shot in the arm for clean energy including natural gas. It would now be in order to connect the discussion in each chapter of this book with India's net-zero related announcements, and how gas while being a fossil fuel itself, might play the role of a 'bridge fuel' to a cleaner energy mix.

2 Natural Gas in India's Energy Mix

2.1 INDIAN AMBITION FOR NATURAL GAS

In this chapter, a brief literature review has been taken up on natural gas and its role in promoting both energy security and economic growth. Thereafter, a detailed status note on natural gas in India has been discussed to contextualise the role of natural gas in enhancing India's energy security. This is expected to help the reader to appreciate the strategic nature of natural gas in meeting India's energy needs, as well as how the country's economy has suffered due to the inability of this fuel to prove its significance in India's energy basket. The chapter also delves deep into the underlying reasons. A detailed discussion on this issue follows in the later chapters. While realising its significance, policymakers have strived through various policy interventions to promote natural gas. In India's energy mix, oil and coal have traditionally held large percentage contribution shares. Initially, there was no natural gas production and the above two fuels along with hydropower played an important part. Natural gas was negligible until the historic discovery of Bombay High in 1974, when a large volume of associated gas started coming out along with oil, the fuel of principal interest. The first major domestic supply from western offshore spurred the fortunes of several urea plants, LPG extraction and petrochemical units, power plants and city gas distribution projects. The share of natural gas in India's PES was 1% in 1974, which quickly grew to 5% by 1990 (BP, 2019). The first internal high-level government committee constituted to consider long-term India's energy security, namely India Hydrocarbon Vision (IHV) in 1999, recognised the value of natural gas in India's energy mix and sought a reasonable increase in its supply, both through domestic production and imports by LNG as well as via pipelines. From a lowly 7% share in PES in 1997–98, it anticipated a share of 20% in 2024–25. It had a 6% share in the PES in 2020–21.

The launch of an auction-based process for oil and natural gas blocks and set-ups of LNG receiving terminal in Dahej (Gujarat coast) in late nineties boosted India's chances further of meeting the aspiration for having a high share of natural gas. The first LNG cargo was received at Dahej in 2004. Subsequently, a number of new LNG-receiving terminals were conceived and the existing terminals at Dahej, Hazira and Dabhol planned for their genuine expansions (Jain, 2011). While the pipeline options, both from Iran and Myanmar have eluded realisation so far, but there is still an enthusiasm amongst investors in setting up a number of new LNG-receiving terminals. This gives a room for confidence that robust LNG supplies could materialise in the coming years. The earlier terminals were all conceived along the west coast to receive LNG from the prolific Gulf countries.

DOI: 10.1201/9781003307693-2

TABLE 2.1
Primary Energy Consumption of India (2020)

	Exajoules	Share (%)
Oil	9	28
Natural gas	2.15	7
Coal	17.5	55
Nuclear energy	0.4	1
Hydroelectricity	1.45	5
Renewables	1.43	4
Total	31.93	100

Source: BP Statistics (2021).

Now new terminals are coming up along the east coast, too, that may receive supplies even from Australia.

In 2018, the government gave a tall call to raise the share of natural gas in commercial PES from 6% to 15% by 2022 (MoPNG, 2018b). In 2020, the share of natural gas was 7% (Table 2.1). Thereafter, the target for 2022 was shifted to 2030 (Pradhan, 2019).

Would the Indian economy gain if, natural gas was to achieve a high share in its PES? A number of distinctive advantages can be quickly counted over other fuels. It emits 50% lesser carbon dioxide than coal and nearly 30% lesser than oil. It can replace oil and its derivatives such as petrol, diesel, LPG, and fuel oil in all the end-uses—transportation, power generation, cooking, heating, etc. In the liquefied state as LNG, natural gas can be conveniently transported over long distances, and also be stored by pressurising as for example is done for compressed natural gas (CNG) in vehicles. Methane is generated from a number of biomass sources, particularly from waste food and sewage in urban settings where city gas distribution (CGD) networks are available and can be transported by commingling in the natural gas distribution pipes. It is also competitive over crude on calorific parity basis. The slope of price curve of natural gas is below that of oil. Even the initial high price of imported gas may not be seen negatively, as policy interventions in local energy markets have been seen in the EU to bring gas prices down (Biały et al., 2019).

Gas-based power generation is 'flexible' and open-cycle gas turbines can come online quickly when electricity demand spurts. In India, there has been a dearth of power supply at the time of evening peak and gas-based generation could prove of much help. The above feature also makes natural gas an ideal companion to intermittently available renewable sources of electricity such as wind and solar power and is very relevant for the futuristic Indian electricity system. India has a large renewable power target of 175 GW to meet by 2022 (MNRE, 2019) with an aspiration to even reach 500 GW by 2030. The 2022 target includes 100 Giga

Watts (GW) of solar and 60 GW of wind power components that belong to the intermittent category. Should the above target be achieved, there would be grid stability concerns, which could be easily addressed by open-cycle natural gas turbines. Hydropower is also a good balancing source, but due to issues linked to displacement of affected population, this source does not look promising. Until battery storage becomes cost-effective, the grid instability from a growing share of renewables will remain a concern. Large capacity energy storage system coupled to the grid is a relatively recent phenomenon in this direction.

India's environmental concerns can also be well-served by substituting both coal and oil with natural gas. As it is, coal-based power meets 76% of India's demand and is responsible for 71% of the country's total energy related carbon dioxide emissions (Mukherjee, 2019). In 2015, natural gas-based power was a mere 4% and if it were to be scaled up, it could play an important role as a cleaner option to coal-based power (NITI Aayog, 2016). The source-wise data is given in Table 2.2. No new gas-based power plants are currently under development, whereas other power generation sources are growing. In due course of time, the share of gas-based power may come down further.

While climate change is a global concern and India is also threatened with its implications, the air quality concern is grave especially in the urban areas. With diesel and petrol being the primary fuels in transportation, the highly populated cities of India face a monumental problem of air pollution. Use of solid fuel, mainly biomass, in cooking also adds to the problem. Both the above challenges are being addressed with some bold measures in rolling-out CGD projects that will replace liquid and solid fuels in the years to come. A recent discussion in the developed world regarding pollution aspect of natural gas (as it is also a fossil fuel), may not be acknowledged by Indian policymakers. The recent bidding out of CGD projects will entail locking-in of large capital, and it will also ease the urban air quality issues from what it is at present. Therefore, natural gas will not be under a severe challenge and is rather being hailed as a clean fuel in Indian energy landscape now.

TABLE 2.2
Power Generation by Source in India (2020)

Fuel	Share (%)
Oil	1
Natural gas	5
Coal	72
Nuclear energy	3
Hydroelectricity	10
Renewables	10
Total	100

Source: BP Statistics (2021).

The successful clean cooking campaign, UJWALA, having a coverage of 90% of households, has placed a huge infrastructure challenge to deliver bottled LPG throughout the country and has also necessitated large imports. India's LPG imports have increased many times over from 6 million tonnes in 2013–14 to 16 million tonnes in 2020–21. Here also natural gas can become a part of the overall sustainable clean cooking agenda and thus substitute LPG. The government aims to extend CGD networks to deliver natural gas conveniently via pipelines and set aside LPG for rural areas (TOI, 2015). As per Petroleum & Natural Gas Regulatory Board (PNGRB), the ninth and tenth CGD bidding rounds have yielded a commitment to extend piped natural gas coverage to 70% of India's overall population besides making a provision of clean cooking/transportation solution to India's urban areas by 2029 (PNGRB, 2019).

2.2   NATURAL GAS AND ECONOMIC GROWTH

Tracing a relationship between natural gas consumption and economic growth has been of a novel interest to researchers. While it has been stated above that natural gas could meet different objectives, but it needs to be noted that the sum total objective to achieve would still be economic growth. (Aydin, 2018) in his study on natural gas consumption and economic growth nexus for ten gas consuming countries showed that there was a long-term positive impact of natural gas consumption on economic growth and associated development. The main finding is that countries should increase the use of natural gas consumption to ensure energy security, reduce energy dependence, reduce carbon dioxide emissions and encourage economic growth. Bildirici and Bakirtas (2014) also discussed that there are causal relationships between economic development and consumption of basic energy commodities like coal, oil and natural gas in emerging economies. They further established that there is a causal relationship between natural gas consumption and economic growth of India, which ascertains the importance of natural gas on Indian economy. A study undertaken for EU has listed multiple gains that a natural gas based energy system might bring forth (Lebelhuber and Steinmüller, 2019). Heidari et al. (2013) examined the relationship between natural gas and economic growth. Based on production model, the results of the study found that natural gas significantly influences economic development. Different studies investigated the causal relationship between use of natural gas for economic prosperity and also its use arising out of economic prosperity and ultimate development. In certain cases, researchers found the bidirectional relationship of natural gas and economic development as well Sinaga et al. (2019), which indicates that economic growth of a country alongside use of natural gas has a close link, and higher the use of the latter, better the prospect of economic development. Alam et al. (2017) have argued that there is a positive correlation between use of natural gas and output growth within developing nations.

Natural gas has been deployed in India for catalysing large capital investment. Due to its unique nature of being a gaseous energy source (other major fuels oil, coal, renewables and electricity are in other forms), it spurs fresh investment along the value chain. Gas flows from the upstream have to be delivered by dedicated pipelines and as LNG receiving terminals for imported supplies. Both these infrastructures are capex heavy and front-loaded. Similarly, city gas distribution grid requires investments in distribution pipelines, piping in building for PNG, and in CNG stations for transport sector. Similarly, for various end-uses in industry and commercial establishments also investments have to be made in burners and heaters. Expectedly in the quest for a $5 trillion economy, natural gas industry is set to make major contributions.

While there is no definitive finding on the above aspects in this book, it must be noted that a more competitive, energy secure and environmentally sustainable economy promotes economic growth over time. On calorific parity basis, natural gas is cheaper than oil. In the bidding held for auction of KG Basin gas supply that took place in 2020, the biddable parameter was discount offered on crude price. This is now quite an accepted norm in international gas pricing. What follows from above is that substitution of crude by natural gas would reduce energy costs and a rise in competitiveness of the Indian economy. Apart from financial and economic benefits of natural gas use in India, there are several technical benefits as well. Besides bringing supply security to the system, there are several other benefits like macroeconomic stability (CII- NITI Aayog, 2018) by reducing oil import, promoting environmental cleanliness and helping in mitigating climate change (Mukherjee, 2019). India's economic and social development is hinged to a stable energy system and currently with very high oil import dependency; it will be difficult for India to achieve the desired level of economic growth and development. Natural gas can improve process efficiency through specific energy consumption (SEC) improvement and by reducing carbon footprint of India's industrial development. Larson (2019) further argued that globally, the natural gas business including use of natural gas for power generation and renewable energy market are growing together, while the coal-based generation business is in the declining mode now. He also argued that natural gas, in most of the cases, works as being complementary to renewable energy business, mostly due to the high energy density of natural gas as compared to other conventional fuels.

2.3   NATURAL GAS AND DIVERSITY IN ENERGY MIX

In order to maintain or improve energy security, a country's energy system needs to meet the demands of its energy services with affordable and preferably environmentally acceptable flows of different sources of energy. The above attributes can be captured in a single term—'diversity'. It is generally agreed that number of energy sources (variety), the evenness in their shares (balance) and differences between the different fuels (disparity) are the key elements in diversity to be measured (Stirling, 2007). In many countries, including India, diversity in energy has often been seen from the key perspective of geographical sources from where imported supplies are being received—more the supply destinations, greater the security of supply. However, what has not received due attention is diversity in its energy mix. The Indian energy mix has traditionally been dominated by coal and oil that has reduced the diversity. Natural gas has the smallest share from amongst the three main fossil fuels and is an eminent candidate that could counter the low diversity by achieving a higher share. Later in the book, it has been established that with a fall in share of natural gas over the last 15 years or so, India's energy mix diversity has suffered. More the number of energy sources (technologies), especially if, all of them have significant share in energy mix, logically make a nation more energy secure from supply security angle. In countries with balanced shares of energy sources, natural gas has helped to achieve this balance. But, in India the small share of natural gas has resulted in disproportionately high shares of coal and oil, thus reducing the 'diversity' in energy mix.

Since diversity can be an important factor in the long-term survival of a system, having a diverse energy flow is frequently treated as a proxy for energy security as well (Ranjan and Hughes, 2014). A body of energy analysts have supported the above view (Kruyt et al., 2009). In energy policy, diversity plays important roles in energy supply security, efficiency of energy use and adaptability of energy system. One view that is often advanced is that if a country is having high import dependency, it is difficult to increase the diversity (number of fuels) of the energy portfolio. The above view seems to be limited in its approach. For example, India has a high energy import dependency and for oil a high level of above 80%. This brings insecurity of supply due to dependence on a particular region (Gulf countries) and also of speculative prices including commercial terms, often as an outcome of the decisions of the oil exporters' lobby (OPEC). If India were to diversify its energy mix by even substituting one imported fuel (oil) with another (natural gas), it may reduce India's energy insecurity. There is already a moderate gas-specific infrastructure available. If, we consider gas-based power plants, they are in a stranded state in India, as are several trunk pipelines. The above may readily spring to life and deliver energy service to consumers. This would enhance diversity and also lead to energy security. There are a few other benefits arising out of the above. On the demand side, diversity opens up the possibility of energy efficiency, inter-fuel substitution and energy conservation related activities that induction of natural gas may bring forth to the Indian energy system. Moreover, diversity in energy supply opens up the possibility of increasing cooperation between different countries (Lo, 2011). All the above attributes are directly relevant to natural gas in India.

In terms of measuring the level of energy security, there are several methodologies available. (Kruyt et al., 2009) described such available techniques in detail and argued that depending on the enunciated purpose of studies and objectives, methodology should be adopted. Here natural gas comes in for a major role in enhancing energy security. Flexibility in the energy system is crucial for a country to adopt renewable energy in a significant way. Increasing share of renewable energy, which is infirm in character, requires additional flexibility in the system to protect the power supply grid. In assessing ASEAN's grid flexibility, Huang et al. (2019) used some multiple indicators to determine grid flexibility. They took the number of sources of power generation for the ten ASEAN countries and by min–max normalisation came to an indicator of grid flexibility, which is important for grid-based integration of renewable electricity. An energy system, especially power system, becomes flexible when it is fed by sources which are quick in generating power from their starting position. Natural gas-based power has been offered as one such solution and especially for India where other sources of balancing are scant.

Natural gas has been playing an important role in enhancing energy security for several decades now, and it has been argued that there should have been greater recognition of this role of natural gas (Cohen et al., 2011). In fact, for energy-importing countries as a whole, diversification in oil supplies has remained constant over the last decade, while diversification in natural gas supplies has steadily increased. In Chapter 3, it has been discussed as to how natural gas has played a major role in sustaining high DI in countries, where it has a high share in energy mix (USA, Germany, Canada and Japan), and correspondingly, countries with low natural gas share had a lower DI (China, Brazil and India). Given the increasing importance of natural gas in energy use, this is an indicator of an increase in overall energy security. While comparing imports, natural gas is considered to be an easier option than oil in order to manage supply and costs. Transportation of natural gas is easier and cheaper as compared to oil and thus import of natural gas is a preferred option for a country having large energy import dependence. Thus, increasing energy supply diversity with natural gas can create an enabling environment for a secure and reliable energy system (Speight, 2013). In the following chapter, there is a discussion on India's DI and role of different fuels in poor diversity with special focus on natural gas.

2.4   UNCERTAINTY AROUND THE ROLE OF NATURAL GAS IN INDIA

In spite of a high requirement, India has not been able to enhance the share of natural gas in its energy mix appreciably. It is notable that globally, the share of natural gas has been 24% and India's natural gas share at a fraction of the above offers a genuine scope for a large increase. In an interesting chronicle of how the expectation of role of natural gas has swung both ways in under a decade of the 'optimistic' IHV Report in 1999, and a 'pessimistic' Working Group Report for Petroleum & Natural Gas sector for 11th Plan (2007–12). When new NELP gas fields became production worthy in 2009, the share of natural gas went up, but then it came down because this production was found to be short-lived. However, India could have gone for imports if, this fuel was found to be superior. Incidentally the share of imported gas remained small, and it is only since 2020 that India has started consuming more of imported gas than the domestic one. Hopefully, there will be a paradigm shift and India's gas story will not remain captive to the domestic gas production scenario alone.

The challenges to raising its share are numerous and they have been addressed in different chapters of this book. Some of them have been listed here. To start with, there has been poor availability of natural gas itself due to low production. As regards imported gas, a robust expansion in the capacity of LNG terminals is happening only now. The price of imported gas is market determined, which is unacceptable to major consumers—urea and power sectors—largely due to sale of these products at a discount to cost and the dual gas pricing regime. The urea manufacturers and power producers sell their products below cost price with the difference being made up by the government through a subsidy allocation. The higher the gas price, the more is the subsidy required. This links the concern of prices with domestic production and forms a loop. With a large share of domestically produced natural gas priced at a discount as per an administrative gas pricing mechanism (APM) and other government-controlled pricing policies, pricing of end products in the related demand sectors such as power and urea is itself distorted. As cheaply priced domestic natural gas production did not rise, its use in the price sensitive demand sectors such as cooking and transport sectors has remained subdued. The dual pricing situation (LNG is sold at international price) has created a challenge for new entrants into the end-use application sectors. As a remedial measure, a maze of policies have been devised to blend the two supplies, prioritise the cheaper gas supply to certain sectors, presenting a complex situation in the market place. In a similar situation in China, researchers have argued that reduction in price spreads between different market segments held the key to an enhanced demand (Rioux et al., 2019).

As regards supply of natural gas, the major focus has been on enhancing domestic exploration and production and lesser on imported supply. Over the past two decades and more, Indian government has carried out several policy reforms to enhance exploration and enhance domestic oil and gas production. One major reform has been adoption of the New Exploration Licensing Policy (NELP) in 1999 which did away with monopoly right of government companies like the Oil and Natural Gas Corporation Ltd. (ONGC) and Oil India Ltd. (OIL) to explore and produce hydrocarbons, and introduced an international competitive bidding (ICB) system for grant of acreages expansions (Jain, 2011). The exploration for the two hydrocarbons—oil and natural gas—is a common pursuit, but there has been higher success in discovering natural gas. Between 2000 and 2019, oil reserves in India fell from 5.3 to 4.7 billion barrels (by production and poor accretion), while that of natural gas rose from 0.7 trillion cubic metres (TCM) to 1.3 TCM (BP, 2019). The latter has been largely due to the discoveries made under NELP contracts. These successes led Indian policymakers to expect a large domestic natural gas supply and this anticipation encouraged a favourable regime to connect the natural gas fields to the markets (MoPNG, 2016). It is evident from Table 2.3 that after the success achieved in 2010, the gas production has been falling and within a decade, it has ended up at nearly half of this value in 2020.

The progressive NELP regime delivered the result, when natural gas production started from the first NELP field in KG Basin in 2009, with an expectation of 120 MMSCMD of peak production, more than the then total domestic natural gas production of the country. The start of supply from this field led to natural gas achieving its highest-ever level of 11% in India's commercial PES in 2010–11 (Abhyankar, 2012)[1]. However, this euphoria too was short-lived as production from this field peaked at 55 MMSCMD in 2010–11, then fell steeply by two-thirds in 2013–14, and became nil in 2018–19 (CSE, 2019). With this swinging fortune,

TABLE 2.3
Natural Gas Production in India (in BCM) 2010–2020

Year	Production
2010	47.4
2011	42.9
2012	37.3
2013	31.1
2014	29.4
2015	28.1
2016	26.6
2017	27.7
2018	27.5
2019	26.9
2020	23.8

Source: BP Statistics (2021).

the share of natural gas has fallen back to 6% at present and an era of uncertainty has begun. It is notable that after development of new discoveries in the same field, additional natural gas supplies have been introduced in the market in 2020.

In India, there has been a historical legacy of pricing and natural gas utilisation policies. Natural gas has been allocated to preferred sectors like urea making and LPG. The above measures have enabled government role into fixing of both upstream prices and allocation of gas to consumers. These policies have now given way to pricing and marketing freedom. However, the gas coming largely from government-owned companies is still governed under the old regime. This is also due to transitional challenge, and may be subsumed soon under the more liberalised dispensation discussed in this book. One progressive early reform has been setting up of an independent, statutory downstream Regulator—PNGRB—that was created in 2006 and has successfully launched a number of CGD bidding rounds that will be a major vehicle for delivering gas throughout the country. With a little role for the Regulator in price determination, it has contributed substantially in creation of downstream infrastructure such as trunk pipelines and urban gas grids. Hence, India has seen a large number of policy reforms and their impact is now beginning to be felt. The rise in LNG supply, setting up of new LNG terminals and beginning of production from deep-water KG Basin gas fields in 2020, can all be attributed to the recent policy announcements.

A number of studies have offered outlook on natural gas uptake in the country. The IHV's projections pertain to the period going up to 2025, and had anticipated high natural gas shares in intermediate years, which though has been missed by a wide gulf. It had projected a 15% share from 2001–02 rising to 20% in 2024–25. With the above early miss, there is a likelihood that the target for 2025 may also be missed by a large number. However, the Petroleum Minister's statement has again aroused some hope that government may give a policy push to attain a high share of natural gas (MoPNG, 2018). The IEA's India Energy Outlook published in 2015 projected a low share, typically between 6% and 8%, under the two scenarios—New Policies and Indian Vision Case scenarios, respectively in 2040. In their 2021 publication, they have projected a higher share, between 11% and 16% for the same year. Another study of likely LNG demand in emerging Asian economies undertaken by Oxford Institute for Energy Studies (OIES) found uncertainty in India's natural gas story, particularly in direct comparison to other Asian economies (Rogers, 2017). It is in this light, that Chapter 7 on natural gas demand scenarios in 2030 helps in bringing clarity. While it is not the intention to predict natural gas demand, however, a discussion around the factors/drivers in the above chapters are expected to help interested readers in demystifying the future for this fuel.

The studies/reports on India's natural gas story have been more in the nature of demand projections and have made recommendations on how could more of this fuel be consumed in India. However, they have lacked an academic fervour. Surely there are some structural reasons that are defying both the public and private efforts to raise the consumption of natural gas in India. Billions of dollars

BOX 2.1   NATURAL GAS AS A BRIDGE FUEL TO NET-ZERO

Post COP 26, natural gas has become a good candidate for adoption in India to help achieve net-zero by 2030. It is a fairly well assimilated fuel in India—while it is certainly a 'new' fuel in comparison to coal, oil and hydropower, yet it has been around for nearly half a century. When 'phasing down' coal in the medium run, natural gas could be a ready alternative. The presence of large corporates in the natural gas business, both public and MNCs, pan-India infrastructure (and growing), and availability of a formal regulatory mechanism (PNGRB) offer fertile ground for it to quickly scale up. Indeed, India is fast aspiring to achieve a higher share of this fuel in the energy mix, from the present low of 6%–15% by 2030. As the global average is 24%, even at the targeted number, experience of other nations indicates that due scope exists for more growth. There is ample availability of literature that links a high share of natural gas with high levels of economic growth and diversity in the energy mix. In the design scheme of this book, a dedicated chapter follows on comparison of fuel diversity across major energy consuming nations, and how India has fared until now. Simultaneously though, this chapter has also raised a doubt or two on the future role of gas. It reflects upon the inability of this fuel to have achieved high share in the past as also due to well entrenched competing fuels, especially coal in both the power and industry segments.

India's clean energy commitments at COP 26 are likely to be seen as a frontal challenge to the policymakers and the country at large. This reaction may not be new and even developed countries have been through this cycle of apprehension, resignation and encouragement. Large investments may be required in clean energy deployment, and there may even be a fear of having to dismantle the existing carbon-intensive energy infrastructure. That is why in this chapter, it has been argued that natural gas offers a viable energy option and may even support economic growth. Hence, in the pathway to a net-zero energy future, natural gas could become a part of the effective solution and also contribute to economic growth. Still ahead in this book, a large expansion is underway in LNG receiving terminals and pipelines, and this upbeat investment climate may get a further boost. Gas demand projections may become a growing reality and possibility improves for issuance of a slew of policies to promote gas demand and supply. However, gas being cleaner than oil and coal cannot be the only factor in its adoption.

There is already a strong advocacy in this chapter for raising the share of natural gas in order to achieve a more diverse fuel mix. Diversity and energy security have been argued for long as being two sides of the same coin. With India's energy demand poised to grow in the near foreseeable future, an increase in natural gas share does not mean rolling back absolute levels of other fuels, such as coal. We already know that natural gas can substitute coal across various end uses, in which coal may be deployed in the future. So, a rising share of gas does not even hurt the existing coal con-suming sectors, mainly coal-based thermal power plants, by denying them fuel. In a nutshell, the proposals in this chapter gel well with the scenario of natural gas as a bridge fuel to net-zero emission attainment.

A number of concerns on domestic gas production, pricing, distortions in downstream sectors, taxation, etc., have been enumerated. Natural gas will have to contend with other fuels, namely, renewables, electricity in general, hydrogen, nuclear energy amongst others that are regarded as sustainable fuels. They do not emit any carbon and are the choice of climate advocates, while natural gas is being touted only as a 'bridge' fuel that must ultimately give way. There is already a clamour against the latter in several European countries, as significant methane emissions are reported during the produc-tion of natural gas, along with at the point of combustion. The challenges faced by gas utilisation in India need resolution, failing which it may not serve as an intermediary fuel between coal and renewables. Notably during the last nine years in India (2010–19), while renewables have grown by a multiple of five from 20 to 100 GW, natural gas consumption has remained more or less static at 52 Mtoe. Therefore, the Indian experience so far has been that is possible to make a transition to a clean energy future without reliance on natural gas. It is only after a detailed discussion on structural and fuel-specific factors (in the following chapters) that one can confidently address the issues raised in the caption above.

spent on setting up gas-fired power plants and trunk pipelines have not yielded the desired returns and lie stranded due to lack of natural gas. Poor domestic production has received a lion's share of attention, but reforms in the downstream sectors that consume gas have still not been reformed. Another area of concern is lack of recognition of the lower carbon emission involved in gas consumption and its possible role in substituting coal and oil. There are many similar aspects that are not directly related to this fuel, but belong to the domain of India's broader energy and clean air policy. These issues have been covered in the later parts of this book.

NOTE

1 As per BP (2019), the share was 9%.

3 Comparative Analysis of Diversity of India's Commercial Primary Energy Supply

3.1 INTRODUCTION

At present, India is one of the fastest-growing economies in the world, with energy consumption growing at a Growth Rate of around 6.74% (2019–20) (Energy Statistics, 2021). While the Covid-19 pandemic has hurt the major economies across the world, India is expected to bounce back strongly in FY22 and the energy growth rate might ultimately sustain. Its energy mix is characterised by a large dependence (above 50%) on coal, which has remained fairly stable over the last couple of decades and has exhibited 'inflexibility' through global highs and lows of relative prices of different fuels, thus far. On the other hand, another large fossil consumer, China, has reduced its coal consumption. This has contributed to India exhibiting the lowest share of clean energy sources amongst the world's large energy consumers, despite some recent efforts to ramp it up. Recently reviewed literature indicates that the criteria for making energy choices has moved from only costs to a greater reflection of opportunity costs of finite resources and health costs attributable to pollution from conventional fossil fuels, and growing recognition of the carbon constraints within which the planetary activities must remain (Bery et al., 2017). For India, several studies that sought to examine its medium to long term energy scenarios, have suggested that fossil fuels and in particular, coal is likely to remain a major contributor for some more time, and that even with policy measures to enhance the penetration of renewable over the course of the next few years, the energy mix is unlikely to change significantly over the next couple of decades (Bery et al., 2017).

India's energy planners are much concerned with the fiscal aspects of energy security owing to high import dependency for its commercial energy supplies. Imported fuels come at market price, whereas domestically produced fuels have been subsidised. The government's focus on reducing import dependence has been a major reason for the persistence of coal in India's energy mix, as it holds the world's fourth largest coal reserves of 319 billion tonnes (GOI, 2018a). India is not an outlier in this as domestic availability of an energy resource was found to lead to high share of that source in the energy mix, also impacting the diversity in energy supply, of many countries. A detailed discussion on this is offered in the

DOI: 10.1201/9781003307693-3

next chapter where share of natural gas in primary energy supply (PES) has been found to be reflective of its availability either from domestic gas fields, or access to pipeline networks as has been the case with Germany and France. Nevertheless, in light of the urgency to mitigate climate change as well as worsening local air quality, the backing out of coal is arguably as critical as the adding of clean energy resources as a policy priority (Jewell et al., 2013). Continued reliance on limited number of fuels with large shares impacts supply diversity, with possible implications on energy security via concerns related to possible over-dependence on a handful of fuels, limited consumer choices, increased imports and the like.

This chapter answers the following key questions:

• How has the diversity of energy mix of leading energy consuming countries including India evolved over the medium term?
• What trends are visible in the energy mix of these countries?

The above questions have been addressed by applying Shannon Wiener diversity index (DI), a statistical tool through which not only has the transition over a period of four decades (1980–2019) been tracked, but a comparison between India and other leading energy consuming countries has also been done. This tool was selected after considering several other options, and this has been discussed later in this chapter. The findings from this exercise suggest that energy supply diversity has improved in all the study scoped countries. While India's energy supply diversity, too, has increased, but others saw a higher increase, pushing India down two notches from 1980 figure, and nearly to the bottom of the list. The results indicate that India's policy planners have overlooked an important aspect of energy system ambition—to keep it flexible, develop new sources and achieve a balance amongst different sources. The research consideration for this study provides new insights into drivers of energy security, and promotes research on energy supply diversity in other similarly placed emerging economies (Babajide, 2018).[1]

3.2   APPROACH ADOPTED FOR ANALYSIS

The choice and mix of fuels adopted by different countries has seen continuous transition over the years. The timing and nature of changes has varied across countries. Accordingly, we seek to track the mix of the commercial PES of India and other top energy consuming countries to make comparisons and draw conclusions regarding common trends and differences to understand this more clearly. In terms of countries included for study, we consider the world's top seven energy consumers of 2019, namely, USA, China, India, Brazil, Japan, Germany and Canada. Although Russian Federation is presently the fourth largest energy consumer in the world, since the data for energy consumption by fuel for the present state is not available for the period before the split of USSR in 1991, it has not been included for analysis.[2] For ranking of countries, by considering the magnitude of energy consumption in 2019 and not 1980, which marks the start of this study, India, gets included in the list of study countries (Table 3.1). In the

TABLE 3.1

Change in Global Rank in Energy Consumption (1980–2019)

Country/Rank	China	USA	India	Japan	Canada	Germany	Brazil
2019	1	2	3	4	5	6	7
1980[a]	2	1	10	4	5	3	11

Source: BP (2019a).

[a] UK, France, Italy and Poland were at 6th, 7th, 8th and 9th places, respectively, in 1980.

discussion throughout this chapter, unless otherwise pointed out, we refer to the aforementioned countries.

Further, in order to overcome the variations in size of their energy systems, it would be useful to undertake the above analysis in terms of percentage share consumption of different commercially traded energy sources. The analysis is conducted over the medium term (39 years extending between 1980 and 2019) that allows reasonable time for changes to take shape in energy mix of any country. The share of fossil fuels in the global PES was as high as 92% in 1980, and after 39 years, the same has reduced to 84% in 2019 (BP, 2020).

The data on energy mix classifies the traditional fuel sources individually. In light of the fast emerging importance more so of solar, wind and small hydro sources within 'clean energy domain', a grouping of these three sources called 'new renewables' has been captured separately. Further, the total energy consumption is also grouped into 'fossil' and 'clean' technologies, where 'new renewables', as above, and mature clean technologies such as large hydro and nuclear have been grouped together as 'clean'. The percentage shares of six fuel sources—oil, natural gas, coal, nuclear, hydro and new renewables—are indicated below for all the seven countries (Table 3.2). The graphs (Figures 3.1–3.7) provide a snapshot of evolution in energy mix on a ten-year basis within the above period.

3.3 ENERGY TRANSITION IN THE STUDY COUNTRIES (1980–2019)

In the following discussion, the question on the trends in evolution of energy mix in above seven countries has been addressed (Figures 3.1–3.7), and salient changes (1980–2019) within the two groups of fuels—fossil and clean fuels—have been discussed.

3.3.1 FOSSIL FUELS

During the last four decades or so, all countries except India saw a decline in fossil fuel shares. In India, fossil fuels surprisingly grew over the last four decades from 87% to 91%. The global energy system is trending towards an enhanced

TABLE 3.2
Energy Mix of Study Countries in 1980 and 2019 (in %)

	Year	Oil	Nuclear	Natural Gas	Coal	Hydro	New RE	Fossil	Clean
Brazil	1980	58	0	1	6	33	2	65	35
	2019	38	1	10	5	29	16	54	46
Canada	1980	41	5	19	10	26	0	69	31
	2019	32	6	30	4	24	4	66	34
China	1980	21	0	3	73	3	0	97	3
	2019	20	2	8	58	8	5	85	15
Germany	1980	42	4	14	39	1	0	95	5
	2019	36	5	24	18	1	17	77	23
India	1980	31	1	1	55	12	0	87	13
	2019	30	1	6	55	4	4	91	9
Japan	1980	67	5	6	16	6	0	89	11
	2019	40	3	21	26	4	6	87	13
USA	1980	45	4	26	21	4	0	92	8
	2019	39	8	32	12	3	6	83	17

Source: BP (2020).

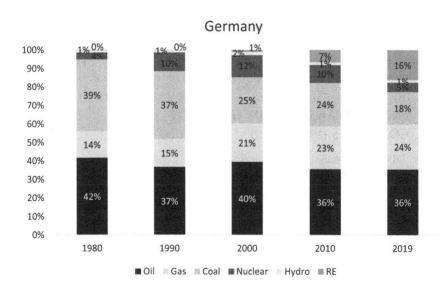

FIGURE 3.1 Energy mix of Germany (1980–2019) (BP, 2020).

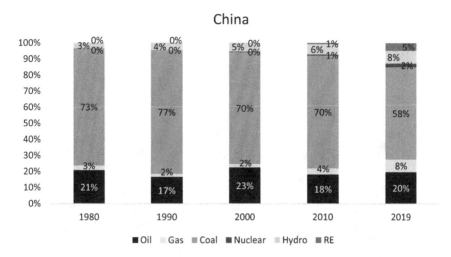

FIGURE 3.2 Energy mix of China (1980–2019) (BP, 2020).

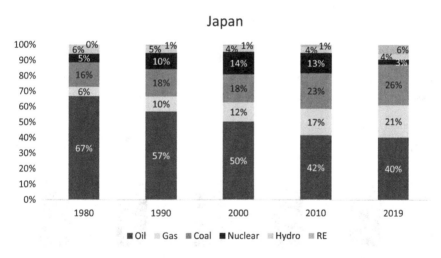

FIGURE 3.3 Energy mix of Japan (1980–2019) (BP, 2020).

use of clean energy. Germany has exhibited the sharpest decline in fossil fuels (from 95% to 77%). Within the three fossil fuels (coal, oil and natural gas), a few interesting differences between developed and emerging economies can be seen. While the share of fossil fuels as a whole has fallen, but the share of natural gas increased across the board. The developed countries generally have a high share of natural gas. USA has the highest share of natural gas within the study group at 32% (up from 28%), while with its least share being in India, it rose from a mere 1% to 6%. Even in Germany, a country where clean energy grew significantly, the share of natural gas still grew, perhaps replacing oil and coal. Overall the rise of

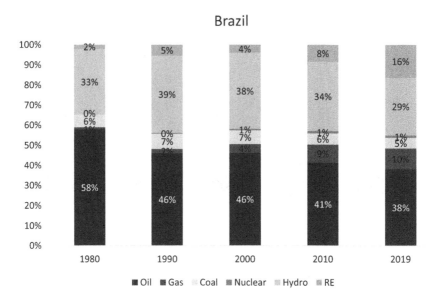

FIGURE 3.4   Energy mix of Brazil (1980–2019) (BP, 2020).

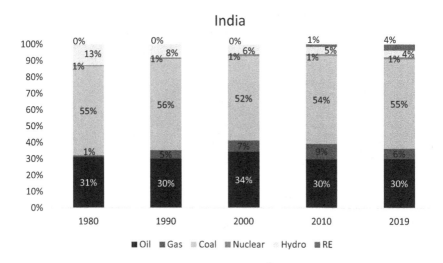

FIGURE 3.5   Energy mix of India (1980–2019) (BP, 2020).

natural gas (a cleaner fossil fuel) while fossil fuels as a whole declined, indicates that there was an inclination in favour of clean fuels.

Coal is an important fuel in most countries albeit its shares fell across the study countries with a lone exception—Japan—where it grew. India is the only country where the share of coal remained the same at a very high level. The highest shares are in China (58%) and India (55%), while the lowest ones are in Canada and

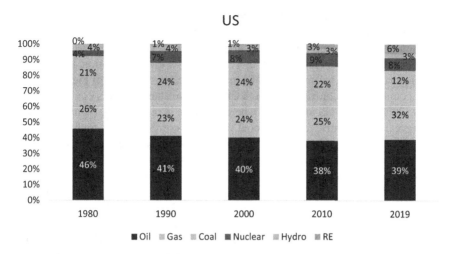

FIGURE 3.6   Energy mix of USA (1980–2019) (BP, 2020).

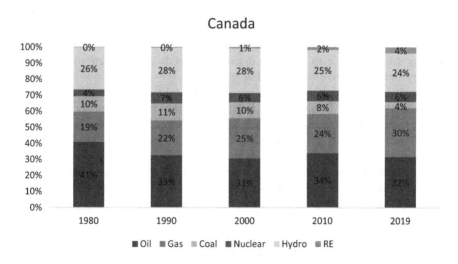

FIGURE 3.7   Energy mix of Canada (1980–2019) (BP, 2020).

Brazil (5% and 4%). In the developed economies, share of coal is lower than what is for the emerging economies. It is 26% in Japan, 18% in Germany and 12% in USA. In Germany, it is only in the last decade that the share of coal has fallen. It is the same story in USA and China, whereas in Japan coal share has actually risen during the last decade while in India it is stubbornly static. India does stand out in comparison to Japan, as the energy mix underwent a transformation in Japan after the Fukushima disaster in 2011. India and China offer a contrasting case wherein while both countries are registering growth in their respective energy consumptions, but in India it is coal and new renewables that are contributing to the new demand but in China, it is not coal but natural gas that is combining with new renewables to meet this increase in demand (BP, 2020).

Oil shares have also fallen in all these countries without exception; however, it continues to remain an important fuel, meeting nearly one-third of the PES in in most countries. The only exception is China where share of oil is comparatively lower (20%). It is in US and Japan, where oil share is rather high. Figures 3.1–3.7 also reveal that countries with low coal shares are correlated with high oil share.[3] As the two fuels meet different end-use demands—oil as a transport fuel and coal in non-transport—the above trend needs further study. China and India have the highest share of coal use with least share of oil as compared to all the others.

3.3.2 CLEAN ENERGY

The share of clean energy has increased in all countries except India with a large range present across the seven countries—46% in Brazil and 9% in India. The steep rise in fortunes of wind and solar stands out in Germany (from nil to 16%). No other country has shown such a dramatic rise in any clean energy source utilisation. Brazil, which started in 1980 with the highest clean energy share of 33% (mainly hydro) amongst the seven countries, is still at the top with 46% share of its PES coming from clean sources. On the other hand, in India, share of clean energy fell from 13% to 9%. Two discernible trends can be seen within clean energy and have been discussed below.

Firstly, clean energy is actually a post-2000 story, and it has been actually boosted after 2005. In India and China, the increase in clean energy share has happened more during the last decade (2010–19). In China, while clean energy share grew from 3% in 1980 to 5% and 8% in 2000 and 2010, respectively, it doubled to 15% in 2019. It is notable that this growth in clean energy has happened due to induction of 'new renewables', i.e. wind and solar (not in nuclear and hydro), whose share has risen appreciably in all countries by 2019. Secondly, we also see a synergy across different clean energy technologies. While penetration of new renewables is rising, so far, no single technology uniformly dominates the clean energy group. Nuclear is the main source in USA, while hydropower leads in Canada and Brazil. Solar and wind energy technologies are the leaders in Germany. It calls for further study as to why one particular clean technology has not emerged as the clear winner across countries. Perhaps the need for diversity, local resource endowment and attributes such as seasonal variability is guiding the choice of technology.

What is clear is that with the exception of natural gas, the energy mix across the countries of study has transitioned away from fossil fuels. In addition, over the last three decades at least one new clean energy source (not the same one) has made its debut in every country with varying shares of these sources across them. As a result, in 2019, we see different fuels performing differently in the energy mix of countries. In the next section we introduce a quantitative tool—DI—to analyse the above developments across countries on a common unit of measurement.

3.4   DIVERSITY INDICES IN ENERGY SYSTEMS

The field of biodiversity, which evaluates the health of ecosystems and the diversity therein, offers different measures of diversity. In order to compare and measure the flexibility of energy systems and transition over time, it is instructive to turn to biodiversity. It is easy to appreciate that abundance of species of plant or animal life in an ecosystem is valued as an insurance against their destruction by any reason that may be partial to a specie. The above varietal spread is, however, only one positive aspect of 'biodiversity' or diversity. Most researchers tend to define diversity in terms of two more terms: balance and disparity (Stirling, 2007b). This has led to the development of a statistical tool (e.g. DI) that quantitatively measures the above three attributes in a single unit, to avail of unique qualities that different participants bring. The main indices have been listed below (Cooke et al., 2013):

- Hill
- Herfindahl–Hirschman
- Simpson
- Shannon Wiener
- Stirling

It is understandable that the concept of 'diversity' may be adapted by other disciplines where richness of spread is valued. Energy systems are one such area especially in cases where there is an excessive dependence on an imported source of energy. In these cases, the pursuit of diversity may even be interpreted as energy security (Cooke et al., 2013).[4] Depending on the preference, as to which aspect(s) of diversity are to be accorded greater importance, or even not to be included in the enquiry, researchers have offered different indices. Hill's index allows weights to be allocated to different sources. While this may be helpful in according higher importance to a preferred source (let us say clean sources), but at times may mute other outcomes such as market neutrality or energy security that comes with even shares of other sources. Simpson DI and its variant, Herfindahl–Hirschman, are well known for measuring concentration (balance), particularly for companies where there is great interest in control over markets via large shares. Simpson index does not reward higher number of sources (or variety); as a result, a higher index is not representative of varietal richness. In this context, as Shannon Wiener measures the varietal spread as well as the balance between them, it is the most popular index for measuring long-term energy security (Ranjan and Hughes, 2014b). Stirling has combined all the three aspects (variety, balance and disparity) to create his own index. While the adoption of an index offers advantage of combining several features in one number, the drawback here is that there is no prescription on acceptable range.

3.4.1   CHOICE OF INDEX

Diversity trends have application both in measurement of absolute position and transition over time (Kruyt et al., 2009). In the following discussion, the transition in energy mix in the seven study countries has been analysed by applying Shannon Wiener DI (or Shannon DI). Hill has been ruled out as it brings bias to the analysis by assigning weights. Herfindahl and Simpson DI are also not chosen as measuring concentration is not the objective of the current study (Chalvatzis and Ioannidis, 2017).[5] The last one, Stirling, is not valid for this study as disparity is not of focal importance as would have been the case if the focus was measuring diversity in sources of power generation. The Shannon DI is simple and transparent and it works on energy share data which is publicly available; it is straightforward as it works on two well-understood levers—number of energy sources and variety; and it is unbiased as neither does it give weights to data and nor does it require subjective categorisation as to what is disparity (Jansen et al., 2004).[6] One comment that brings out the superiority of Shannon DI has been quoted below (Grubb et al., 2006):

> Diversity itself comprises at least three subordinate properties (Stirling & Waxman, 1998; Jansen et al., 2004). Variety refers to the number of categories into which the quantity in question is partitioned (e.g. gas, coal, wind, etc.). Balance refers to the pattern in the apportionment (spread) of that quantity across the relevant categories. Given the number of categories, the more even the spread, the greater is the diversity. Finally, disparity refers to the nature and degree to which the categories themselves are different from each other. For example, coal and gas generation are more closely related (via linked fuel prices) than wind and nuclear. Stirling (1994) reviewed the ecological literature and found no measure of diversity that addressed the property of disparity. The Shannon–Wiener index, defined below, was considered to be the most satisfactory since although it does not take account of disparity, it does incorporate the concepts of variety and balance.

Given the above qualities, this study considers the Shannon DI to address the trends in energy mix of the study countries by quantifying them.

3.4.2 APPLICATION OF SHANNON DI IN MAJOR ENERGY CONSUMING COUNTRIES

Shannon DI has been defined as the ratio of the species to their importance values within a community. The same is transformed in the context of energy systems within countries with the Shannon DI for energy calculated using the following formula:

$$H = -\sum_i p_i \ln p_i$$

Here p_i represents the share of fuel i in the energy mix, while $\ln p_i$ is the natural log of p_i. The respective shares of different fuels in energy mix are multiplied by their natural logarithm and summed up. The higher the value of 'H' the more diverse the energy mix is. While it is granted that use of just one attribute—energy share—to measure a complex issue like diversity is inadequate, however, the availability of different fuel sources in an energy mix offers many benefits including the prospect of fuel-switching if necessary, thereby, promoting energy security. Additionally, the above formula also addresses the aspect of 'balance' through the natural logarithm function. The index ascribes different values when fuel shares rise. When there is rise from a small share, the index rises disproportionately initially, and then the rate tapers off.[7] Hence, it rewards moderate shares but not disproportionately large ones.

A graph tracking DI over a medium-term transforms the static diversity outcomes to one that measures transition (Table 3.3 and Figure 3.8)

TABLE 3.3

Shannon Wiener Diversity Index of Seven Leading Energy Consumers (1980–2019)

	1980	1985	1990	1995	2000	2005	2010	2015	2019
Brazil	0.98	1.19	1.18	1.19	1.21	1.30	1.37	1.45	1.46
Canada	1.40	1.48	1.50	1.52	1.49	1.50	1.51	1.52	1.49
China	0.77	0.72	0.71	0.77	0.85	0.81	0.89	1.02	1.12
Germany	1.20	1.28	1.31	1.36	1.41	1.47	1.51	1.53	1.52
India	1.03	1.05	1.08	1.09	1.12	1.13	1.16	1.11	1.17
Japan	1.06	1.27	1.26	1.29	1.35	1.38	1.46	1.31	1.44
USA	1.30	1.36	1.40	1.42	1.40	1.40	1.46	1.47	1.45

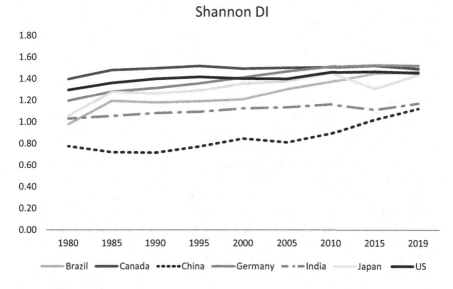

FIGURE 3.8 Shannon Wiener diversity index graph (1980–2019). (Derived from BP, 2019b.)

(Wu and Rai, 2017).[8] The indices in this study have been derived by applying the Shannon DI formula to percentage shares of different energy sources available in BP Statistics. In Table 3.3, in 2019 Germany is at the top rank with maximum diversity with Canada just behind, while India and China are at the bottom positions. In 1980, Canada was at the top rank and Germany was at the fourth place. So, Germany's climb is remarkable. USA was at second rank, and is now at fourth position. In 1980, China, Brazil and India occupied the three receding positions. In 2019, while China is still at the bottom, Brazil has zoomed up beyond India and Japan, thus pushing India to the second last position and Japan to the third from the bottom. (Japan lost it diversity due to closure of nuclear plants.) Over 2005–2019, China's Shannon DI has risen at a rapid rate, and has closed the gap with India of 0.26 to just 0.05 points. What is remarkable that while India's absolute DI improved by just 15% over 1980, China improved the same by over 45%. While Japan's DI may be third from the bottom, but it is not faring poorly with the countries above whose DI varies in a small range. It is notable that in the study under reference, Japan's energy system has indeed been found to be rather inflexible which is confirmed by the Shannon Weiner DI (Kucharski and Unesaki, 2018).[9]

While every country improved its DI (one new source of energy increased in all countries), what caused the DI of some countries to improve more than others? The natural logarithm used in calculating the DI favours those with more energy sources (options) with sources being evenly spread (called 'balance'). The following illustration explains the interplay of these two levers. The shares of the dominant fuel—oil in Brazil and coal in China—were disproportionately high at 58% and 73% in 1980, respectively, which resulted in imbalance and low DI. However, in comparison to Brazil, the share of oil in Japan was higher at 67%. Yet the DI of latter was higher than both Brazil and China because while they had four energy sources each, Japan had five sources (additional source was nuclear energy). During the last 39 years, both Brazil and China expanded their energy sources to six each (nuclear plus new renewables), and also reduced the weight of their dominant fuel sources to 38% and 58%, respectively, resulting in substantive improvement in their DI (Table 3.3). Japan, however added new renewables as the sixth source and also brought down the oil share to 40% and continued to remain diverse (except for the nuclear story). It is, therefore, an outcome of application of both levers—number (varietal spread) and balance—and not of one lever alone. For the same case specifics, at four fuel sources each in 1980 in China and Brazil, the DI of Brazil was higher due to a lower share of its dominant fuel.

Given that all countries in the study group have six common sources of energy in their resource base, it is indeed the balance aspect that drives DI. The three countries at the bottom of Shannon DI (China, India and Japan) are the only ones to have one source of energy at above 50% or so share (oil in Brazil is at 40%). This imbalance pulls their DI down to be at the bottom of the study countries.

In addition to the above discussion of two levers working simultaneously, it is also notable that the relationship between percentage share of a fuel in PES and

TABLE 3.4

Share of Coal and Its Weight in Shannon DI (2019)

	% In PES	% In DI
Brazil	5	11
Canada	4	9
China	58	28
Germany	18	20
India	55	28
Japan	26	24
USA	12	17

its share in DI is non-linear. The above feature of this tool is explained by the following illustration of coal shares and DI given in Table 3.4

It can be seen that the shares of coal in Brazil (5%) and USA (12%) in 2019 were in the ratio of 1:2.4 but the values in Shannon Wiener index (percentage of coal sub-index in overall Shannon DI) are not in the above proportion, but lower at 11:17. While the Shannon DI provides useful insights regarding trends and relative rankings, any insights into the underlying causes may require use of other statistical tools like correlation and multi-variate analysis. While we do not use statistical methods further, based on insights from a range of scholarly articles and literature, we stress on the need for a carefully measured and deliberated view towards diversity in energy mix, while keeping other country specific consideration in view. In the following section, outcomes of consultation with experts on diversity related aspects have been discussed, followed by a comparative analysis of India's DI with the other major energy consuming countries. The same has to be seen in the light of the above-mentioned caveats.

3.5   CRITICAL ANALYSIS

Before getting into a detailed discussion on comparison of India's fuel diversity with other countries, it may be instructive to refer to the views obtained from subject-matter experts during the consultation undertaken for this study.

3.5.1   What Are the Reasons behind Low Diversity of India's Energy Mix?

The respondents were asked to assign a suitable rank within the four offered reasons. The first rank was given by an equal number of respondents to three options. Government policy and poor endowment of resources were ranked as the highest, followed closely by lack of energy markets. Due to lack of a clear verdict, it may be useful to see which option has got more responses of second rank.

Experts have opined that the government has had a major role in perpetuating the existing energy mix, and perhaps, this was a consequence of the natural resource endowment (the third option in the questionnaire). Even the findings in this chapter indicate similar outcome. The poor endowment of resources predicated the government policy with a mindset of self-dependence. The fourth option of high prices of fuels has received the fourth rank.

3.5.2 WHETHER DIVERSIFYING INDIA'S ENERGY SOURCES MIGHT ENHANCE INDIA'S ENERGY SECURITY?

Nearly all the respondents have endorsed the above position in an affirmative—19 out of 21 experts responded affirmatively to the above question. This is a major endorsement for the findings coming out of this chapter that India's energy security might receive a boost, if there was a genuine balance in its energy mix, towards which natural gas could be a major contributor.

3.5.3 WHETHER SHARE OF NATURAL GAS IN PES WILL EXCEED 10% BY 2030?

A rise in the share of natural gas will give the desired boost to India's DI. With the present share within commercial PES at 6% and an aim to reach 15% by 2030, the likelihood of attaining 10% share is a mid-way possibility. Majority of the responses endorsed the above possibility (Figure 3.9). A rising share is a positive vote for natural gas, and calls for a favourable policy support to make it happen. Even the research findings in this study have indicated that natural gas share might increase.

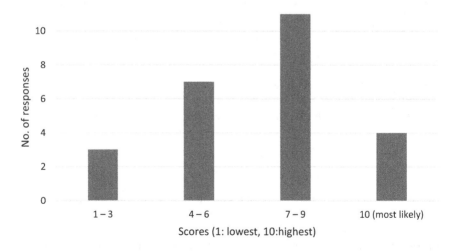

FIGURE 3.9 Likelihood of rise in share of natural gas to 10% or more by 2030 (by number of responses).

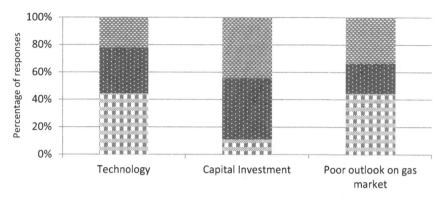

FIGURE 3.10   Deterrents of natural gas penetration in supply mix.

3.5.4 DETERRENTS OF NATURAL GAS PENETRATION IN INDIA'S ENERGY SUPPLY MIX

While investigating the market deterrents for penetration of this fuel, it was suggested by experts that there could be three major factors: (i) technological hindrance, (ii) financial hindrance and (iii) poor outlook for gas (policy hindrance). The outcome of the consultation was that technology and indifferent outlook/unfavourable gas policy could be amongst the big hindrances. More than 40% of the respondents argued in favour of removing such hindrances in these two areas. Interestingly, financial or investment barrier is not considered as a major deterrent for natural gas penetration in PES (Figure 3.10). The analysis in this study has revealed that it is the poor outlook on market competitiveness of natural gas in major consumption sectors that is the real negative.

3.6 COMPARISON OF DIVERSITY IN INDIA'S ENERGY SUPPLY WITH OTHERS

Here, the trends existing in the six major fuels (coal, oil, natural gas, nuclear, hydro and new renewables) have been pursued in detail for a comparative analysis. Different fuels yield their own Shannon Wiener sub-index (they total up to make the main index) whose trends over time (1980–2019) have been tracked below. For a specific fuel, the trends in its sub-index can be compared across countries as to their contribution in determining the overall DI. Further changes in the trend over time can be compared to see which countries saw a rise or fall in a particular fuel's sub-index. The above analysis is useful owing to the following salient reasons:

- A rise in sub-index of a fuel(s) is always a welcome development as it would lift the composite Shannon DI.

- The role of the Inverse log in yielding a higher or equal sub-index with a change in share of a fuel in PES is a useful policy message.
- A fuel-wise trend line is definitely instructive as it captures the energy supply transition.

3.6.1   OIL SHANNON SUB-INDEX

India's oil sub-index has been high, and over the last 39 years it has been static (Table 3.5 and Figure 3.11). Oil's share in India's energy mix has fallen while the sub-index remained the same (at 30% share in PES, it is well-balanced). This shows that with a moderation in share of oil, the diversity did not fall (India's overall DI has improved). Other countries with a higher oil share have a similar oil sub-index as that of India (impacted by other fuels in their energy mix). The

TABLE 3.5
Shannon Wiener Oil Sub-Index

	1980	1990	2000	2010	2019
Brazil	0.32	0.36	0.36	0.37	0.37
Canada	0.37	0.37	0.36	0.37	0.36
China	0.33	0.30	0.34	0.31	0.32
Germany	0.36	0.37	0.37	0.37	0.37
India	0.36	0.36	0.37	0.36	0.36
Japan	0.27	0.32	0.35	0.36	0.37
USA	0.36	0.37	0.37	0.37	0.37

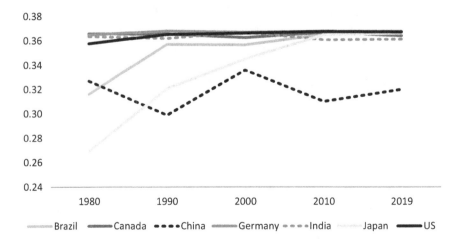

FIGURE 3.11   Graph of Shannon Wiener sub-indices of oil (1980–2019).

key message is that a falling oil share has helped in keeping the sub-index static, otherwise a rising oil share would have resulted in a lower DI.

3.6.2   COAL SHANNON SUB-INDEX

Coming to the second fossil fuel, coal, only two countries have registered a rise (or stability) in their respective share over 1980—Japan and India. Coal grew in Japan from a share in PES of 16%–26%, while in India it remained static at 55%. In all other study countries, coal declined in relative importance over the four-decade period (Figure 3.12 and Table 3.6).

Here is a contrasting effect on Shannon DI with the same stimulus. The high share of coal in India has retained its DI (Figure 3.12). However, a rising coal share in Japan only helped it achieve a better balance, and resulted in a higher

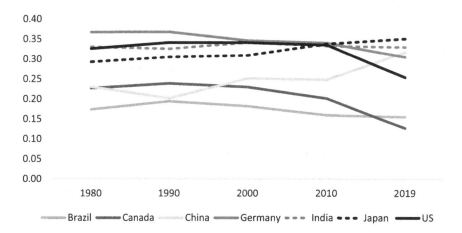

FIGURE 3.12   Graph of Shannon Wiener sub-indices of coal (1980–2019).

TABLE 3.6
Shannon Wiener Sub-Index of Coal

	1980	1990	2000	2010	2019
Brazil	0.17	0.19	0.18	0.16	0.16
Canada	0.23	0.24	0.23	0.20	0.13
China	0.23	0.20	0.25	0.25	0.32
Germany	0.37	0.37	0.35	0.34	0.31
India	0.33	0.33	0.34	0.33	0.33
Japan	0.29	0.31	0.31	0.34	0.35
USA	0.33	0.34	0.34	0.34	0.25

sub-index (As Shannon Weiner DI only measures diversity, it is agnostic to whether the sources are clean or fossil fuels). This is because oil had a dispropor-tionate high share in 1980. Therefore, in 2019, while oil share fell and coal rose, leading to a better balance. With lower coal shares in PES than what it is in India, the coal sub-index of Japan and Germany is higher than India's. China has, in fact, been able to achieve a growth in its coal sub-index by decreasing coal share (Kruyt et al., 2009).[10] Any decrease in India's coal share would actually enhance its overall DI.

3.6.3 NATURAL GAS SHANNON SUB-INDEX

In the case of third fossil fuel, natural gas, due to low share in India's PES (6%), its Shannon sub-index is very low. India's natural gas story was expected to be bright when gas share rose in 2010 to 9%—it raised the sub-index from 0.18 in 2000 to 0.22 in 2010 (Figure 3.13 and Table 3.7). As the share fell back to 6% in 2019, the

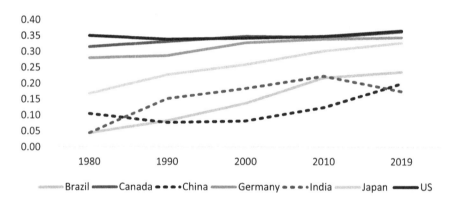

FIGURE 3.13   Graph of Shannon Wiener sub-indices of natural gas (1980–2019).

TABLE 3.7
Shannon Wiener Sub-Index of Natural Gas

	1980	1990	2000	2010	2019
Brazil	0.04	0.08	0.14	0.22	0.24
Canada	0.31	0.33	0.35	0.34	0.36
China	0.10	0.08	0.08	0.12	0.20
Germany	0.28	0.29	0.33	0.34	0.34
India	0.04	0.15	0.18	0.22	0.17
Japan	0.17	0.23	0.26	0.30	0.33
USA	0.35	0.34	0.34	0.35	0.36

sub-index also fell to 0.17 and thus impacted India's Shannon DI adversely. The countries with high Shannon DI—Canada, USA, Germany and Japan—appear to have a high gas sub-index in the band of 0.3–0.35. The rising share of natural gas has also boosted China's DI in 2019. It is also notable that the countries with poor Shannon rating also have lower natural gas sub-index (below 0.3). This indicates that this fuel enjoys a unique status due to its ability to influence the DI, particularly because it has a moderate share in the study countries. A small increase in its share would have a high upward impact on sub-index. This is also a key message of this chapter.

3.6.4 CLEAN ENERGY SUB-INDICES

In India, clean energy occupies a marginal role (9%), which is lowest amongst the study countries in 2019 as the clean energy group of fuels, fell during 1980–2019. In 1980, India had an additional energy source—nuclear energy—over China and Brazil. This also contributed to a higher DI for India. Hydro had a reasonably high share of 12% in 1980, third highest amongst the countries. The falling share of hydro and with no increase in nuclear, it is only new RE that has enhanced the share of clean energy rise even though marginally (Figures 3.14–3.16 and Tables 3.8–3.10). During the study period, all the other countries in the study group registered substantial increase in their Shannon sub-index for clean energy except India where it grew by just a whisker (from 0.29 to 0.30). A similarly placed large fossil dependent consumer, China, increased its clean energy sub-index to nearly two and a half times, from 0.11 to 0.28.

While the percentage share of clean energy sub-index (sum of clean energy sub-indices as a percentage of total Shannon Wiener index) in India's Shannon

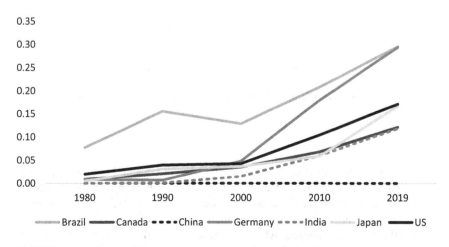

FIGURE 3.14 Graph of Shannon Wiener sub-indices of New Renewables (1980–2019).

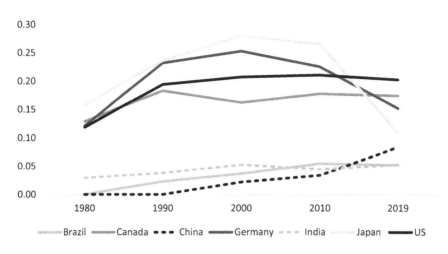

FIGURE 3.15   Graph of Shannon Wiener sub-indices of nuclear energy (1980–2019).

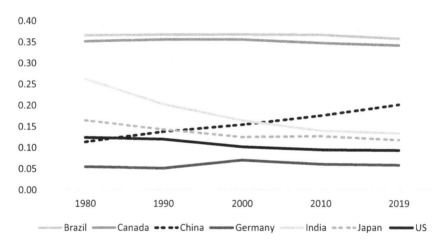

FIGURE 3.16   Graph of Shannon Wiener sub-indices of hydropower (1980–2019).

DI was 28% in 1980, even higher than what it was in USA and China. The same has now fallen to 24%. It is clear that in terms of enhancing supply diversity, clean energy in India may also hold the key to future energy use along with natural gas. It is notable that the Government has now committed a large increment to the renewable agenda, which may result in a different outcome for clean energy shares.

TABLE 3.8
Shannon Wiener Sub-Index of New Renewables

	1980	1990	2000	2010	2019
Brazil	0.08	0.16	0.13	0.21	0.30
Canada	0.01	0.02	0.04	0.07	0.12
China	0.00	0.00	0.00	0.00	0.00
Germany	0.01	0.01	0.05	0.18	0.29
India	0.00	0.00	0.02	0.06	0.12
Japan	0.01	0.03	0.04	0.06	0.17
USA	0.02	0.04	0.04	0.10	0.17

TABLE 3.9
Shannon Wiener Sub-Index of Nuclear

	1980	1990	2000	2010	2019
Brazil	0.00	0.02	0.04	0.05	0.05
Canada	0.13	0.18	0.16	0.18	0.17
China	0.00	0.00	0.02	0.03	0.08
Germany	0.12	0.23	0.25	0.23	0.15
India	0.03	0.04	0.05	0.04	0.05
Japan	0.16	0.24	0.28	0.27	0.11
USA	0.12	0.19	0.21	0.21	0.20

TABLE 3.10
Shannon Wiener Sub-Index of Hydro

	1980	1990	2000	2010	2019
Brazil	0.37	0.37	0.37	0.37	0.36
Canada	0.35	0.36	0.36	0.35	0.34
China	0.11	0.14	0.15	0.18	0.20
Germany	0.05	0.05	0.07	0.06	0.06
India	0.26	0.20	0.16	0.14	0.13
Japan	0.16	0.14	0.12	0.13	0.12
USA	0.12	0.12	0.10	0.09	0.09

3.6.5 INDIA'S SLOW GROWTH IN DI AND ROLE OF NATURAL GAS

As derived from Table 3.11, India's DI grew in every five-year interval since 1980, but fell during 2010–15. In fact, it was the only other country to have registered a decline in the above time interval (Japan is an outlier due to Fukushima event in 2011). This was exactly the period when clean energy shares remained stable

TABLE 3.11

Changes in Shannon Wiener Diversity Index on Five-Year Basis (1980–2019)

	1980–1985	1985–1990	1990–1995	1995–2000	2000–2005	2005–2010	2010–2015	2015–2019	1980–2019 Change in Index	Change in Percent
Brazil	0.16	-0.03	0.02	0.05	0.09	0.04	0.08	0.01	0.49	50
Germany	0.08	0.03	0.05	0.05	0.05	0.05	0.03	0.00	0.33	27
China	-0.06	-0.01	0.06	0.07	-0.03	0.11	0.18	0.10	0.35	45
USA	0.06	0.05	0.01	-0.01	0	0.04	0.01	-0.01	0.16	12
Japan	0.22	-0.01	0.03	0.06	0.03	0.08	-0.15	0.13	0.38	36
Canada	0.09	0.01	0.02	-0.02	0.01	0	0.02	-0.03	0.10	7
India	0.03	0.03	0.01	0.03	0.01	0.03	-0.06	0.06	0.14	14

or grew for every country including India. The above fall is not owing to fossil versus clean energy debate, but due to inter-se changes within these groups. A glance at India's energy mix in Figure 3.5 indicates that a significant change was the decline in natural gas share by 3% (from 9% in 2010 to 6% in 2019), which also saw a decline by 0.05 in the Shannon sub-index of natural gas (Table 3.7). In 2010, India's DI was satisfactory (it was well above China and not far behind that of Brazil), but in the subsequent years, decline in Shannon natural gas sub-index brought it to nearly the last place. Barring hydro where DI fell by 0.1, in no other source of energy did India see a decline in DI sub-index in the 2010–2019 period. It had earlier risen in every ten-year cohort and the overall Shannon DI had always remained above China. During 2010–19, while all other countries raced upwards, the decline in natural gas sub-index, held India back to almost where it was in 2010. It is only when new RE grew during 2010–19 that India's overall DI rose, albeit dampened by the fall in natural gas sub-index.

3.7   SUMMING UP

Energy security is a major driver of energy policy across countries with the policy being tailor-made to achieve the specific objectives that are adopted to advance the chosen understanding of the term 'energy security'. Be that as it may, high diversity in PES has been acknowledged to be a good indicator of energy security. This diversity may be in terms of variety present in energy sources, evenness in shares of sources, and high disparity between them. More the sources, lesser the dependence on one or few of them, and higher ability to deploy divergent technologies, making an economy resilient to cope up with shocks of multiple kinds. From the field of biodiversity, the statistical tool—DI—has often been applied to quantitatively evaluate energy supply diversity as a proxy for energy security. Amongst various indices, Shannon Wiener DI has generally been found to be most acceptable when variety and balance are adopted as goals of a diverse energy system. Over time, it rewards rise in fuel options and reduction in size of large sources (and conversely rise in share of smaller sources).

The study took into fold the world's top seven energy consumers of 2019 and tracked evolution in their energy diversity since 1980. In the beginning, Canada, USA and Germany were the most diverse while India, Brazil and China were the least. By 2019, with induction of at least one new source of energy (New RE that includes mainly wind/solar) variety increased and DI also increased across the countries. However, the knock-down effect of differing growth rates in fuels was passed on to their DI. As a result, inter-se position of countries changed. Now, Germany (with large share of new renewables) is the most diverse with Canada and Brazil at the second and third places. Brazil's upward climb is most dramatic and is fuelled by an effective mix of biodiesel and new RE. Japan is surprisingly at the third from bottom, but the decline of nuclear has cost it some diversity. There has been movement at the bottom, too. India has moved down one rank and is now just marginally above China which is at the bottom.

The fuel-wise evolution in energy mix of leading energy consuming countries during 1980–2019 is summarised below:

- Move away from fossil fuels: All countries except India reduced their fossil shares as a group versus clean energy. Oil shares have universally fallen.
- Rising share of natural gas: Although a fossil fuel, natural gas grew in all countries.
- Sharp reduction in share of coal: Except Japan, all countries registered a decline in coal share. In India the coal share has remained static.
- Increase in clean energy share: Nuclear, hydro and new renewables as a group have enhanced their share across the study countries except for India.
- New renewables is the new story: It is only after 2005 that new renewables have started growing across countries.
- Interplay between different clean energy technologies: It was found that no single clean technology dominates across countries. Nations made their choices as per local circumstances.

So far, just a few studies have been done on measuring the diversity of energy supply of emerging economies, thus denying policymakers an insight into virtues of introducing new fuels and thereby achieving balance amongst fuels in energy mix. In many cases dominant fuels are domestically produced, and there is an obsession of sorts with 'self-dependence' that perpetuates large shares of such fuels. This point has been further reinforced via a case study of natural gas in the following chapter. Such an approach may diminish diversity and even defeat the intended goal of energy security rather than enhancing the same. The debate regarding achieving higher diversity with higher import dependence or lower diversity with lower imports of fuels has not been settled in this study, and merely an analytical tool has been provided to the policymaker. It may, however, be suggested that with the trend shifting towards renewables such as solar and wind power, it is now possible to achieve higher diversity and even reduce imports. In the above discussion what might be the approach in India towards imported fuels including natural gas has been left to the policymaker, who may strategise towards achieving long-term security as is the case in biodiversity, which is explored through DI studies.

India's lacklustre Shannon Wiener DI performance, which has rated its energy supply diversity last amongst the study countries, has been underpinned by differing trends in its energy mix vis-à-vis others. India could not dislodge the share of its dominant fuel—coal. China and Brazil, two similarly placed emerging economies with the same number of fuel sources, were able to reduce the dominance of a particular fuel. As regards India's inability to effect major improvement in its DI, it also has to blame itself for not having retained the rising share in natural gas whose share rose between 2000 and 2010, but then fell thereafter (Hydro shares

BOX 3.1   DIVERSITY INDEX, ACHIEVEMENT OF NET-ZERO AND NATURAL GAS

As has been explained in this chapter, DI measures 'flexibility' in the energy system to adopt new fuels or dislodge an existing one. It also measures as to how balanced a country's energy mix is in terms of variety and respective shares of different sources. It offers an important diagnosis in the present scenario, on how difficult or easy would it be for India to move towards net-zero emission status. We saw that in the last four decades, India has not enhanced its diversity the way other leading nations did. Higher DI anyway indicates a diversified energy mix which is made possible by national energy policies and markets. In the absence of markets that allow consumers to exercise preferences, or transition to a more competitive or cleaner fuel, the energy mix is likely to remain rigid. In this chapter we saw that India's energy mix has inherently been rigid. We have seen as to how the share of natural gas did not grow over the last 40 years, with a small uptick for a year or two in the middle. The share of coal has remained where it was, and did not allow any appreciable increase in share of clean fuels.

If India is to achieve net-zero by 2070, it will have to allow consumers to switch to clean fuels. For a shift to lower emissions, natural gas and clean energy sources ought to replace coal. This chapter did not go into the specific reasons as to why countries display a particular scenario of fuel diversity. In the following chapter this has been discussed taking natural gas as a test case. For natural gas to play a role in India's steady march to net-zero, a comprehensive analysis is needed on the structural reasons that have inhibited a higher diversity. In the case of natural gas, sheer unavailability has been a big obstacle and may remain so in the future. Availability of adequate capacity in regasification terminals and cross-country pipeline are other important reasons. Imported supplies could surely make a difference, and there is a recent impetus towards pipelines. More of this is discussed in following chapters.

The key message here is that while fuel specific reasons may have to be gone into, however, there is an unseen hand of structural reasons that impact a nation's energy mix, and India needs to fix this for an evolution in its energy mix. At individual fuel level, there may be merits and demerits in each one of them. Contrasted with this, macro level factors such as free markets, subsidies, energy policy, and taxation on fuels are common to all and influence their fate regardless of what fuel it is. During the period when natural gas share fell in India, the share of clean energy grew at the slowest rate amongst the seven nations. This happened only because the Indian energy policies did not give any preference to use of clean fuels. For the achievement of net-zero, there will have to be positive discrimination in favour of cleaner fuels. If, the policies reward lower or no emissions like those from renewables, maybe, even gas would get a chance to edge out more polluting fossil fuels. In the following chapter, a comparison between leading energy consumers reveals as to what measures were taken by some of them to enhance the role of gas.

As the caption in this box suggests, the three terms (DI, net-zero and natural gas) are inter-linked. A higher share of natural gas would make the task of net-zero easier, and also enhance India's DI in the process. The other side of the coin of a low DI/high share of few fuels, is that the task of moderating the share of the dominant fuel becomes easier. A candidate, and in the case of India, it would be coal be would the target fuel for reduction. It would also be easier for India because to achieve an energy transition, India does not need to rollback a fuel sub-system, but just control its further growth in the rising energy demand scenario. Further, a mature fuel usually may not decline in technology costs as no innovation takes place in a fuel that is ebbing. On the other hand, the incoming fuel is usually a new fuel wherein cost reductions are more likely due to innovations taking place. Once the newer fuels get a foothold, then energy mix is likely to achieve a fair balance thus resulting in high DI as well. This intersection of three aspects of India's energy system would make the task of achieving net-zero easier. The current status of India's DI hints that it may not be that easy either for natural gas or renewables to dislodge fossil fuels in a significant manner. In the last chapter on policy recommendations, it has been purported that a revamped integrated energy policy alone may be the answer to some of the issues faced by India to realise its cherished energy agenda.

have been falling consistently since 1980). As regards the outlook for the future, India and China have a large share of coal and are also bracketed at the bottom in terms of Shannon DI (2019). China has drastically reduced its share of coal and enhanced clean energy shares, which is helping its diversity. At this rate, it may not be surprising if, China overtakes India in this relative ranking in the next couple of years.

India is a major energy consumer, and as per IEA, post-2020, it will contribute to the largest annual increments to energy demand in the world. It is also a large fossil fuel consumer which compulsively draws the attention of climate change analysts. As revealed in the present analysis, its supply diversity has grown at the slowest rate, which does not even serve its energy security objectives. This research is perhaps first of its kind to offer an insight into the poor growth in diversity in Indian energy system in direct comparison with other large consumers. The need to introduce the concept of DI in energy security debates of large energy consuming emerging countries, can reveal new insights for bringing in reduction in fossil fuel shares accompanied by uptake of clean energy.

NOTES

1 Babajide (2018) has offered a short analysis of energy insecurity arising out of India's large oil import dependence by applying DI. Even Koyama (2012) has offered a limited analysis of diversity of India and several East Asian countries, without looking at fuel-wise sub-indices that has been attempted in this chapter.

2 The data for undivided Germany is available seamlessly, mainly by BP, even for the period before its re-unification in 1990.

3 It is notable that coal contributes high share in supply terms (PES) but after suffering large conversion losses as compared to other fossil fuels, its share in final (delivered) energy much reduces.

4 Cooke et al. (2013) argued that diversity is 'context specific' particularly when addressing 'disparity'. In this chapter we do not take up 'disparity' as an indicator of diversity.

5 Chalvatzis and Ioannidis (2017) used both Shannon and HH to measure supply diversity for EU. However, they were looking at market concentration for oil and natural gas.

6 Jansen et al. (2004) based on their study of Stirling's work on Diversity, they found Shannon Wiener to be the 'most attractive simple' index.

7 This output is similar to Law of Varying Proportions in Micro-Economics.

8 Wu and Rai (2017) have tracked diversity of power generation sources in electricity supply of states and regional entities in the US over a two-decade period (1990–2010).

9 Kucharski and Unesaki (2018) have examined the institutional analysis of Japan's energy transition and stated that Japan had 'a stable but rigid and inflexible energy system'. However, a statistical analysis with DI reveals flexibility in energy shares.

10 Kruyt et al. (2009) have discussed how fall in China's coal share increases its diversity while a similar drop in Europe decreases it due to the differences in size of coal shares.

4 Growth of Natural Gas in India
A Comparative Study

4.1 BACKGROUND

India's large import dependence in the energy sector may be addressed in near time as the government assigns high priority to the domestic production of hydrocarbons. The government had earlier aimed to reduce oil import dependency to 67% by 2022 (at the time of declaration of this intent it was 77%), reduce coal imports, and enhance domestic natural gas production for which an attractive pricing policy for the producers was announced (Shishir Sinha, 2018; ET, 2020). While the achievement of the above targets may be missed out, the policy direction is clear. Natural gas-related objectives have always been central to the energy strategy. India Hydrocarbon Vision (IHV) 2025, formulated in 1999, and the Integrated Energy Policy of 2008 had both laid emphasis on enhancing the role of natural gas in the primary energy supply (PES) (Srivastava, 2009; MoPNG, 2010). Even the present government has made a bold announcement that its share would be raised to 15% by 2030 (it was 6% in 2015). To achieve this goal, interventions have been made across the value chain—upstream, transportation and marketing.

Many analysts observe that a high natural gas share in India hinges on domestic production, and this has been discussed earlier. There is the option of imported LNG, too. India has for long followed a dual natural gas pricing policy for domestic and RLNG, and it is often held responsible for the subdued demand for the latter. In the light of price distortions, it is not easy to assess the future role of natural gas especially of market-priced RLNG, and this is acknowledged in scholarly articles (Rogers, 2016). Pricing in the Indian energy sector has a long demonstrated history of subsidies and the government has found it difficult to transition to free energy markets. However, a good beginning has recently been made by implementing reforms in petroleum pricing (Jain, 2018). The above move is likely to pave the way for a level playing field for natural gas. Natural gas forms a significant portfolio in many countries and it is not that all of them have significant domestic production. Some of them are large importers, too. Both supply and demand side factors seem to have helped achieve significant natural gas share. An enquiry into the above might help in identifying any common factors that support natural gas, and also as to whether the absence of these factors has hampered its progress in India.

The price competitiveness of natural gas has been taken up later in this book, and only structural drivers that have worked over a period of time figure in this chapter. A historical perspective might help analysts and policymakers to devise supportive policies for the future. The study has been undertaken on the seven largest energy-consuming countries of the world for 2019, and compares the Indian case for an in-depth enquiry. This chapter takes up three questions briefly stated below:

- What factors/consuming sectors are responsible for higher growth in demand for natural gas within major energy-consuming countries?
- Has the impact of the above factors been consistent across countries?
- Which of the above factors have been responsible for lack of growth of natural gas in India?

By specifically answering the above questions, the building of India's natural gas demand scenarios in Chapter 7 may be better appreciated.

4.2   APPROACH ADOPTED FOR ANALYSIS

The main approach followed herein is analysis of documents, particularly of data and literature relating to natural gas demand and supply in the study countries. Here again, the world's seven top energy consumers ranked as per consumption of commercial energy in 2019 have been selected (on the same lines as in Chapter 3).[1] Figure 4.1 offers the ranks of the top energy consumers of 2019, along with their energy consumption. The top seven consumers comprise a balanced mix. Four of them are OECD countries (USA, Canada, Japan and Germany) and the remaining three are emerging economies (China, India and Brazil). They include natural gas

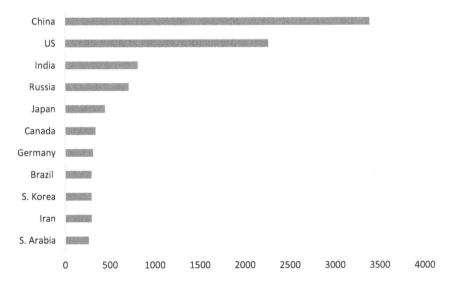

FIGURE 4.1   Top energy consumers in 2019 (in Mtoe) (BP, 2020).

producers and importers as well as countries with low and high share of natural gas. We have seen in the last chapter that most of them have over last several decades undergone major transition from fossil to clean energy. The definitions of clean energy and New Renewables are the same as what has been followed in the previous chapter.

As in Chapter 3, to accommodate for adequate time for an energy system transition and development of new sources, the study covers a medium term of nearly four decades (1980–2019). A number of studies exist where a sample of countries has been taken and their energy system fully analysed over a three-decade long period (Atalla et al., 2017). The start of study from 1980 allows for the upheaval caused by the 1973 oil crisis to have settled down, and the tenure of the study being 39 years ending in 2019, allows sufficient time to note the medium-term structural transition that may have taken place.[2] Table 4.1 offers a snapshot of natural gas-related data of the currently chosen countries.

For this study, a number of supply and demand side factors have been identified as possible drivers of natural gas in energy mix. On supply side, the need for diversity was discussed in the previous chapter. Furthermore, the role of domestic production of natural gas and availability of pipelines, particularly for expansion of CGD networks, were identified as critical factors for growth of natural gas. On

TABLE 4.1
Natural Gas-Related Parameters of Major Energy-Consuming Countries

		Natural Gas (in Mtoe)		
	Year	Production	Exports	Consumption
Brazil	1980	0.9	0	0.9
	2019	22	(−8.4)	31
Canada	1980	61	18	43
	2019	149	42.3	103
China	1980	12	0	12
	2019	153	(−113.9)	264
Germany	1980	17	(−35)[a]	52
	2019	5	(−94.2)[a]	76
India	1980	1	0	1
	2019	23	(−28.3)[a]	51
Japan	1980	1	(−22)[b]	23
	2019	0	(−90.7)[b]	93
USA	1980	451	(−8)	459
	2019	792	0.5	728

Source: BP (2019) Export of natural gas in 1980 has been derived from production/consumption numbers.

[a] by pipeline; [b] as LNG; others by both.

Note: Consumption numbers do not add up due to internal use, etc.

the demand side, it was discussed that in several countries particularly China and Russia, power sector drew large volumes of natural gas. Hence, the link between anchor demand sectors and significance of natural gas to a country is evident. Further, the low emission property of natural gas, and what was seen in Germany regarding the impact of the clean energy policies in encouraging natural gas, was also acknowledged. Rising energy demand in India has also been factored in the scheme of things. However, this may not be valid for developed economies where energy demand has now stabilised, but when historical perspective is taken, it becomes relevant because energy demand did grow in the past within all the study specific countries. Following the key findings of previous chapter, the role of the supply and demand side factors as under have been taken up—first two are of supply side and latter three of demand origin:

Supply side

- Role of domestic natural gas production
- Availability of natural gas supply infrastructure

Demand side

- Role of anchor demand sectors
- Association between clean energy and natural gas
- Is rising energy demand a driver of natural gas demand?

In the discussion below, first the supply levers are discussed to be followed by the demand ones across the seven countries, and concluded by a dedicated section on India.

4.3   ANALYSIS OF IMPACT OF SUPPLY AND DEMAND SIDE LEVERS ON NATURAL GAS CONSUMPTION

Natural gas is a naturally endowed resource and domestic production is an important factor. It can also be imported, but price goes up due to costs involved in liquefaction/regasification (for LNG) and transportation. Supply-related factors have historically played an important role, with healthy growth of natural gas initially restricted to the nearby markets (Rogers, 2012). On demand side, too, consumer category with specialised process equipment such as compressed natural gas (CNG) vehicles, urea plants, gas-based power plants and petrochemical units is a must. There may be policy factors, too, particularly related to promotion of clean energy.

4.3.1   Supply Side Drivers

Until 1970s, natural gas was consumed largely within natural gas producing countries. Gradually pipelines were setup and natural gas trade grew in the neighbourhood of the above countries. In 1970, trade through pipelines accounted for

43 BCM, while LNG was a mere 2.7 BCM (Stern, 2012). The combined natural gas trade in 1980 through both these means of export comprised 14% of total natural gas consumption, which has now grown to 33% of total natural gas consumed in 2019. In the meanwhile, countries that did not have any natural gas option developed other sources of energy. Globally in 1965 itself, the first year for which data is freely available, oil and coal already had an individual share of 42% and 37%, respectively in global energy mix, while natural gas was at 14.6% which by 1980 gradually grew to 18.4%.[3] Therefore, depending upon local factors, early commitment to fuel types, seems to have shaped up the energy mix of countries. This aspect has been examined in this study. Globally there is ample natural gas availability and as per IEA, 'The stage appears to be set for natural gas to thrive, at least in relative terms, over the coming decades' (IEA, 2019). While availability of natural gas in international markets is expected to be sufficient, but how much imported gas might India receive, will be directly dependent on the capacity of the infrastructure at ports and transnational pipelines to deliver natural gas to the country. As far as overland overseas supplies are concerned, there is no indication of its realisation in the near future. However, there is an expectation of a large LNG regasification (or regas) capacity coming up in the future. Two important supply side factors—domestic production and availability of infrastructure for imported supplies—are taken up below.

4.3.1.1   Role of Domestic Natural Gas Production

Globally, natural Gas production grew from 1,228 in 1980 to over 3,431 Mtoe by 2019, raising its share to 24% in global energy mix (BP, 2020). Incidentally, the major producers were also the major consumers—in 1980, two-thirds of world's natural gas consumption and production took place in two countries only, namely, USA and USSR (BP, 2019). Other large natural gas producers of that time such as Canada, Netherland, Romania and UK, were also large consumers. Even presently, over half of global natural gas consumption takes place in nine countries that also happen to be the captive producers—USA, Canada, Russia, UAE, Malaysia, Indonesia, Qatar, Iran and Saudi Arabia. Natural gas trade at 33% of total natural gas consumption enforces the point that local production is a major driver of its consumption. In the study specific countries, a high correlation of 0.91 existed between local natural gas production (represented by share of domestic natural gas production in PES), and share of natural gas consumption in PES in 1980, which has now come down to 0.7 in 2019 (Table 4.2). Hence, large capacity domestic natural gas producers did not export it, but mostly used it locally—also establishing yet again that production and consumption patterns are interlinked (there may be other reasons, too). At the same time, the decline in the above correlation indicates that with growing trade in natural gas, production and consumption are now lesser linked than earlier times.

Coming to the world's top seven energy consumers, in Table 4.2, the relationship between domestically produced natural gas and share of gas in PES has been presented. In 2019, the top two natural gas consumers (and large gas producers), Canada and USA had a share of domestic gas production in their PES at 44% and

TABLE 4.2

Natural gas production and share of gas consumption in PES (1980 and 2019)

Country	Natural Gas Production (A) Mtoe		PES (B) Mtoe		Natural gas Production in PES A/B in %		Natural Gas Consumption in PES in %	
	1980	2019	1980	2019	1980	2019	1980	2019
Brazil	1	22	91	296	0	7	1	10
Canada	64	149	218	339	29.4	44	22	30
India	0	23	102	813	0	3	1	6
Japan	1	0	356	446	0	0	6	21
USA	502	792	1,811	2,260	27.7	35	28	32
Germany	17	5	358	314	5	1	15	24
China	13	153	417	3,384	31/3	5	3	8

Source: BP (2020), correlation has been calculated.
Correlation of share of domestic natural gas and its consumption in PES: 0.91 (1980), 0.7 (2019).

35%, respectively. Natural gas share in PES of Canada may have been even higher if, there had been no natural gas exports (export data is in Table 4.1). In the UK, too, when natural gas production was rising (until 2000), consumption also grew alongside (Skea et al., 2012). Thereafter, both parameters peaked together and started falling. On the other hand, countries without substantial natural gas production in comparison to their energy demand, namely, India, China and Brazil, have historically had low shares of natural gas. In Japan and Germany, however, with insignificant domestic production, imports helped achieve a significant share of natural gas in their PES. The factors which made this happen are discussed later.

4.3.1.2   Availability of Gas Supply Infrastructure

Even with negligible natural gas production, Germany's high share of natural gas was made possible by early development of pipelines thus connecting it with gas producing countries in the region. In fact, Germany (and Austria) funded the construction of trunk pipelines through barter trade with USSR, supplying pipes to the latter on credit for term sale of gas (Högselius et al., 2010). As early as in 1982, West Germany was receiving 43 BCM natural gas from western Europe and Soviet Union through pipelines against its total consumption of 54 BCM (Högselius et al., 2010; BP, 2019b). Another country in Germany's neighbourhood, France, has had a similar natural gas story without any captive production. France was receiving 21 BCM out of its total natural gas consumption of 24.6 BCM via pipelines from western Europe, Soviet Union and Algeria. On the other hand, Japan owes its large natural gas consumption to LNG, a technology of which it was an early adopter. It received its first LNG cargo way back in 1969 from Alaska, and is now one of the world's largest LNG importers (DOE, 2013; IGU, 2019). While pipelines were a natural monopoly earlier, but LNG infrastructure, both for liquefaction and regasification, has become vital for countries that do not have pipeline connectivity. In Europe alone, between 1999 and 2016, the LNG import capacity grew by nearly 350% from 64.3 to 225.6 BCM/year (Chyong, 2019). China and Brazil have now built both pipeline and LNG capabilities that support a growing share of natural gas in their PES. Globally, LNG now comprises of more than 10% of the total natural gas consumption (2016) (IGU, 2019).

The construction of pipelines and LNG terminals has provided a head start to countries to enable a large natural gas supply even without domestic production. The provision of surplus supply capacity in the above infrastructure for future growth has helped to attain large growth in natural gas uptake. In five-member countries of the EU (Greece, Spain, Lithuania, Portugal and Sweden), even though there were other supply sources of natural gas, a large LNG regasification capacity was created that was enough to cover the entire natural gas consumption of 2017 (Biały et al., 2019). Large requirement of capital in building up such infrastructure is an investment hurdle, but once committed for, it pays to exploit it fully. In its 1998 edition of World Energy Outlook (WEO), the IEA has stated as below (IEA, 1998):

> Once the substantial capital investments in gas delivery systems have been made, the marginal cost of delivering gas in the short term is low, provided spare capacity to deliver exists. Hence demand will be encouraged until full capacity is reached.

In contrast, natural gas distribution in various cities within India is of recent vintage.[4] A handful of cities in Gujarat were the first to receive natural gas through a CGD network in 1990. Delhi and Mumbai got covered only around 1995. On the other hand, USA and European countries had fully developed urban networks much earlier.

BP Statistics (2020) show that domestic production of natural gas has a significant link with its consumption pattern and high share in PES. IEA (1998) has described that natural gas infrastructure also played a crucial role in terms of increasing share of natural gas in the energy mix. IGU (2019) argued that LNG use is increasing, mainly due to its ease in transportation. LNG terminals are being built all across the world and this has helped in increasing its utilisation. In Europe alone, the LNG import capacity increased by 350% between 1999 and 2016. There are few other reasons, too.

4.3.2 DEMAND SIDE DRIVERS

Multiple fuel supply options including natural gas, offer fuel choices and enable consumers to shift to natural gas. While it is difficult to state which came first, supply side factors or demand side ones, presently it is quite clear that several demand side factors are available in countries with large gas consumption. The latter would be needed in any country aiming for a large gas consumption. This has been examined in some detail below.

4.3.2.1   Role of Anchor Demand Sectors

Power, industries, buildings and non-combustible use (urea) are amongst the main natural gas-consuming sectors, in that order. The analysis below classifies total natural gas demand by consuming sectors in the study countries. It is notable that there is no one particular sector that can be identified with large natural gas consumption. In countries that were early adopters of natural gas, it was essentially the industry that laid the foundation of a vibrant natural gas sector (even globally). USA, Canada and Germany, where natural gas had already assumed a high share in PES in 1980 (also China), it was industry that in the initial stages was the largest consuming sector (Figure 4.2a–g). In due course, other sectors grew, and by

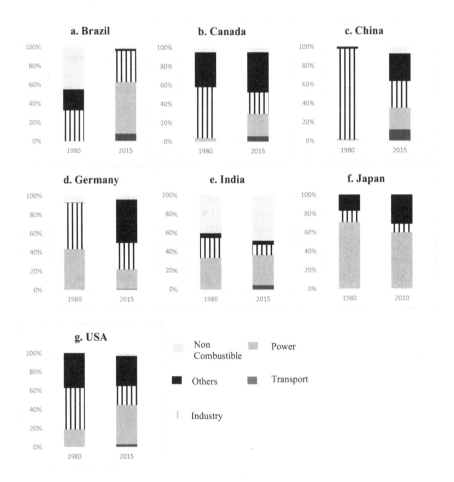

FIGURE 4.2 (a–g) Natural gas consumption by sectors (in %) (1980 and 2015). *Note:* IEA classifies natural gas used as feedstock in industries as non-combustible (IEA, 2017).

2015 industry had been toppled by power generation from the first position globally. Even in countries where natural gas has become important only recently, it is not industry but different sectors that took the first lead. In India and Brazil, it was non-combusted natural gas use (in urea manufacture, etc.), while in Japan it was power generation. Presently, too, different sectors dominate across both categories of countries—those that took an early lead to take up natural gas and others where natural gas is a recent phenomenon. This has been discussed below.

Due to the desirable properties of lesser emissions and ability in gas turbines to start-up and back-down quickly, natural gas is often hailed as a preferred source of power generation (BP, 2019).[5] In the case of yet another major natural gas consumer, UK, both system stability and price have played a major role. Pye et al. (2015) have conducted sensitivity analysis of selected important parameters of energy systems of the UK to understand the impact of uncertainty on system costs and subsequent achievement of the targeted objective. It revealed that natural gas price is the most sensitive parameter for the UK in terms of its power generation to achieve lower GHG emissions target. They argued the importance of natural gas in a low carbon power generation scenario and subsequent impact of natural gas on an overall energy supply security of the country.

Globally, the share of natural gas-based power in total generation has nearly doubled between 1980 and 2015, from 12% to 23%, respectively (IEA, 2017). At the same time, it does not necessarily mean that in countries that have a high share of total natural gas consumption going to power, natural gas comprises a major source of power generation. In Brazil, nearly 45% of all natural gas consumed went into power, but natural gas-based power comprised only 14% of all power generated. From Figure 4.3a–g, it is evident that large energy-consuming countries have a diversified power sector.

Presently, natural gas-based power does not play an important role in most of the large countries, except in Japan and USA where it contributes to nearly one-third of all power generated (Figure 4.3f and g). With different consuming sectors dominating consumption of natural gas in different countries, the overall thrust of the argument is that for natural gas to grow in a country, the presence of a particular anchor consuming sector (least of all power) is not essential.

4.3.2.2 Impetus to Clean Energy and Its Impact on Demand for Natural Gas

Looking to its low carbon intensity accompanied by calls for adoption of natural gas over other fossil fuels, it needs to be examined whether this aspect has ultimately helped natural gas to grow or not. Conversely, with impetus to newer clean technologies in the recent past, it also remains to be seen whether natural gas has faced headwinds from them. From Figure 4.4 it is apparent that it is only after 2,000 that new renewables (wind, solar and small hydro) started growing at a rapid rate, and are now leading to an uptick in the overall share of clean energy (including large hydro and nuclear). Figure 4.4 captures the data for multiple time spots over the period 1980–2019, and it is evident that up to 2,000 the market shares of new renewables such as solar and wind were almost negligible.

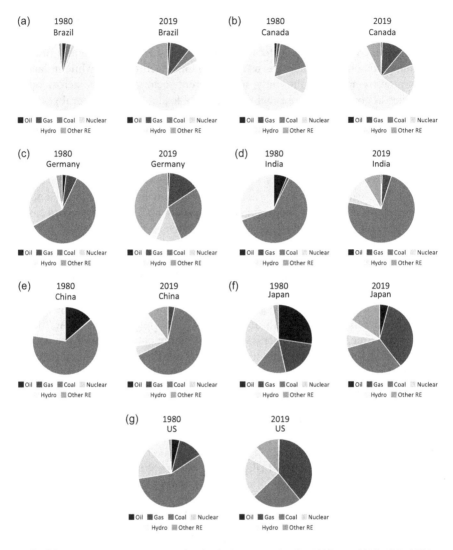

FIGURE 4.3   (a–g) Power generation by fuel sources (in %) (1980 and 2019) (BP, 2020).

As the new renewables are a post 2,000 phenomenon, they have helped the share of clean energy grow in relative importance in the 21st century itself. The above transition can be well appreciated by dividing the period of the instant study (1980–2019) into two phases that distinguish the developments prior to their induction on a rapid rate—pre-2005 (1980–2005) and post-2005 (2005–19). In the graphs below (Figure 4.5a–g), the association of natural gas with clean energy has been tracked. Even though the time period in these two phases of the instant study is dissimilar (25 and 14 years), as merely trends and not absolute numbers are being evaluated, the above phases may be useful to examine whether these

TABLE 4.3

Increases in PES and Natural Gas Demand During 1980–2005 and 2005–2019 (%)

	PES	Natural Gas Demand	PES	Natural Gas Demand
	1980–2005		2005–2019	
Brazil	132%	1,700%	40%	78%
Germany	−7%	49%	−7%	−2%
China	332%	238%	87%	554%
India	286%	3,100%	106%	74%
US	30%	12%	−2%	42%
Canada	48%	87%	7%	39%
Japan	46%	227%	−16%	31%

Source: Data sourced from BP (2019b).

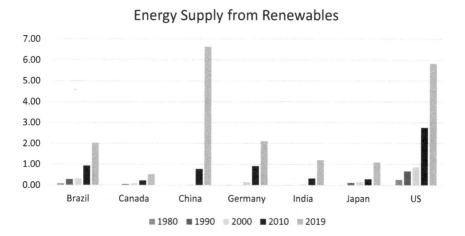

FIGURE 4.4 Growth trends in new renewables (1980–2019) in Mtoe. (Data sourced from BP, 2020.)

new sources helped in growth of natural gas.[6] The answer to the above question is generally in the affirmative for both the phases.

At the outset, it may be mentioned that induction of new renewables that drove clean energy shares has not dramatically changed the profile of clean energy in the study specific countries in the post-2005 era. Barring India, shares of both have grown. Furthermore, growth in clean energy has been higher in all countries over India. The growth in natural gas appears to complement clean energy, which is interesting because it is a fossil fuel and is thus not a member of the clean

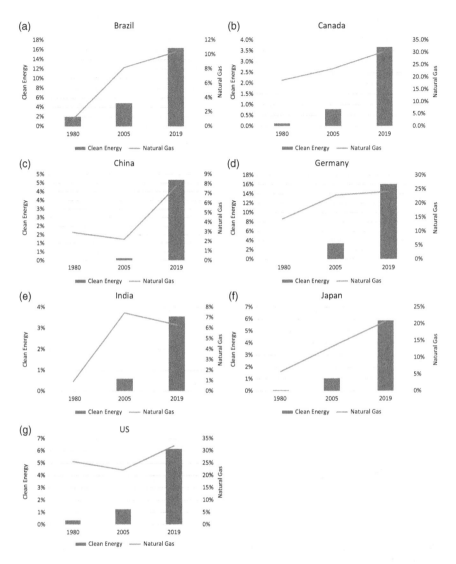

FIGURE 4.5 (a–g) Trends in share of natural gas and clean energy 1980–2019 (%) in PES. (Data sourced from BP, 2020.)

energy family. USA shows an interesting trend of a decline in natural gas in the pre-2005 era even when clean energy was growing. It is notable that availability of the former increased only in the post-2005 era when the shale gas-related developments took place. In Germany, now at higher shares of clean energy, share of natural gas is flattening. It may then be generally concluded that within the basket of all fuels, with the growing share of clean energy, natural gas has also received the much-needed impetus—a positive association.

4.3.2.3 Adoption of Natural Gas in Countries with Rising Energy Demand

Rising energy demand offers a significant opportunity to different fuels to grow their volumes, and particular fuels may even enhance their share in total energy availability. It needs to be seen whether natural gas demand grew in those countries where PES has increased. During the overall study period of 39 years, it is seen that overall energy demand grew in six out of seven countries during pre-2005 period, and thereafter it grew in four countries.[7] Table 4.3 charts the growth in total demand for energy, and natural gas demand, both in percentage contribution terms.

During the first phase (pre-2005), with increase in energy demand, natural gas demand grew in all countries. In the second phase (2005–19) also natural gas demand grew in all countries, with Germany as a lone exception, where demand fell. As the percentage increase in natural gas was correspondingly higher than an overall growth in PES within the five countries, natural gas share in PES also rose in these five countries. India is an outlier where energy demand grew but consumption of natural gas did not grow in the same or larger ratio (connects with the role of natural gas in restraining the DI of India). In this period, three countries registered a decline in energy demand (Germany, USA and Japan). Within EU, in the recent years particularly between 2008 and 2018, natural gas share in PES has been steady at 22%–26% (Biały et al., 2019).

The above data also indicates that regardless of energy demand growing or not, natural gas demand has grown in the study countries during 1980–2019. The above discussion establishes that natural gas demand grew faster than the growth in demand for overall energy demand in most of the study countries, perhaps because they included more of cleaner fuels including natural gas in their kitty. In post-2005 phase, it was only in Germany and India that natural gas shares fell.

4.3.3 DEMAND SIDE VERSUS SUPPLY SIDE

It then follows that enhanced availability of natural gas through domestic production, and to some extent even via pipelines, had led to its early uptake. Japan is the only country with a high natural gas share, where the supply comes from LNG and not via domestic production. China, yet another large energy consumer like India, is unable to meet natural gas demand through domestic production alone, and has a high ambition to raise its share in PES from 6.4% in 2016 to 15% by 2030. But, the above target is not expected to be met even if, imports were augmented (Rioux et al., 2019). The earlier discussion has also indicated that while supply factors have mattered for sure, demand side factors have largely had an indifferent role to play. Additionally, no particular consuming sector has been found to drive natural gas demand—all sectors are amenable to substantial natural gas uptake.

Clean energy shares are displacing fossil fuels but not natural gas (also a fossil fuel). Lastly, energy demand is both rising in some countries, and falling in several others (especially in OECD). However, natural gas demand does not depend on any new energy demand for it to grow—but it has been found to grow regardless of—and is displacing other fuels across the study countries with some exceptions.

4.4   COMPARISON BETWEEN INDIA AND OTHER COUNTRIES

The analysis undertaken in this chapter offers a good opportunity to examine the historical growth of natural gas in India's PES and thus compare it with other leading countries of the world. Within the cohort of the seven study countries, both Brazil and India had a low natural gas share of 1% each in their PES in 1980. In contrast, by 2019, Brazil had raced ahead with a 10% share while natural gas in India was still at 6%. On the other hand, China, another slow starter has grown on the same lines as India at a small rate, with its natural gas share rising gradually from 3% in 1980 to 8% in 2019. The other four countries have much higher use of natural gas than what it is in India. Small natural gas production and no pipeline connectivity with overseas gas fields in India, has resulted in a poor share of natural gas in commercial PES.

The following few are the major points of differences between India and other countries:

• Natural gas share easily grew in those countries that had domestic gas production. India has suffered from the absence of a robust domestic production, and even at present, India does not have a favourable indigenous gas production outlook.
• In countries with poor domestic production but availability of natural gas in the neighbourhood, transnational pipelines helped develop a large natural gas portfolio. However, in spite of large natural gas reserves in India's neighbourhood, and even when there was an early start of LNG, India has not been able to develop these options in a significant manner.
• For natural gas to achieve a higher share, the presence of a particular demand sector was not found to be essential in the study countries. For a country like India with a diversified presence of all consuming sectors, the low share of natural gas in PES does stand out.
• It has been seen that supported by new renewable technologies (mainly wind and solar), shares of clean energy as a group as well as natural gas have been growing across most of the developed countries studied in this chapter. However, in India clean energy has not grown robustly, (particularly between 1980 and 2005 period), and natural gas share has been negatively correlated with clean energy during the entire 39-year study period with a moderately higher share than what existed in 1980.
• Demand (and share) of natural gas has been found to be rising across study countries, regardless of PES growing or not. However, despite a sustained

growth in energy demand in India, in the last decade while natural gas demand (Mtoe terms) has gone up, its share in commercial PES has fallen.

The volatility in share of natural gas in PES have led many observers to conclude that the clue to India's natural gas story lies on the supply side. There has been the LNG option also, which has, however, not fared well so far. On the demand side, even the large presence of anchor natural gas-consuming sectors such as buildings and power has not boosted LNG supply in India. On the other hand, policymakers have been tinkering with policies on both the supply and demand sides, in an expectation that natural gas share might somehow rise. The debate continues as to whether it would ever assume its due importance in the Indian energy system. The historical perspective analysed in this chapter might help in examining the issues closer in the following chapter.

4.5   SUMMARY

Three relevant questions were identified for examination in this chapter. The first and second ones are being addressed together. Domestic production has been found to be an important factor in promoting natural gas. A high correlation (moderating in 2019) exists between the volume of domestically produced natural gas and its consumption. Import infrastructure such as transnational pipeline is an important factor, too. Some countries without substantial natural gas domestic production could achieve its high share via pipelines, but this option is not available to all (there needs to be natural gas in neighbourhood). In recent years, LNG is also helping, but only Japan has exhibited an LNG-led natural gas story. An important outcome of this study has been that anchor consuming sectors have not been found to play a defining role in natural gas demand growth. Coming to the next demand factor, it has been seen that the recent global impetus for clean energy has not impacted natural gas demand adversely, and both have prospered together in most of the countries. Lastly, energy demand and natural gas consumption have not been found to be a necessary trigger for growth—natural gas demand and its share in PES have grown regardless of rising overall energy demand or not. What follows from above is that with demand side largely being supportive, it is the supply side, mainly domestic production, that has played a bigger role in promoting natural gas.

The third question has been discussed below and the following main outcomes have been found:

- India's case is consistent with such countries as did not have a comfortable supply position—poor supply scenario leading to low natural gas share.
- On demand side, all anchor sectors exist—power, industry, non-combustible and buildings. But, despite their presence, natural gas share has remained static—an inconsistency with the findings of the study for other countries.

BOX 4.1   ROLE OF NATURAL GAS IN
SUPPORTING ENERGY TRANSITION

This chapter continues the analysis of comparative growth of natural gas in major energy-consuming countries and its role in helping achieve a cleaner energy mix. Here the chapter attempts to draw messages from the experience of other countries that might be relevant for India in the context of the wholesome attainment of the target of net-zero.

There is adequate evidence that natural gas does support clean energy transition. The share of natural gas and that of clean energy in the PES of most large energy-consuming countries (except India) is high. On the other hand, India's low clean energy share corresponds with its low share of natural gas (Table 3.1). While the two may not be correlated, in other countries studied in this chapter, the relationship was found to be quite strong. It is noted that both fuels have grown over the study period of the last four decades. There is also an acknowledgement that the two are not antagonistic to one another. In India, the share of both these fuels have grown over the years, albeit they are lower than the shares for other countries. Perhaps, at higher levels, share of natural gas gets de-linked with clean energy (there may be a pushback as it is also a fossil fuel). Having attained high share in Germany, natural gas seems to have plateaued.

Delving into the hidden variable that links natural gas with clean energy, it can be observed that natural gas is itself 'cleaner' than other fossil fuels, and countries that prefer clean energy sources also encourage natural gas. Gas-fired power plants can operate flexibly and thus help balance intermittent renewable power. It is also evident that natural gas was already established as an energy source several decades back, whereas New Renewables have grown in importance only in the 21st century. In 1980, the share of natural gas was already 20% in the global energy mix. As regards the future, there is a buzz that the infrastructure created for natural gas such as pipelines may find a second use for clean energy sources. Hydrogen can be pumped into natural gas pipelines up to a certain degree of blending (around 20%). And when hydrogen costs come down substantially from their present levels and technology improves, it may substitute natural gas entirely, and be piped in the same pipelines to consumers. With an imminent expansion in natural gas pipelines in India, this possibility may further encourage CGD investors to go ahead with their investment plans, and thus not worry about the net-zero commitments of India that might eventually impact natural gas adversely.

At Glasgow while the world agreed for a 'phase down' of coal, there was no commitment on natural gas. It is quite likely that soon the world's attention will converge on natural gas, too. For India, a question will engage some attention, whether to increase this fuel or not, especially as more of this is being imported with a large outflow of foreign exchange, and is not domestically well endowed, as well as it being a fossil fuel. This issue will be clarified only when India launches its strategy/road map for steps to be taken towards fulfilling the target of net-zero.

It, therefore, follows that in the quest for net-zero goal, India needs to consider the option of natural gas carefully. It was also shown in this chapter that a fall in share of natural gas, in fact, brought down the diversity of the Indian fuel system and enhanced energy insecurity. Hence, natural gas corresponds positively with higher diversity, and supports the assertion that natural gas may be a bridge fuel to net-zero.

- The phenomenon as observed elsewhere of clean energy and natural gas demand growing together has not been seen in India. When clean energy share fell initially, natural gas share rose, and in recent decade the two fuels have reversed the trend in direct terms of clean energy share rising and that of natural gas falling.
- A robust growth in energy demand in India has also not helped the cause of natural gas—other fuels grew at a higher rate than natural gas in the last decade (2005–19).

In the initial stage, the supply side has to be strong for a fuel to prosper, and India's natural gas supply scenario has been weak. Lack of domestic production and absence of transnational gas pipelines has indeed made it difficult to develop a natural gas-denominated story. Now LNG receiving terminals have come up and this is helping make up for poor domestic production. Earlier, the rising energy demand and presence of natural gas-consuming sectors were supportive. Another desirable demand side factor—impetus to clean energy—was earlier absent, however, in the past decade an ambitious new renewables capacity is underway. While natural gas and clean energy have generally been found to have grown together particularly in post-2005 phase, natural gas has not been found to have benefitted in India by the moves made in favour of clean energy. This raises a doubt on the case for natural gas, a 'clean' fossil fuel. For India, it calls for a deeper study on the supportive role or otherwise of natural gas especially in light of the ambitious targets set for renewables.

In the light of both supply and demand side enablers being present, natural gas does seem poised to grow. In the following chapter, an incisive analysis has been undertaken exclusively on the Indian natural gas supply options, followed by a discussion on prices and demand scenarios.

NOTES

1 Unless specified otherwise, all references in this chapter pertaining to PES refer to commercial energy supplies.

2 For example, the 1973 oil crisis led to a conscious decision in Japan to reduce oil consumption, resulting in decline from 77% share in PES in 1973 to 67% in 1980 (40% in 2019). Even USA undertook a major overhaul of its domestic energy policy.

3 Historical energy data is available freely in BP Statistical Review of World Energy, which gives data from 1965.

4 Local distribution to townships and tea gardens near gas-fields in north eastern India had begun earlier.

5 In 2015, power sector consumed 38% of total gas consumption.

6 In Atalla et al. (2017) different time periods (even number of years) for analysing uptake of fossil fuels in the study countries have been decided on the basis of developments relevant to specific countries.

7 Germany has registered reduction in its energy demand in both phases.

5 Natural Gas Supply Outlook

5.1 INTRODUCTION

As discussed in the previous chapter, India does not have significant proven reserves of natural gas. With nearly 17% of the world population, India's oil and natural gas reserves are just 0.4% and 0.6% of the global reserves (BP Statistics, 2020). Natural gas had become a serious option for India amongst different stakeholders nearly two decades back, largely due to the emergence of R-LNG as an option (India received its first LNG cargo in 2004 even before China did). This was supplemented by the world-size discovery of natural gas reserves in the offshore Krishna Godavari (KG) Basin (in the Bay of Bengal) during the same year. When the domestic production scenario became encouraging, it was perceived to be a game changer. The regulatory environment was quickly provided by the government in the following years by the announcement of the Gas Utilisation Policy and Gas Pipeline Policy. While the former was meant to prioritise consuming sectors, the latter opened up the possibility of laying gas pipelines by the private sector, which was hitherto an exclusive preserve of GAIL, the government-owned gas company.[1] The PNGRB was set up with passage by the Parliament of a dedicated Act in 2006. While anticipating the availability of domestic gas, a number of gas-based power plants were announced by the private sector, especially in the coastal region close to KG Basin, and even the Fertiliser Ministry took a key decision to convert all naphtha-based urea plants to natural gas feedstock. The above moves were accompanied by a race within consumers, to stake claim to be the first recipients of this fuel, and may be called the Indian version of the British 'Dash for Gas'.

As has been experienced in the succeeding years, the above supply scenario did not match the real expectations. Both supply options—domestic production and R-LNG supply—did not grow appreciably after an initial burst of activity. With the start of production from KG Basin fields, there was a spurt in share of natural gas in commercial PES in 2010, reaching 9%, the highest ever. But, when production from the same fields fell in the subsequent year itself, share of natural gas fell to its earlier level and even lower in later years. After a decade or so in 2021, with start of new production, KG Basin has re-emerged as a major gas producing basin. Production has started from new fields giving a significant boost to India's domestic gas production. While other gas producing fields are ageing, the new supplies are likely to sustain the present levels and even increase. Two other domestic supply options, CBM and from gasification of coal, are yet to register their significance. On the lines of the New Exploration Licensing Policy (NELP) for oil and natural gas, the Government had launched a competitive bidding policy for CBM

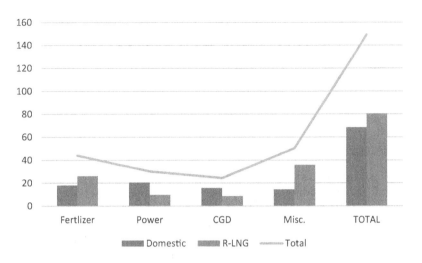

FIGURE 5.1   Natural gas consumption by sectors (2019–20) MMSCMD. (PPAC, 2020).

blocks in 1998 itself. However, even after two decades, this source has not yielded even 1% of India's total natural gas consumption. On the other hand, coal gasification has received serious attention only recently and one has to wait to see the actual outcome. The natural gas supply both from domestic and imported sources, and its consumption in different sectors in 2019–20 may be seen in Figure 5.1.

International natural gas supply—as LNG and via overland pipeline—also holds a potential for India. In the previous chapter, it was brought out that internationally traded gas has grown at a rapid pace across the world. India is advantageously placed for receipt of both LNG and overland piped supplies (also via sub-sea pipelines). Iran, Qatar and central Asian republics that have one of the world's largest natural gas deposits, are in India's proximate western neighbourhood. Even the eastern neighbour, Myanmar, has considerable deposits and is already supplying natural gas via overland pipeline to China. India's bold appearance on the global LNG scene was much hailed when it signed a long-term LNG supply contract with Qatar in 1999, and the first cargo was received at the Dahej LNG terminal in 2004. However, RLNG demand did not pick up much and the growth in regas capacity has been tepid, with China going much ahead even after a late start. It is only after 15 years since receipt of the first LNG cargo, that is in 2019 that LNG imports have exceeded supply from domestic gas fields (33 BCM of R-LNG versus 30 BCM of domestic gas). Now there is flurry of activity on both eastern and western coasts of India towards setting up of new terminals. The government's impetus towards natural gas, and softening of international prices of LNG during the last two years have given a boost to RLNG (in 2021, LNG prices have shot up to a new high). In this chapter, the above two import options have been discussed in some detail.

It is acknowledged that domestically produced natural gas is preferred over R-LNG, particularly in the price-sensitive sectors that offer subsidies to consumers for their products, such as cooking/transport, power generation and urea manufacture. Domestic natural gas is cheaper than R-LNG. Other reasons are an assured supply, and lesser uncertainty around price owing to insulation from international factors. If domestic natural gas was abundantly available, India could even consider setting up export-based urea plants. Prior to a discussion around sectoral demand later in the book, a detailed background of natural gas supply projection for 2030 is desirable. A probabilistic scenario of domestic natural gas availability has been offered here on the basis of discoveries under development/announced. As far as LNG is concerned, the likely growth in capacity of regasification terminals and capacity utilisation of the same, will determine as to how much of imported gas might be actually available. A discussion on natural gas import infrastructure—LNG regasification terminals and domestic natural gas pipelines—has also been undertaken.

5.2   NATURAL GAS EXPLORATION REGIMES

Until late nineties, the government owned upstream companies, ONGC and OIL, were the main companies engaged in E&P operations. They were the extended arm of the government, with the right to explore on whatever area they desired on a nomination basis purely, and the fiscal regime was one of statutory royalty payment. As owner of these companies, the government recouped the surplus via dividends. Starting from the eighties, several auction rounds were conducted to attract private companies for exploratory and discovered blocks/fields, but they were small acreages and did not add much value to the country's oil and gas supply. Only three pre-NELP contracts—two in offshore areas (Panna–Mukta–Tapti and Ravva) and one onland Block (Cairn's fields in Rajasthan, now owned by Vedanta)—have yielded substantial supplies. The nominated acreages of the government companies have been the major oil and gas producing properties and in late 1980s, when the country's energy needs were smaller, they comprised of nearly three-fourths of the total oil consumed in the country. Domestic crude oil supplies now comprise only 12% or so of oil consumption, within which a quarter comes from private sector. Gas has been a late and slow starter, and state-owned companies comprise of nearly half of domestic production. As stated earlier, imported supplies now exceed those from domestic sources.

Faced with rising crude imports and indifferent domestic crude oil and natural gas production, it was in 1998 that the government abolished the monopoly of government-owned companies and opened up the sector for private participation. There was a consensus among policymakers that the exploration business required cutting-edge technology, particularly in deep-water offshore, which was not available with the Indian companies. A transparent and incentivised auction methodology for award of acreages was launched called NELP. This policy provided for a 'risk-reward' regime wherein the successful bidder had to invest his own capital. If, discovery and production took place, then the contractor was allowed to first recover the expenses (cost recovery), and then share the surplus with the government as per an agreed upon investment multiple based ratio.[2] In order to incentivise these companies, while complete marketing and pricing freedom was given for crude, in the case of natural gas, the same was subject to a regulatory framework. NELP did bring in a number of private companies, both Indian and international oil companies (IOCs) into natural gas exploration. The above measure has had the desired effect, and major increments to domestic natural gas production are now maturing from the above contracts.

A still further reformed policy, Hydrocarbon Exploration and Licensing Policy (HELP) was launched in 2016, and offered as a superior regime over NELP. It provided a unified licence to explore all forms of hydrocarbons (oil, gas, CBM and shale gas) under a revenue sharing regime with an extended period of exploration. To operationalise the HELP, a mechanism that allows interested companies to choose their own acreage has been operationalised called the Open Acreage Licensing Policy (OALP). This involves placement of data of unawarded areas in public domain within a National Data Repository (NDR), and the bidders are free to bid for any block on offer. As regards the fiscal regime, instead of Investment Multiple Linked production share (under NELP), now the total revenue from sale of hydrocarbons has to be shared as per a bid formula without any reference to costs involved. Hence, while NELP was a production sharing contract (PSC), the latter is a revenue sharing contract (RSC), and has lesser red tape with no government approvals required for capex and cost recovery. While there are merits and demerits in both these regimes, many commentators believe that the RSC does not incentivise risk-reward, which is very much needed to incentivise exploration in an under-explored country like India. Simultaneously, there is minimal interface with the government in this regime as costs do not have to be approved, which otherwise used to be a bone of contention in administration of previous contracts.

5.3 DOMESTIC SUPPLY

5.3.1 FROM GAS FIELDS

Domestic gas has been available in select States of the country in the east, north-east and west, and both eastern and offshore. The gas-producing fields are located in Gujarat, Andhra Pradesh, north-eastern India, Tamil Nadu, eastern offshore (both off the coast of Andhra Pradesh and Tamil Nadu) and Mumbai offshore. These are the regions where gas consumption has a long-recorded history as local supplies were not dependent on laying of interstate pipelines to deliver gas, which are still being developed on pan-India basis. On an overall basis, Indian natural gas production has not fared well in the last decade – during 2010–20 net production has actually fallen at a CAGR of (–) 5.69% (MOSPI, 2021). The production has steadily fallen almost every year during the above period (but it is poised to increase from FY22 onwards). As is evident from Table 5.1, the domestic production has been falling over the last several years.

After the launch of the NELP bidding rounds, a large number of discoveries were announced (Jain, 2011). But, most of them did not reach the stage of development

TABLE 5.1

Production of Natural Gas from Different Sources

	Production of Natural Gas (Nominated Acreages and Private Producers) in BCM					
	2015–16	2016–17	2017–18	2018–19	2019–20	2020–21
ONGC and OIL	23.2	24.3	25.7	26.8	25.7	23.7
Private/JVs	7.9	6.5	6	5.2	4.5	4
Total	31.1	30.8	31.7	32	30.2	27.7

Source: PPAC.

and production. The above lacunae have resulted in uncertainty regarding the prospectivity of the Indian sedimentary basins. The discoveries do hint at the presence of natural gas, but not on the volume or viability of production basis. This riddle of gas having been discovered but discoveries not being developed leads many analysts to observe, that the governmental control on price that the developers could charge for their production was disincentivising producers. In 2016, the government removed most of these restrictions, and now developers can charge market price as per a given formula. For deep-water production, there is a different formula that yields a yet higher price (discussed in the next chapter). This has given a boost to production and new supplies have begun by BP–RIL combine from their discoveries in KG Basin this year (FY22). However, there is no major new discovery from the NOC–ONGC. It is simply idling on its deep-water discovery in KG Basin for over a decade and thus needs to start the promised production. Incidentally, even this one is expected to yield only 2 MMscmd or 0.72 BCM/year to start with, and may go up to 3 BCM/year in the next two years or so. ONGC has been the major gas producer (24 BCM in FY21) and accounted for 72% of country's domestic production. Even the discovery made in KG Basin by a state-government entity, GSPC, has been taken over by ONGC with no sign of production in the near future. ONGC's production has been falling, and as per the available projections, it is only the private producers that are likely to bring major new supplies to the market. In FY21, natural gas production fell by 2.8% over the previous year to 31.2 BCM. In the light of above, there is not much hope of the NOCs bringing any major increment to the domestic natural gas production.

In the discussion with several experts, the general view has been that India may not see a major increment to domestic production of natural gas. While a growth is expected, however, on the possible realisation of a substantial increase, only 12% of the experts who responded to the questionnaire, sounded highly optimistic that it will increase substantially. 21% of them are moderately optimistic, while 42% are only optimistic about the situation. The rest felt that the domestic gas production outlook might simply be dismal. The results have been presented in Figure 5.2.

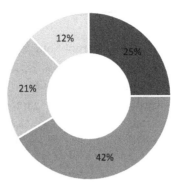

■ 1 − 3   ■ 4 − 6   ■ 7 − 9   ■ 10 (highly optimistic)

FIGURE 5.2   Percentage share of optimism on likely growth in domestic gas production (2030) on a rank of 1–10 (1 being lack of optimism, and 10 being high optimism).

The government's projections have been optimistic, and official reports in the last few years have stated that annual natural gas production might more than double from 33 BCM in 2018, to 72 BCM by 2022 (MoPNG, 2019; Lok Sabha, 2018; Reuters, 2018). However, in the year 2020–21, production was a mere 31.2 BCM. New production from KG Basin fields began in December, 2020, with some addition made in April 21 and further increase is proposed by the producers during 2022–23. With this new production, gas production in April 21 grew by nearly a quarter (22.7%) over April 20. In all, these new supplies are expected to add 30 MMscmd of gas supply by 2022–23, thus reaching a production level of 51 BCM. The supply from KG Basin fields has boosted the outlook for 2030, and a total of 90 BCM/year (65 MMTPA) equivalent domestic production has been projected, which appears to be highly exaggerated (Delloite, 2019). Another consideration would be depleted supply from existing fields which seem to have plateaued. It may be seen in Table 5.1 that production from nominated acreages has been falling, and no new major discovery of ONGC is presently under active development. Production from ONGC's KG Basin deep-water discovery (including the one in shallow water that it acquired from GSPC) is highly uncertain as it has not been developed even after 15 years of its discovery. The BP Energy Outlook, 2020 has projected a low level of production at 43–49 BCM for 2030 under its two built-up scenarios (Rapid and BAU). In its recent publication, India Energy Outlook 2021, IEA has projected that India's domestic gas production (including CBM) may range between 52 and 65 BCM in 2030 (IEA, 2021) (Table 5.2).

Domestic production hinges on discoveries that are highly probabilistic. Therefore, it is difficult to offer any firm estimations other than the production figures available from announced discoveries. In the light of the above, a realistic projection of natural gas production in 2030 would be 50 BCM/year, which is 60% more than the current production, and quite close to the projections of IEA and BP.

TABLE 5.2

Natural Gas Supply Projections by Different Agencies (in BCM/year)

	2022	2030
Petroleum Ministry	72	
Deloitte		90
BP Energy Outlook		43–49
IEA		52–65

Source: Given in the text.

5.3.2 CBM

India has the world's fourth largest coal reserves. CBM is a naturally occurring methane trapped in the coal seams, which can be obtained by depressurising them. With prognosticated reserves of 91.8 TCF of CBM (PPAC), India was touted as an ideal candidate for substantial production of this source of natural gas. The Petroleum Ministry had approved the CBM Production Level Payments (PLP) policy, wherein the bidder for CBM blocks had to commit to an incremental share of payment to the government at different slabs of CBM production. Therefore, as production increased and thereby pushing the contract into a higher slab of production, the contractor would have to allocate a higher share to the government. After approval of this Policy in 1998, a number of CBM blocks specific bidding rounds have been conducted and as in April, 2021, roughly 10% of the prognosticated resources have been established. However, even after the lapse of more than two decades, not even 1 BCM of gas is being produced per annum. Hence, it is clear that the future production from this source is highly uncertain.

The problems encountered so far have been the following:

- Poor quantity of reserves established after exploration
- Land and other local issues including forest clearance delays
- Disinterest on the part of several block allocatees, particularly state-owned enterprises, who have not met the contractual milestones
- Land overlap issues with coal block allocatees (rights of CBM and coal have been given separately for the same chunk of land)

In 2017 the government came out with a policy to incentivise CBM block allocatees, thus granting pricing and marketing freedom to them, so that they may be encouraged to quickly bring this resource to the market. Even Coal India Ltd (CIL) could be a major producer of CBM from their prolific coal mines. They were earlier left out of the policy of grant of CBM blocks, and only unallotted virgin coal bearing areas were covered under the CBM Policy. In 2020, CIL took CBM as a business option, and offered three blocks in eastern India under a liberal production sharing policy drafted on the basis of existing CBM Policy of the Petroleum Ministry. The newspaper reports indicate that the contract for one block has been signed. Expectedly more coal blocks held by CIL may be brought to the market. It may thus be concluded that as of now CBM does not seem to be a promising source of natural gas for the next five to seven years and may yield only a very limited volume of gas. As such, it may not be realistic to project substantial CBM production for 2030. IEA's domestic natural gas production projection includes CBM.

5.3.3   COAL GASIFICATION

While several major coal consuming countries like China and USA are exploiting their coal reserves towards converting coal into synthetic natural gas and chemicals, India has so far been unable to do so. One reason for this has been the presence of high ash (mostly above 40%) in Indian coal that makes it technically challenging and uneconomic to gasify. Indian Government has been keen to promote coal gasification, but it could so far achieve marginal success only in terms of approval of one unit, Talcher Fertilisers Ltd (in Odisha State) in 2016, where coal will be the raw feedstock for ammonia. It has overcome the ash problem by blending coal with pet coke to be sourced from the nearby Paradip Refinery of Indian Oil Corporation. While this has been a pioneering event for coal gasification agenda, one must note the caveat that the likely price of urea from TFL is expected to be higher than that of imported urea. As it is a first project of its kind in India, the government has in May, 2021 approved a special subsidy scheme for this higher priced urea, so that this technology can be firmly established. Thanks to such government support, due to which this project has been able to achieve financial closure, and the plant may indeed come up. The need for such fiscal support to achieve viability has put a dampener on future growth of the coal gasification technology, unless similar subsidy is made available.

Against the above backdrop, the future roadmap of synthetic natural gas is currently being shaped up by CIL, which wishes to secure its future as a coal mining company by putting coal to selective few non-polluting uses including coal gasification. The government has launched an ambitious plan to gasify 100 MT of coal by 2030, yielding an equivalent of roughly 40 BCM of synthetic natural gas. In this direction, CIL has adopted the Build Own Operate (BOO) model wherein the contracted party would receive coal from its mines as per a tolling model, and the gasification products would be transferred back to CIL. The BOO partner would receive a conversion fee on the basis of gas/products delivered. As the price bids have so far not been opened, it is as yet uncertain whether the entire operation would be price competitive or not. However, while the technology and investment prone risks are to be taken by the BOO operator, CIL has taken the marketing and financial risk. CIL has already received a bid for its 1.6 MTPA coal gasification project for production of methanol at Dankuni in the eastern state of West Bengal. It is only when the final outcome of this initiative is made public, will it become clear whether this project may also need subsidy support as in the case of TFL or not. Methanol could be blended with petrol as a transport fuel and is duly supported by approval of M15 specification by Burteau of Indian Standards (BIS), the Indian Government agency authorised to approve standards. CIL is also working concurrently on several other gasification projects where coal mines and possible locations have been identified, and pre-feasibility reports are currently under preparation. These projects will test the viability of conversion of coal to other products such as DME, glycol and ammonia. It is notable that the first output of coal gasification is synthetic natural gas, which may be then converted to other chemicals such as the ones listed above. As synthetic natural gas has the same properties as that of natural gas, coal gasification has been discussed here as a possible source of the latter.

The initiatives of CIL and TFL are not the only ones as even NLC, the Government-owned lignite mining major, is also experimenting with gasifying lignite. They are identifying a relevant technology. The Government has also encouraged coal gasification by providing rebate on the bid revenue share under the commercial coal mining auction round. The coal mined and sold by the successful bidder, or even consumed by the bidder in gasification end-uses, would receive a discount in the revenue share agreed in the contract at the time of bidding of commercial coal mining blocks. Indian government hopes that with the CIL's multiple pilots underway that might establish the financial viability of this technology, there will be a heightened impetus towards coal gasification. In some States of India like Odisha, the stripping ratio of coal (ratio of overburden to coal recovered) is so low that coal can be mined under Rs. 500/tonne, which is the bare minimum cost anywhere in the world. This makes coal an eminent raw material for conversion to synthetic natural gas. For now, we may not make tall assumptions on the possible growth of this end use, and restrict to the earlier mentioned likely achievement of the target of 100 MT of coal gasification by 2030 yielding 40 BCM of gas per annum.

5.4   IMPORTED SUPPLY

5.4.1   LNG

Despite India making an early beginning in commissioning a LNG receiving terminal in 2004 itself, the regas capacities have not grown significantly. China's LNG story also started in 2004, but has fared much better—its LNG regas capacity grew by 2017 to 54 MMTPA against 27 MMTPA in India. For RLNG to materialise, there needs to be an adequate import infrastructure available in LNG import terminals (for regasification). Estimations of regasification capacity are available from the LNG industry—International Gas Union (IGU) and Petronet LNG Ltd. (PLL). Beyond it, some expert agencies have also projected LNG imports. In Table 5.3, the projections have been offered—two for LNG demand and three for regas capacity in LNG terminals.

While a variety of future capacity numbers are in public domain, all projections are robust. IEA has noted that in the IVC scenario, an import of 93 BCM of LNG may happen in 2030. This is the highest capacity projection amongst the three scenarios (76 BCM in STEPS). On the regas capacity, there may be a 115 BCM regas capacity, out of which 58 BCM existed in 2020 in India, and an

TABLE 5.3

LNG Demand/Regas Capacity Projections by Different Agencies (BCM/year)

	2030	
	Demand	Regas Capacity[a]
OIES	66	NA
IEA (IVC Scenario)	93	115[b]
IGU	NA	248
PLL[b]	NA	150[c]

Source: Given in the text below.

[a] Includes sites under construction or planned in the year of publication of Reports.

[b] The terminal year for completion of construction has not been given.

[c] projection includes author's extrapolation, as discussed below.

addition of 57 BCM was 'planned' with no indication of timeline for the latter (IEA, 2021). OIES has projected a lower demand (Low Demand Scenario) to be met by LNG supplies (in high case, a demand of 79 BCM has been indicated)) (Rogers, 2016).[3] IGU has projected a much higher regas capacity of 248 BCM/ year (181 MMTPA). It has supported the above scenario on the available infor- mation that new regas projects of 135 MMTPA have been identified over and above the 27 MMTPA of existing capacity in 2017, and 19 MMTPA are currently under construction.[4] By 2021 beginning, the operational regasification capacity had increased to 39.5 MMTPA with 27 MTPA under construction (IGU, 2021). Figure 5.3 shows the location of LNG terminals and trunk pipelines connecting them with consumption centres, mainly in western and northern India. The last two numbers add up to 86 BCM/year. Therefore, IEA's projection of 115 BCM regas capacity (without any terminal year) is quite realisable. In January, 2020 PLL, the dominant Indian LNG terminal operator, projected a smaller growth in capacity to 72.5 MMTPA within which 62.5 MMTPA was already constructed or nearing completion, and balance ten MTPA was under construction (Petronet, 2020). However, they have not offered any projection for 2030. It is notable that from the commissioning of the first terminal at Dahej in 2004, it has taken 16 years to achieve 62.5 MMTPA in 2020 (yearly growth of nearly 4 MTPA). Perhaps, at the same linear growth rate, a further growth of nearly 36 MMTPA in the next nine years (until 2029–30) to reach nearly 110 MMTPA (151 BCM/year) capacity by 2030 is a credible estimation. Out of the above four agencies, as PLL is the only one entity that has made investments on the ground in India and actu- ally operates LNG terminals—so their growth trajectory may be taken as a good estimator. In this study, a likely regas capacity of 110 MMTPA or 151 BCM may be taken for 2030. It is in between the other two estimates (Table 5.3).

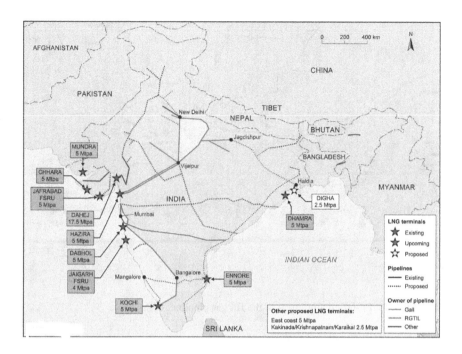

FIGURE 5.3   LNG terminals and trunk gas pipelines.

The LNG regas capacity is the outer limit in the terminals of as to how much natural gas can be received, but the actual availability depends on the cargoes received, also measured in terms of likely utilisation percentage of the regasification capacity. There is a large variation of utilisation rates noticeable across the world. While in 2019, the terminals in India reported a near 67% utilisation (it was 87% in 2018) and 65% for 2020, the global average is 43%, both for 2019 and 2020 (IGU, 2021). CRISIL expects a 50% capacity utilisation in 2023–24 in Indian terminals. Looking at the comparative higher utilisation rates in India, for the purpose of this study, after the large increase in regas capacity, a utilisation of 60% (lesser than what is the present rate) may be taken of PLL's estimated regas capacity of 110 MMT/year by 2030. This yields an imported natural gas supply of 66 MMT of LNG or 250 MMSCMD of natural gas (91 BCM), in the same year. Further, it aligns with IEA's higher end of estimated 76–93 BCM imports of LNG in 2030. A higher utilisation of the available regas capacity, could always make an additional supply available to meet still higher demand.

5.4.2   TRANSNATIONAL GAS PIPELINE

As discussed in the previous chapter, as supplies by pipeline (and LNG) have provided a viable, secure, long-term fuel option, lack of domestic natural gas reserves has not been an impediment in different parts of the world, for development of

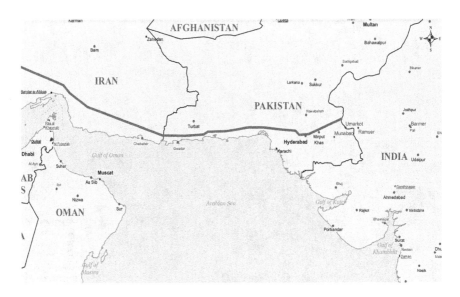

FIGURE 5.4   Proposed alignment of the IPI gas pipeline.

natural gas as a fuel of significance. This has been the case in Europe, South America and now also in Asia where China receives natural gas via pipelines from Russia, central Asia and Myanmar. Even in India there has been a buzz around receiving natural gas from Iran and also Turkmenistan, through over-land pipelines (Jain, 2011). Central Asian republics like Kazakhstan, Uzbekistan, Turkmenistan and Azerbaijan have been traditional exporters of natural gas via Russian pipeline system to Europe. While Iran–Pakistan–India (IPI) gas pipeline has been acknowledged as a viable option but for geopolitical issues (Figure 5.4). Even Turkmenistan–Afghanistan–Pakistan–India (TAPI) gas pipeline has been touted by a credible agency like Asian Development Bank (ADB) for a while (Figure 5.5). During the first decade of this century, there were a number of meet-ings between the nations concerned, and some commercial talks had also been held (some between Iran and Pakistan without India), including international roadshows to attract investors, but nothing has materialised on ground. However, the prospect of a large energy hungry market like India receiving a large natural gas supply from a large producer in the neighbourhood like Iran, it still remains in the realm of a possibility. IEA had in its earlier India Energy Outlook in 2015 projected 2030 as the likely year for receipt of natural gas via IPI gas pipeline in India. But, in its 2021 publication, while it has acknowledged the positive gains of this supply, but has discounted the likelihood until 2040. In the past, another pipe-line had emerged as a possibility—Myanmar–Bangladesh–India pipeline. But the option got quickly ruled out when the Myanmar's natural gas got committed by the military junta to China, and an overland pipeline got completed to deliver the

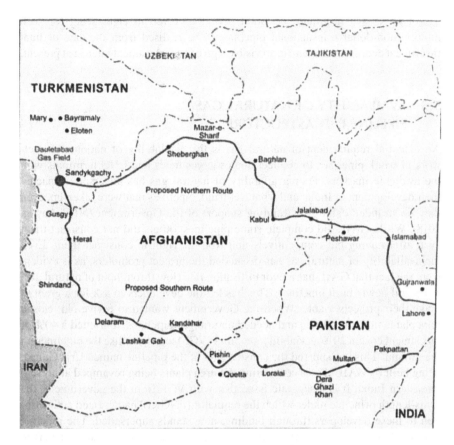

FIGURE 5.5   Proposed alignment of the TAPI gas pipeline.

same. This happened in spite of the fact that GAIL, was a part of the consortium that developed this offshore gas reserve, and India had even offered higher price for the natural gas in the price discovery process. Therefore, non-commercial reasons prevailed in this case, and the eastern pipeline option for India evaporated in the thin air. There were some issues with Bangladesh as well, over whose territory the pipeline would have crossed.

Based on the reasons given below, for the purpose of this book, we do not look upon transnational pipeline as a likelihood in the medium-term timeframe of 2030. One reason is the present environment in the western neighbourhood. Any supply from Iran/central Asia will have to traverse through Pakistan and/or Afghanistan that have a long-standing history of strife and lawlessness in their own western region, from where the natural gas might enter these countries. Second, there is a deep sense of suspicion regarding the role of Pakistani state in assuring an uninterrupted supply from the pipelines, which will pass through their territory into India.

Third, there is a minimum gestation period of seven to eight years for such multi-billion-dollar transnational pipelines to be realised from the date of final investment decision, and there is no visible sign of any investment interest at present.

5.5   AVAILABILITY OF NATURAL GAS PIPELINE INFRASTRUCTURE

An essential requirement of natural gas is the availability of nation-wide network of trunk pipelines to connect domestic gas fields and LNG terminals with the available markets. Poor availability of natural gas has adversely impacted their development in India, and whatever trunk pipelines that were taken up, even they lie stranded calling for funding support of the Government (NITI Aayog, 2018). While GAIL did complete some pipelines, others did not construct them even after having bid competitively and won the right to construct them. Even the availability of natural gas has dissuaded the project promoters, as is evident from the fact that GAIL has a poor utilisation rate (low throughput of natural gas) in several newly built pipelines. This has led the developers to ask for a grant to make their projects viable. When the Government wanted to revive old, closed urea plants in eastern India and needed natural gas pipelines, it granted a 40% of investment cost in 2016 as viability gap fund (VGF) to help realise the pipelines on the ground. This has spurred the construction of the pipeline named Urja Ganga, being built by GAIL that is connecting the urea plants being revamped at present in eastern India. It is a separate issue that with VGF from the government, the arms-length principle under which the regulator (PNGRB) had granted authorisation to these developers through bidding, now stands superseded. The pipeline business was first opened to the private sector through a policy announcement in 2006, when surplus capacity for third party use was also mandated (MoPNG, 2006). The PNGRB, has now been assigned the responsibility of authorising new pipelines and approving the tariff to be charged by pipeline owners for third-party use of the spare capacity. Many commentators believe that India developed the regulatory, third-party regime for development of pipelines too soon, even when the backbone of natural gas grid had not been laid down by the state itself. This has resulted in 'natural gas first or pipeline first' debate and thus has hampered the achievement of full coverage of interstate and spur pipelines. A detailed discussion on above aspects is beyond the scope of this book.

In the initial years, when natural gas production was marginal (1 Mtoe in 1980), the pipeline network was dedicated—connecting the natural gas fields with nearby consumers. The upstream company (ONGC/OIL) itself laid the pipeline. And, no surplus capacity existed in these dedicated pipelines. The slow growth of trunk pipelines may be seen in Table 5.4. A major expansion came only after GAIL was formed in 1984 and it set up the Phase 1 of the Hazira–Vijaipur–Jagdishpur (HVJ) pipeline in 1987–88. Following its successful completion, the above pipeline now covers a distance of 1,700 km, and connects a number of industrial and urban consumers in different states.[5] Its Phase 2 of nearly 505 km was completed in 1994.

TABLE 5.4
India's Commercial PES, Domestic Natural Gas Production, LNG Supply and Pipeline Length

Year	PES (in Mtoe)	Domestic Natural Gas (in Mtoe)	LNG Supply (in Mtoe)	Natural Gas Pipeline (in km)[a]	CGD Cities
1980	102	1	0	0	4
1985	134	4	0	0	9
1990	195	10	0	2,050	10
1995	252	15	0	2,500	11
2000	316	22	0	4,800	12
2005	394	24	6.8	6,039	19
2010	537	41	11.5	9,283	41
2015	685	24	21.6	16,241	67
2019	813	23	29	16,324	92[b]

Source: (PPAC, 2018b), (PNGRB, 2013), Open Govt Data and various sources.
[a] Trunk pipelines.
[b] comprises Geographical areas or Gas.
Note: There has been marginal growth after 2015. As on 31st December, 2020 the operational length was 17,126 km.

The above expansion resulted in a capacity of 33.4 MMSCMD, again fully utilised due to dedicated sale to pre-identified consumers. This underscores the point that even as late as at the turn of the 21st century, India's pipelines were designed only to connect identified natural gas sources with consumers and not for future market growth. Therefore, even if, a supplier did venture out to bring imported LNG, there was little choice in delivering it to consumers. This refers to the poor growth of LNG option in India until recently. Even when LNG supply began in 2004, the Dahej–Vijaipur–Jagdishpur pipeline was laid to deliver this new supply to markets in western and northern India. For India's geographical size and energy market, the pipeline coverage is small. Against 500,000 km length of trunk natural gas pipelines in the USA, and 314,000 km in China, only 16,789 km exists in India in 2018 (PNGRB, 2013; MoPNG, 2018b; Zhang et al., 2016).

After creation of PNGRB, a number of pipelines were announced, but they are yet to be completed and include the ones that are stranded (discussed above). They are considered crucial for one consumer segment, CGD sector, for which the PNGRB has obtained commitments from successful bidders of delivering natural gas to urban consumers, as CNG and PNG. Laying down of trunk natural gas pipelines that might connect the CGD networks is considered an area of concern for the success of natural gas in urban areas. Poor development of pipelines has hindered its availability upcountry. Helped by LNG terminals, imported supplies have been dominant along the western coastline—earlier all terminals have come up on the west coast. For the last two decades, it was the Hazira–Vijaipur–Jagdishpur (HVJ) pipeline, which comprised the bulk of pipeline-delivered natural gas supplies from the LNG terminals and Bombay High gas fields to north India. It may be seen that natural gas pipelines are largely absent in large parts of India[6]. Slow growth in both cross-country pipelines and LNG supplies, resulted in poor natural gas availability in central, eastern and most parts of southern India. With emergence of new LNG terminals and pipelines connecting the industrialised eastern India (Dhamra in Odisha and Ennore in Tamil Nadu), the situation is likely to change. Another development in the LNG sector has been the development of a new gas storage and regas technology in Floating Storage Regasification Unit (FSRU), which is a virtually a floating LNG terminal. It can be quickly brought in a ready shape from another location anywhere in the world where it may be available, and stationed offshore at a place where pipeline exists and natural gas can be directly pumped onland. One FSRU is coming up on the western coast near Mumbai at Jaigarh. A snapshot of growth of the natural gas sector in India has been presented in Table 5.4 wherein the growth in commercial primary energy from all sources has been compared with natural gas supply from domestic and imported sources. It is evident that the latter being a new fuel did not grow at a rapid rate to achieve high shares in overall commercial energy.

It is evident that consumption of commercial energy has grown robustly creating opportunity for natural gas, and the same has grown in tandem albeit not at a faster rate to raise its share in commercial PES. Second, it also appears that pipelines have grown and connected new cities at a fast pace. However, the steep decline in domestic production of natural gas after 2010, has probably left the pipeline sector in a difficult situation during which the pipelines grew rapidly, leading to poor utilisation rates and a dampening of interest in pipeline contractors. The new supplies from KG Basin and upcoming LNG terminals may infuse new life into pipelines.

5.6   SUPPLY PROJECTION FOR 2030

From a late start in India only in the eighties, natural gas production rose at a fast rate during 1980–1990, and its share in PES rose from 1% to 5% in this period. The production saw another spurt in 2010–11 reaching 9% share, only to fall back to previous levels in the succeeding years, and presently natural gas comprises nearly the same share in total energy demand as it did three decades back (6% in 2015). The LNG option emerged in 2004 and has grown at a fast rate to have even out-stripped domestic supply. With the pace in construction of new LNG terminals, the above trend is likely to be maintained. On the basis of the discussion earlier in this chapter, a realistic assessment of the natural gas scenario from both domestic and imported sources in the year 2030 has been given in this chapter.

IEA projects a high of 52 BCM of natural gas production in 2030 from *all* domestic sources including unconventional ones, along with LNG imports of 93 BCM or so in the higher demand case (IEA, 2021). This yields a supply of around 145 BCM/year of total gas supply in 2030. This seems to be realistic as until new discoveries were under development, it is unrealistic to include them. On the

TABLE 5.5
Natural Gas Supply Projections for 2030
(in BCM)

Domestic	
From gas fields and CBM	50
Coal gasification	40
RLNG	**91**
Total	181

other hand, IEA has not taken coal gasification into consideration from which, in this study, around 40 BCM is estimated (gasification of 100 Mt of coal). There is broad agreement with IEA on RLNG, wherein maximum import of 93 BCM of RLNG is assumed. Based on PLL's projections and others in close proximity, a projection of 91 BCM/year of RLNG supply is assumed for 2030. The above three sources add up to 181 BCM in 2030 (Table 5.5).

5.7 CONCLUSION

As discussed in the previous chapter, few nations have scripted their natural gas story on the basis of imported supplies. Even in India while imported supplies form a higher proportion of total supply, we have noted how the domestic supplies have been falling, and this seems to be the reason for the rising appetite for R-LNG in the Indian market. The outlook for domestic production has consistently disappointed the protagonists of the natural gas story. Earlier hopes were pinned on NELP, and now after two decades since the launch of this regime, hopes are pinned on the reforms in pricing for NELP and launch of a new exploratory/fiscal regime (OALP). A new source, coal gasification has definitely appeared on the domestic horizon. It would be fair to see this in a different light than earlier hopes that were belied, perhaps, because domestic coal is now available in abundance for this end-use. Earlier, India had coal shortages and with power sector holding the first claim to domestic supply, coal could not be diverted to other sectors, least of all to gasification. With the sharp decline in price of renewable power vis-à-vis coal-based one, and the impetus being given by the government to the former, it is quite likely that availability of cheap coal will spur gasification. But, in this book we will only leave this at a sanguine note of expectation especially as the first contract for gasification of coal on commercial basis (TFL has received subsidy and is not commercially viable on its own), is yet to be signed and a tender has been received for the same.

For natural gas to be delivered, pipelines are a natural monopoly. And for imported supplies via LNG tankers, there is a need for LNG receiving terminals that may regasify and deliver natural gas via pipelines. As regards the first infrastructure, we have seen that the government is willing to assist pipeline developers

BOX 5.1   WILL THE DRIVE TOWARDS ENERGY
TRANSITION HELP IMPROVE NATURAL GAS SUPPLY?

In energy debates, particularly around natural gas in India, supply aspect is an important topic. Energy transition is about carbon intensity, and does not relate to a particular fuel but a group of fuels. If a fossil fuel is to be substituted then a variety of fuels such as biofuels, new renewables, hydro-power, and even hydrogen when it is available at competitive prices may be the possible candidates. Natural gas faces headwinds in India due to low domestic production and if the supply scenario does not improve, other fuels may fill the gap. In this chapter, it was brought out that due to higher price and limited infrastructure (to receive LNG and deliver it across the country), imported supplies did not receive impetus. This is now changing. But, it cannot be said with confidence whether the recent increments to natural gas demand and supply are entirely due to its low emission property or for other reasons. If it is due to the former, then the recent commitment of India at Glasgow will definitely boost its demand. It is only the future energy roadmap of India to net-zero that might clarify the policymakers' outlook on this.

The discussions in this book are around the energy landscape for the period until 2030, whereas India's energy transition is likely to take shape over a longer timeframe (commitment is for 2070). Should natural gas be adopted as a key contributor to the national energy strategy, supply scenarios may change. Adequate LNG supply is available and the lack of domestic production would not matter. While carbon intensive fuels such as coal and oil are already targeted for reduction (oil not as much as coal), natural gas is perceived as a substitute. The demand sectors where it might replace the above are discussed in a later chapter. However, lack of availability of domestic gas may be a dampener, and energy planners might be more oriented towards readily available domestic fuels, and natural gas may lose out. The Indian Government lays a lot of emphasis on 'Atmanirbhar Bharat' or self-reliant India. Coal gasification was discussed in this chapter as an emerging option, also because coal is abundantly available and fits into the political economy very well. It may not be easy for the energy policy-makers to ignore the import dependence versus local debates. Even New Renewables are receiving encouragement because of India's tropical loca-tion, with over 300 clear sunny days that augur well for solar power. Hence, the poor domestic endowment is a negative for natural gas.

even financially. A liberal, open regime already exists for authorising new trunk pipelines as well as CGD networks via an independent regulator. We believe that if there were an appetite for natural gas, there would be investors including the state-owned entity, GAIL, willing to lay the pipeline. Coming to LNG terminals, there is already a flurry of activity and the regas capacity is poised to undergo a steep rise in the next decade (up to 2030). The emergence of FSRUs that can be erected and be up and ready in no time offers further comfort to prospective consumers. The general decline in LNG prices over the recent years has boosted its demand (prices have again risen in 2021). Therefore, from infrastructure perspective, we do not expect major hurdles in the way of delivering natural gas.

As regards imported supply via pipelines, the prospect of supply from the west has defied expectations for several decades. It is a viable option particularly because this source of natural gas does not need to undergo expenses like liquefaction and regasification that LNG requires. Hence, while there is a sustained growth projected in LNG supply, if the overland supply could be made possible by surmounting the geopolitical concerns, it would definitely be a game changer. As of now, for the 2030 timeframe, the projections of LNG seem to be realisable. India is a growing energy market which is an attraction for the new LNG projects. In the next chapter, we discuss price competitiveness of natural gas with greater granularity in different sub-sectors. From the above discussion it follows that availability of natural gas especially from imported sources will not be a concern. Should there be demand for natural gas especially as with higher capacity utilisation of regas capacity, and emergence of new technologies such as FSRUs, a spurt in demand can be met from imports with a short time lag.

NOTES

1 A detailed discussion on these policies is available in 'Natural Gas in India: Policy and Development' by Anil Kumar Jain.

2 What percentage of the yearly revenue would be first charged to cost recovery (even 100%) was bid at the time of auction. The balance was shared with the government as per the bid formula.

3 Rogers (2016) has anticipated 'High case' LNG demand of 79.2 BCM/year. Also see Sen (2015) who has estimated LNG supply of 60 BCM/year (58 BCM/year) in 2030.

4 Many agencies have not given a definite timeline for the realisation of the planned/ underway capacities, perhaps, due to frequent delays in construction. For conversion, we have taken 1.37 BCM = 1 MMTPA.

5 This was executed by GAIL, a dedicated gas pipeline company formed for evacuation of this gas.

6 Indian Petroleum & Natural gas Statistics 2017–18, http://petroleum.nic.in/sites/default/files/ipngstat_0.pdf.

6 Price Competitiveness of Natural Gas

6.1 INTRODUCTION

A discussion on energy prices assumes significance because India has a long-standing history of subsidising various fuels. All commercially traded fuels—petroleum products, natural gas, coal, electricity—have been subsidised in the past, either through government budget or by energy companies via cross-subsidy. These subsidies were meant to promote social objectives and could be implemented conveniently through the large state-owned companies in the energy sector. State governments have also applied differential rate in taxes to promote their social objectives by moderating the end consumer price of fuels. For example, natural gas used for cooking/transport gets taxed lower as compared to its use in commercial and industrial sectors. It is a separate story that fossil fuels have been taxed heavily in the country. Importantly, in the interplay of subsidy and tax, India does not have any net subsidy to a fuel from the public exchequer. Even in power sector where there are budgeted subsidies, when compared with the overall taxation on power via taxes on coal and electricity, there would be no net subsidy outgo. Significantly enough, subsidies do impact price and demand, as well as sheer attractiveness to invest for the private sector. The differential pricing regime has been examined in this chapter, while its impact on demand is included in the following chapter. Taxes on hydrocarbons are levied at various stages—production stage (royalty), processing stage in refineries (excise duty) and then on sale (VAT, GST, etc.). Similarly, coal and electricity are taxed at various stages of their transfer of hands (including across state borders) and value addition. Notably, in case of some fuels like natural gas, it is subsidised as input to downstream processor, and then again in the pricing of the final product. Urea is a good example for which natural gas price is administered by government (from upstream producer to fertiliser unit), and then subsidy is further advanced to the farmer to lower down even the manufacturing cost. This has made it quite difficult for the government to carry out pricing reforms in the upstream sector, without carrying out similar reforms in the downstream pricing of final products.

As we know, natural gas has a versatile use and thus can be put to virtually all energy-related end uses including as a raw feedstock material. Resultantly, it faces competition from different fuels as are relevant to that sub-sector. This calls for a detailed pricing analysis across sub-sectors. The exercise gets further complicated as natural gas coming from different contractual regimes is also priced differently. The above complication arises from different pricing provisions in the PSCs signed at different time periods. Some of them grant pricing freedom to upstream producers, while others require just the government approval under its Pricing Policy as notified from time to time. On the other hand, imported gas is sold as per commercial contracts usually struck between seller and buyer. Hence, natural gas as becomes available from different sources (domestic, imported) is priced differently. It is only from FY20 that the share of imported natural gas has exceeded the domestic share, with the result that more of this fuel is now being sold on market principles than ever before.

In the light of government involvement within the Indian energy sector through taxation/subsidy policy as well as due to the presence of government-owned energy companies, role of energy security policy assumes greater significance. This aspect was briefly touched upon in previous chapters particularly in Chapter 3 wherein the 'stickiness' of India's energy mix was brought out, which in turn has owed its origin to the 'self-sufficiency' motive. The attractiveness of taxing energy sector to garner additional resources for centre/state remains high, with the result that India has one of the highest tax rates in the world on fossil fuels. Even when GST was adopted in 2017 and all taxes were subsumed in it, the clean energy cess was retained on coal by yet another name (GST compensation cess). Hence, coal still suffers an additional burden of Rs 400/ton, expressly to help the Centre compensate those States that might lose revenue during their transition to the new taxation regime. The non-inclusion of petroleum (and natural gas) in GST has left the states totally free to fix their own tax rate on these two fuels, which have been kept at a high pedestal to simply shore up their finances. In this regard, oil and gas consumer industry has suffered because unlike other fuels (like coal) that are included under the GST regime, no input rebate is available for VAT levied on oil and natural gas. Therefore, while India may not have adopted 'carbon tax', however, taxes on fuels including natural gas are substantial. Also, while the energy taxation policy is not within the defined scope of this book, suffice it to say that a positive move in India towards clean energy could recognise the low carbon emission property of natural gas and thus promote its uptake by moderating the tax rate on it.

6.2   PREVALENT PRICING POLICIES

Facilitated by the proliferation of government owned entities in the larger energy sector, fuels have been historically priced as per the guidance emanating from the government policy. Energy was treated as a public good and only an administratively approved post-tax return was allowed to these entities in lieu of price determination. Within this overall policy, those fuels such as diesel, LPG and kerosene that were reckoned to be used by 'vulnerable sectors', namely transport, households, farmers and poor, were priced lower with a cross subsidy extended by other fuels such as petrol and ATF, that were priced higher. The above petroleum retail pricing policy has recently been reformed with cost-reflective petroleum product pricing (Jain, 2018). It is notable that the government has not back-tracked on the reforms even after crude prices have shot up to $75/barrel or even higher, and is now passing on the rise in crude price to the consumers. However, the policy for determining the price of natural gas to be paid to the upstream companies for

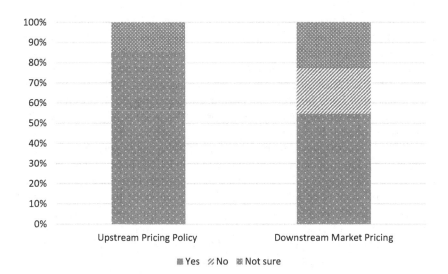

FIGURE 6.1   Policies affecting the gas market in India.

production from domestic gas fields remains subject to government regulation (which is now becoming liberal), while crude producers are given international prices, without any role at all for the government.

In the discussion with experts on whether it is the upstream or downstream pricing policy that might play a bigger role in evolution of a natural gas market in India, the overwhelming response was towards upstream pricing policy.[1] Due to subsidies and other methods in vogue, such as cross-subsidy and pooling of price from different streams of gas, there is a difference between the two in India. As presented in Figure 6.1, is found that more than 80% of the experts have averred that price realised by natural gas producer is more important as a trigger for domestic production rather than the price charged to consuming sectors.

As mentioned elsewhere, the E&P contracts provide pricing terms with the provisions having evolved over time when auction rounds for gas fields were conducted. It being consistent with the overarching energy pricing policy, these contracts limited the freedom to charge market prices. Over the last decade, the natural gas pricing policy under E&P contracts was assailed for disincentivising upstream companies, leading to several interventions that have now liberalised the terms.[2] Broadly there are two sources of domestic supply—from nominated acreages belonging to government owned companies (ONGC and OIL), and other from gas fields developed under PSCs that were signed under auction regimes. Both government and private companies have signed PSCs as contractors, wherein they share production with the government as per the percentage share bid available at the time of auction rounds. It is notable that recently the government has substituted PSC regime with revenue sharing (the sale proceeds are shared), but blocks under this regime are still under exploration and are yet to come into actual production.

It was in 2014 that a major pricing reform was carried out and, under the above pricing guidelines, all domestic natural gas prices are now being fixed on six-monthly basis and are arrived at through a formula based on volume-weighted average of four international natural gas prices. The latter are those of US Henry Hub, NBP (UK), Russian and Alberta natural gas prices. With this, a common regime has been given for government companies and private producers (only for those contractors wherein government approval for price is required under their PSCs). As is evident from the choice of the four markers, they pertain to prolific gas producing regions, and the price so derived for a gas importing country like India is rather low especially when compared with RLNG prices. It has, therefore, not changed the fortune of NOCs who are the main suppliers under this category. In June, 2021 they were getting $1.79/MMbtu, even lower than what they were receiving a decade back! On calorific parity basis, this gas price translates to under $12/barrel of crude oil when the latter was trading at under $50/barrel. Nearly 85% of domestic gas production of the country was priced as per the 2014 formula. Further pricing reforms have been effected in 2016.

Looking to the unattractiveness of the above gas pricing formula, in 2016 a special pricing provision was issued for domestic production that might come from deepwater and difficult fields (high temperature, high pressure conditions). The above measure was conceived to attract investment in deepwater exploration, and also incentivise production from existing discoveries that were unviable. Under these guidelines, the government has allowed market price that may be determined on the basis of open bids for sale of natural gas, but subject to a 'ceiling' as might be achieved by the formula provided in the notification. Instead of international natural gas price markets, the latter has incorporated prices of imported fuels including LNG (GOI, 2019a). While it does translate into a higher price than the 2014 guidelines, but due to inclusion of low-priced fuels like coal and fuel oil, this formula does not yield a much higher price than worked out via the earlier formula. Further, the prices realised might not incentivise production of gas from new projects, especially from the deepwater basins in India, where cost of production is high, especially when compared with other prolific basins of the world. In June, 21 the above formula had yielded a natural gas price of $3.62/MMbtu, while spot LNG prices were above $10/MMbtu. What is of immediate relevance is that the new supplies that have begun this year from Krishna Godavari Basin are priced as per the above formula and will be priced much above the price of natural gas coming from nominated acreages of ONGC and OIL (Business Today, 2020).

As a result of the above guidelines of 2016, there are now broadly two main pricing regimes, and the ills of Indian natural gas pricing system of multiple prices coming from different PSCs have to a large extent been sorted out by now. Additionally, an attractive price has been allowed particularly for deepwater/difficult basins which are likely to be the main producing areas of the future. Hence, there are now two main prices for domestic natural gas—one for deepwater/difficult gas fields and another for all other domestic supply, without distinction having been made between government-owned or private producers.

The price paid by consumers varies as per the source of supply and whether it originates from domestic or imported sources. In Table 6.1, the historical gap in domestic price has been indicated as per the formula-based pricing of government. In 2019 the weighted average price of natural gas sold in India (domestic and RLNG) was $6/MMbtu. After levy of taxes and other costs such as transportation, the price at retail end was between $6/MMbtu and $18/MMbtu. This makes the higher priced supply (imported) unaffordable in India, and IEA acknowledges that on price competitiveness basis, natural gas 'is much less compelling' for India. The competitiveness in different sub-sectors has been discussed later.

Two features stand out clearly in the above discussion. First, do the above formulae yield higher prices as compared to international prices, and second, what is the share of the two main domestic supply (and pricing) streams in the overall supply? From Table 6.1, it is evident that the domestic gas prices are much below the ceiling prices fixed for supply from 'difficult' fields. And even the formula derived ceiling price that determines the price for domestic natural gas coming from deepwater fields is lower than LNG price. Second, at present, the supply of gas from the first stream comprises the major share. But, going forward, additions to domestic supply are expected almost entirely from the deepwater regime. The prolific Krishna Godavari Basin gas fields of ONGC and RIL–BP combine (from where new supplies have begun) are in the deepwater. As we will see later, for those price-sensitive sub-sectors where gas was acceptable only due to the administratively determined price, now even the new gas supply from domestic fields will not be available at much discount. In the following pages, the competitiveness of natural gas has been discussed vis-à-vis the relevant fuels.[3]

It is notable that energy prices in the international market have undergone ups and downs due to the pandemic since 2020, due to which it becomes difficult to use recent prices (in 2021) as the reference prices. Therefore, it would

TABLE 6.1

Yearly Approximate Prices of Natural Gas in India (US $/MMbtu)

	Domestic[a]	Ceiling Gas Prices[b]
2015–16	4.66–3.1	5.8
2016–17	3.1–2.5	5.3–6.61
2017–18	2.5–2.9	5.56–6.3
Apr–Sept 2018	3.06	6.78
Oct 2018–March 2019	3.36	7.67
Apr–Sept 2019	3.69	9.32
Oct 2019–Mar 2020	3.23	8.43
Apr–Sept 2020	2.39	5.61
Oct 2020–Mar 2021	1.79	4.06
Apr–Sept 2021	1.79	3.62

[a] On GCV basis
[b] Calendar year average

be useful to take pre-pandemic prices. In an ongoing analysis, the prices of late 2018 (November 2018) have been taken and a reference to prices of 2021 have also been offered.

6.3 COMPETITIVENESS OF NATURAL GAS IN DOMESTIC COOKING

The government subsidises the domestic LPG consumed in households, while Industrial and commercial consumers of LPG do not get any such subsidy. Here, we discuss the competitiveness of natural gas both with the economic price (pre-subsidy) as well as the subsidised one. There is, however, no subsidy on PNG used by households for cooking. It is also notable that natural gas produced by state-owned companies such as ONGC and OIL comes from fields other than deepwater/difficult ones, and is priced at a discount to the second stream (discussed above) as well as LNG. These supplies at administered price have been subject to allocations made by the government to priority consumption sectors. With transport and domestic cooking having been prioritised for receipt of this supply, natural gas becomes competitive in domestic and transport sectors against competitive fuels (Tables 6.2–6.4). As a way forward, more gas supplies are likely to mature from imported sources and a comparison has also been made between LPG and PNG coming from RLNG.

In domestic cooking sub-sector, the comparison of cost implication has to be made between LPG (both pre- and post-subsidy) and energy equivalent volume of PNG (again both for administered-priced gas and RLNG prices). In different tables below these three comparisons have been offered. On the basis of field survey, Gujarat prices have been taken as representative price for comparison, also because CGD market is well established in Gujarat due to its early introduction in 1990, (even earlier than in Delhi). In Table 6.2 the price build-up of domestic gas sold as PNG has been derived from retail selling price. In the tables below, the recent prices (June, 2021) have also been given and it is evident that the prices are nearly the same as those three years back, i.e. in 2018, thus making the old data relevant for a discussion.

While in Table 6.2, the comparison has been offered with price of administratively priced gas, however, for a comparison with economic cost of the fuels, it would be prudent to compare it with RLNG because the latter is market-driven. This will also be useful to analyse competitiveness of RLNG supplies in future Geographical areas (GAs), the market area awarded to licencees on competitive basis for sale of natural gas by the PNGRB, where domestic natural gas, especially of the first stream, may not be available (in light of poor domestic production scenario). In Table 6.3, the price build-up of PNG based on RLNG has been given. The cost of RLNG varies by contracts between the parties, and this information for different CGD entities is not available in public domain. Therefore, based on a web reference of prices in July 2018, an estimation of the likely price for November 2018 has been done on pro-rata basis as selling price for RLNG in this chapter. As noted in Table 6.3, the retail prices for RLNG as recent as in

TABLE 6.2

Price Build-Up of Domestic Natural Gas Sold as PNG (Rs/SCM) in Gujarat (November 2018)

	In Rs/SCM	In Rs/MMbtu
Cost of gas	13.77	395.71
Supply & distr. cost	10.44	300.02
Margin	0.57	16.38
Basic selling price	24.78	712.11
VAT[a]	3.72	106.82
Retail selling price (Rs/SCM)	28.50	818.92

[a] Current VAT assumption (Gujarat: 15%).

Calorific Value in kcal/SCM 8770.

Note: Retail prices in May, 2021 are nearly the same at Rs 27.5/SCM in Gujarat and Rs 28.41/SCM in Delhi.

TABLE 6.3

Derived Price Build-Up of RLNG sold as PNG (Rs/SCM) in Gujarat (November, 2018)

	$/MMbtu	(Rs)
Gas cost $ Mmbtu/GCV	11.3	26.95
Selling & distribution cost	-	9.95
Entity margin	-	
Basic cost (A+B+C)	-	36.90
VAT (6%)	-	2.21
Selling price (Rs/SCM)	-	39.11

Notes: 1. In the above web reference, sourcing cost of RLNG gas in July 2018 including VAT and transmission, was derived as Rs 31.5/SCM at RLNG CIF price of $10.03/MMbtu. With rise in RLNG price by $1/MMbtu in November 2018 over July (PPAC), a pro-rata 10% increase may be taken, which pro-rated yields an input cost of Rs 34.7/SCM ($1 = Rs 69). Retail selling price after adding margin was Rs 39.11/SCM.

2. *In June 2021, the retail selling price was Rs 36.46/SCM.*

June 2021 are even higher than what they were in 2018. In a later analysis, it will become evident that higher RLNG prices do not affect the outcome of the analysis based on 2018 prices, and natural gas still remains competitive.

Using the information of prices of PNG given in Table 6.2, the impact of substitution of LPG by PNG has been determined, both at economic price of LPG and at subsidised price of LPG (Table 6.4). On the basis of market survey of PNG usage in cooking, an average yearly consumption of 186 SCM has been derived in domestic household sector. On the other hand, no standard LPG consumption number is available especially, as there is a diversion in subsidised LPG and the demand for this supply is not truly representative of energy needed for cooking. Therefore, LPG consumption of 11.25 cylinders which is equivalent to the PNG supply of 186 SCM in energy terms has been taken in Table 6.4. As regards recent prices (June 2021), there is an enhanced attraction for having domestically sourced PNG, as its prices are lower than what they were in 2018, while LPG prices have continued to increase due to high crude prices (noted in Table 6.4).

In the first case of comparison between non-subsidised LPG and domestic-gas-based PNG, there is an annual saving of nearly Rs 8,785 per household (see Table 6.4). But, when compared to subsidised price of LPG, the consumer would find the switch to PNG cheaper by Rs 796, on an annual basis (difference between serial numbers 2 and 3 in Table 6.4). Another comparison could be that of RLNG-based PNG with LPG. At a higher gas price of Rs 39.11 per SCM (as derived in Table 6.3), it would still be cheaper for the consumer to purchase PNG than non-subsidised LPG, but the cost competitiveness would turn around when compared to subsidised LPG. Hence, the subsidy policy and taxes play an important role in the economics of domestic cooking fuel (as does the supply of domestically produced PNG versus RLNG). The government ought to consider the impact on its fiscal position by continuing with subsidy availability from Union Budget on LPG. Unless the consumers are charged market price for LPG, there would be little impetus to migrate to natural gas.

TABLE 6.4
Competitiveness of PNG in Domestic Cooking versus LPG (Economic Cost) in Gujarat (November 2018)

		Assumed Consumption of 11.25 LPG Cylinders (@14.2 kg/cylinder)	Price (cylinder) Rs for 14.2 kg (one cylinder)	Price per kg	Total Cost (Rs)
1.	LPG (11.25 cylinders) non subsidised	kg 160	936.5	84.30	13,488
2.	LPG (11.25 cylinders) subsidised	kg 160	488	34.37	5,499
3.	PNG[a]	SCM 186	-	28.50	4,703
4.	Difference between Sl. 1 and 3 is Rs 8,785.				

[a] Equivalent in energy terms to 160 kg of LPG (1 SCM of PNG = 0.86 kg of LPG).

Note: In June 2021, with a marginal reduction in PNG price and a moderate increase in LPG prices, the savings by substituting LPG by PNG has further increased.

6.4   COMPETITIVENESS OF NATURAL GAS IN TRANSPORT

In the transport sector, a complex set of concerns have to be addressed when estimating the cost competitiveness of natural gas. On the lines of the cooking sector, even transport operation receives the cheaper supply of natural gas, whose prices are at a discount to market-determined prices. Firstly, the competing fuels are different from cooking fuels—diesel and petrol (EV is still not a major contender). Second, there are different vehicle types—two wheelers, three wheelers, cars and truck/bus—each with different levels of fuel economics. Third, acquisition cost of differently fuelled vehicles varies, and lastly the salvage value is also not same. In Table 6.5, all the above concerns have been factored in and results presented. In the transport sector, prices as in Delhi (November 2018) have been taken for liquid fuels as well as CNG.[4] The results indicate that CNG is a competitive option across the three fuels and vehicle types too. Here again as domestic natural gas has been allocated as CNG, the cost of domestic gas (and not RLNG) has been taken. For economic costing, domestic natural gas is substituted by RLNG at \$11.3/MMbtu, leads to a CNG price of Rs 60/kg in Delhi (instead of Rs 44.7/kg with APM domestic gas). At this price, the economics still stays favourable for natural gas in all vehicle types except for buses where the fuel and usage cost becomes higher to diesel-fuelled vehicles by 25% (Table 6.5). Here again, with a significant increase in petrol prices in June 2021 competitiveness of CNG has become even stronger.

6.5   COMPETITIVENESS OF NATURAL
GAS IN COMMERCIAL USE

In the commercial segment, major PNG consumers would include institutions, hotels and restaurants. These consumers have traditionally been using the alternately available fuel—commercially priced LPG. As these consumers are located in urban areas, they are also required to use cleaner fuels and LPG fits in the scheme of things in terms of its low emission.

However, with roll-out of CGDs across the country, they are now converting to PNG. In this consumer segment, CGD licensees sell RLNG and not domestic natural gas. In Table 6.6 cost comparisons have been made between RLNG and the closely competing fuel—commercially priced LPG (prices of Gujarat). For ease of analysing a large set of consumers in this segment whose consumption volumes vary a lot, two categories have been made—those who consume less than 1,000 SCM/month with an average of 600 SCM/month, and another category of more than 1,000 SCM/month with an average consumption of 2,400 SCM/month. As this comparison is based on a per unit of energy, the results for both categories would be similar with a different range of savings or otherwise.

The results indicate that RLNG has a clear edge. With the combustion equipment for both LPG and PNG being the same, there is no capital cost variation for the two fuels. As consumption rises from small consumers to larger ones, the absolute savings also rise, simply because on a calorific parity basis natural gas

TABLE 6.5
Competitiveness of Domestic Gas in Transport Sector versus Petrol and Diesel in Delhi (November 2018)

	Vehicle Type	Fuel Economy (km/L and per kg for CNG)	Price of Fuel (Rs/L and per kg for CNG)	Fuel cost/km (Rs)	Cost of Vehicle (Rs)	Cost[a] (Less Salvage Value)	Useful Life	Annual Usage (km)	Total Usage	Usage Cost Rs/km	Fuel and Usage Cost (Rs/km)
					Car (Hatchback)						
1	CNG	22	44.7	2.03	578,000	520,200	15	11,560	173,400	3.00	5.03
	Petrol	21	76.52	3.64	541,000	486,900	15	11,560	173,400	2.81	6.45
	Diesel	24	71.39	2.97	679000	611,100	10	11,560	115,600	5.29	8.26
					Car (Sedan)						
2	CNG	20	44.7	2.24	925,000	832,500	15	11,560	173,400	4.80	7.04
	Petrol	16	76.52	4.78	877,000	789,300	15	11560	173400	4.55	9.33
	Diesel	25	71.39	2.86	111,0000	999,000	10	11,560	115,600	8.64	11.50
					Auto Rickshaw						
3	CNG	42	44.7	1.06	213,376	192,038	15	39,055	585,825	0.33	1.39
	Petrol	21	76.52	3.64	200,000	180,000	15	39,055	585,825	0.31	3.95
	Diesel[b]	32	71.39	2.23	200,000	180,000	15	39,055	58,5825	0.31	2.54
					Bus (12m, non AC)[c]						
4	CNG	2.5	44.7	17.88	3,000,000	2,700,000	15	91,800	1,377,000	1.96	19.84
	Diesel	4	71.39	17.85	3,300,000	2,970,000	15	91,800	1,377,000	2.16	20.00

[a] Salvage value is assumed at 10% of the acquisition cost.

[b] Diesel taxis/autorickshaws not allowed in Delhi.

[c] Average daily run is 306 km, and 300 days per year. See http://www.indiaenvironmentportal.org.in/files/file/Review%20of%20the%20Performance%20of%20State%20Road%20Transport%20Undertakings%20(SRTUs)%20for%202015–2016.pdf.

Note: Even in June 2021 the price of CNG in Delhi is nearly the same at Rs 44.3/kg. The prices of diesel and petrol are much higher enhancing the competitiveness of CNG.

TABLE 6.6

Derived Cost Benefit of Using RLNG vs LPG in Small/Large Commercial Establishments in Gujarat (November 2018)

S. No.	Fuel/Unit/Month	Volume	Price (Rs)	Total (Rs)
Small Commercial Segment<1,000 SCM/month Assuming 600 SCM/month				
1	PNG (SCM)	600	39.1	23,468
2	LPG (kg)[a]	516	84	43,344
3	Savings (monthly)	-	-	19,876
4	Yearly	-	-	238,512
Large Commercial Segment>1,000 SCM/month, Assuming 2,400 SCM/month				
5	PNG (SCM)	2,400	39.1	93,874
6	LPG (kg)[a]	2,064	84	173,376
7	Savings (monthly)	-	-	79,502
8	Yearly	-	-	954,024

Notes: 1. Assumed CIF price of PNG to non-domestic is $11.3/MMbtu, $1=Rs 69.
2. Only LPG has been taken as alternative to PNG.
3. [a]1 SCM gas has equivalence in calorific terms with 0.86 kg of LPG.
4. Price of packed LPG (November 2018) is Rs 1,601 for 19 kg cylinder (Ahmedabad).
5. As per prices in June 2021, the results are similar to 2018 in terms of competitiveness but only savings are marginally lesser.

is cheaper than liquid fuels. It was mentioned earlier in this chapter that gas is generally cheaper than liquid fuels (LPG also being a liquid fuel).

6.6 COMPETITIVENESS OF NATURAL GAS IN INDUSTRIES

The discussion in this sub-sector is a bit complicated because akin to the transport sector, there are a number of variables involved that impinge on fuel economy in industries. First, there is the question of size of the industry: small and moderate, classified by volume of fuel consumed. However, this has been simplified by analysing only small sized ones, as the bigger ones are covered under Industries sub-sector of CGD (the large industries have been discussed separately). Then comes the variable of which fuels are to be compared with. Fuels vary as per process requirement. This issue has been addressed by reducing different fuels to a common platform on the basis of their energy equivalence. There may also be issues of capital equipment dedicated to different fuels. As the variety of industries in urban and peri-urban areas is quite diverse, this cannot be simply addressed through a short analysis here. Moreover, due to long life of equipment

TABLE 6.7

Derived Cost Benefit of Using RLNG vs Liquid Fuels in Small Industries (PNG < 5,000 SCM/month) in Gujarat (November 2018)

S. No.	Fuel/Unit/Month	Volume	In INR (Minus Sign Denotes Saving)	
			Price	Total/Month
1	PNG (SCM)	5,000	39	195,000
2	LDO (kg)	4,200	48	201,600
3	FO (kg)	4,357	43	187,351
4	HSD (L)	5,100	71	362,100
5	LPG Bulk (kg)	4,300	84	361,200
PNG vs competing fuel (in INR)			Monthly	Yearly
6	LDO		−6,600	−79,200
7	FO		7,649	91,788
8	HSD		−167,100	−2,005,200
9	LPG		−166,200	−1,994,400

Notes: 1. Assumed CIF price of PNG to non-domestic is $11.3/MMbtu, $1 = Rs 69.
2. 1 SCM of PNG has calorific equivalence of 0.86 kg of LPG and 1.02 L of HSD, 0.91 kg of furnace oil and 0.84 kg of LDO.
3. RLNG price of PNG price is ($11.3/MMbtu). LPG at market price of Rs 84.3/kg.
4. As per prices in June 2021 due to high oil prices, savings have further increased across the competing fuels.

and small depreciation on an annual basis, the impact on final costing on energy terms may not be much. Finally, there is the vexing issue of pollution especially due to heightened concerns of urban air quality. Consequently, these industries have come under the lens of various courts/tribunals, and the environmental cost though not formally added in this viability analysis is seen to be working to the advantage of natural gas. It may also be noted that this analysis is based on price of RLNG (domestic gas is not allocated to this category). On the basis of the above discussion, the costing of different fuels has been showcased in Table 6.7 (Gujarat prices).

It is evident from the above data that barring furnace oil, natural gas is a cheaper option across all fuels. As use of furnace oil is much restricted due to its highly polluting nature, it doesn't pose a major challenge to utilisation of gas in Industries. Its consumption has consistently been coming down from over 9 MT in 2011–12 to below 7 MT in 2018–19 (PPAC, n.d.). In a first of its kind analysis done to compare natural gas price with average price of main competing fuels in end-use sectors, the IEA found that natural gas competes well in 'other industries' (IEA, 2021). This end-use is poised well to uptake LNG in the coming years.

6.7   COMPETITIVENESS OF NATURAL GAS
IN POWER GENERATION

India's power sector has traditionally been coal-based and even in 2020, nearly 75% of the power supply has come from coal. It is notable that the government had in 2015 announced its ambition of achieving 175 GW of renewables-based capacity, when the existing capacity of the latter was 25 GW and share of coal in total generation was same at three-fourths. Thereafter, a higher ambition of 500 GW of renewables by 2030 has been announced by the government. Natural gas-based power has generally been more expensive than other sources due to fuel price. Most of the country's gas-based plants came up after 2004 when large domestic natural gas discoveries were announced. This shows that LNG was not the preferred fuel for power generation as its supplies could have even come earlier at international prices. Indian power market has been price-sensitive thus far. The comparative difference in prices of domestic and RLNG is rather high, thus making power from the latter unviable. With majority of the new natural gas supplies likely to come from deepwater in future, there would be little difference present between domestic gas and imported LNG. In view of this, the domestic gas price scenario cannot be expected to become favourable (particularly for power sector) even when more domestic supply comes on stream.

Typically, power prices are fixed in terms of two key components—capacity charge (fixed cost) and energy charge (variable cost). The latter varies much in accordance with price of fuel. In a submission made to the Parliamentary Standing Committee on Energy in 2018, NTPC informed that the energy charge of their natural gas-based power plants varied between Rs 2.86 and 6.53/kWh, while the capacity charge varied between Rs 0.5 and 1.84/kWh (Lok Sabha, 2019). Such a wide variance in energy charge was due to price of APM gas being government regulated while the upper limit was of RLNG price. At a delivered price of RLNG of \$12.35/MMbtu the energy charge from their Dadri plant near Delhi was Rs 6.53/kWh (2017–18). (Even in June, 2021, RLNG prices continue to be high and same prices/cost may be assumed as what prevailed earlier in November, 2018.) This was much higher than final coal-based prices for some of their new TPPs at Rs 5/kW as informed by the Ministry of Power to the concerned Committee. In 2015, the (levelised cost of electricity) LCOE of power generated from a new coal-based power plant of super critical technology was Rs 3.79/kWh (Reddy, 2018).[5] Presently, the cost may have gone up to Rs 4.25–4.50/kWh, also because of requirement of emission control devices, i.e. FGD system. Only hydro-based power turned out to be cheaper at Rs 3.16/kWh. However, due to the difficult resettlement and land submergence issues woven around it, this is not a viable option for making large increments. In contrast, price of power from natural gas-based power plants that received domestic gas was estimated at Rs 4.50/kWh (assuming Rs 1.50/kWh as capacity charge) (Lok Sabha, 2019). At RLNG price of \$10/MMbtu, the energy charge was stated to result in Rs 6/kWh of energy charge in the above reference.

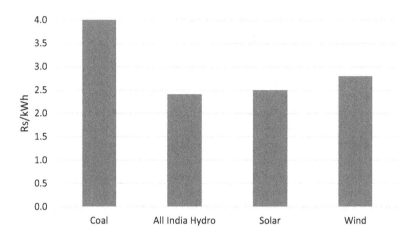

FIGURE 6.2 Weighted average sale price of power from different sources (2019–20) (Rs/kWh). (*Source:* As per Information collected by Author from Various Public Sources.)

The weighted average sale price of power made from other sources in 2019–20 may be seen in Figure 6.2. Due to large difference existing between prices of domestic natural gas and RLNG, weighted average of gas-based power may not be a true indicator and thus has not been shown.

As recent as in June 2021, RLNG price were very high and close to the November 2018 price. Table 6.1 gives ceiling prices for upstream natural gas producers, fixed by government on the basis of international prices for gas coming from identified offshore fields, and they serve as a good marker for LNG prices. With RLNG still indexed in 2019 above $7/MMbtu especially for the long-term contracted supplies, gas-based power may also be assumed to cost Rs 5.5/kWh or so inclusive of Rs 1.5/kWh as capacity charge. It is notable that demand for RLNG is still low vis-à-vis the Indian power sector, and it is APM that is preferred as it is cheaper. As domestic gas supply is lesser than an overall demand, large gas-based power capacity remains stranded. Simultaneously, cost of renewable energy technologies has come down. In several recent tenders in 2021 for solar and wind power, utilities have received below Rs 2.5/kWh rates. In January, 2021 the Gujarat Urja Vikas Nigam Limited (GUVNL) signed a PPA for a 200 MWp solar project with NTPC at a price of Rs 1.99/kWh. In other recent tenders, the price has gone up marginally, but is still below Rs 3/kWh. The above prices fluctuate as per international price of solar cells much because India has still a marginal domestic cell production, and that too relies heavily on price of imported silicon wafer. For wind power, in the same state of Gujarat, the GUVNL received the lowest bid of Rs 2.77/kWh for 300 MWp. The above prices of solar/wind have to be seen in the light of the requirement of having to buy expensive balancing power from other sources during peak evening hours when solar generation stops, or in the off-windy season. Even then, these prices are very competitive against all other sources barring coal. Thus, the price of power is cheap

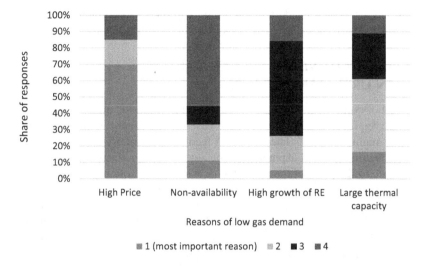

FIGURE 6.3 Reasons for lower natural gas demand in Power Generation. *Note:* 1: Most important, 4: Least important.

when produced from coal (after taking into account the balancing cost of variable renewable power) and relatively expensive from natural gas. For a more detailed understanding of market competitiveness of power, one will have to look at the base-load and peaking power aspects of both thermal and renewable power.

In the power sector, even though domestic natural gas production has not grown much, but imported supplies could have filled the demand–supply gap. However, experts feel that that the high price of the latter has been the number one deterrent (Figure 6.3). Four major choices were offered to the experts (i) high price of gas, (ii) non-availability of gas, (iii) high growth of renewable energy and (iv) large thermal capacity addition in the system. Consistently with the findings elsewhere in this study, high price for imported supplies has been duly acknowledged by them to be a more significant reason than merely being about non-availability of natural gas.

The cheapest source of power until recently has been based on coal, and now while its price is rising, renewable power is emerging as a cheaper source. On the other hand, natural gas-based power prices are trending to be on a higher side. Once battery storage prices come down, even the present challenge of meeting peak demand in the case of the intermittent renewables (solar and wind) will be overcome. Therefore, the climate change imperative and pricing are now in favour of solar/wind power. In fact, now the challenge to natural gas in power is not so much from coal as much as from renewables. While coal is assailed for being a fossil fuel and new TPPs are less likely, renewables are on the ascendancy. Hence, climate policy will not support natural gas-based power generation as it is also a fossil fuel, and it is now renewables which will be the new challenger to it. The only question is at what pace the latter will grow. India's power needs are rising and renewables need to both replace fossil fuels and augment supply, at the same time. These issues have been discussed in the following chapter.

6.8 COMPETITIVENESS OF NATURAL GAS IN UREA MANUFACTURE

The cost of domestically manufactured as well as imported urea has been higher than the retail price. This has been the case despite supply of domestic natural gas at a regulated price. The two main feedstocks available for urea manufacture are natural gas and naphtha, and the cost of urea production is directly proportionate to the price of the feedstock. Earlier, when natural gas prices tracked crude prices, there was not much difference in the prices of the two competing feedstocks (naphtha is a derivative of crude). In the recent past, the demand–supply for naphtha in international markets has seen major mismatches that might lead to volatility in its price, but this has not been the case in natural gas. The demand for the latter has been by and large rising over the years, with a seasonality factor (higher demand in winter) and other macro-economic reasons. On the basis of available information available in public domain, it is found that the cost of producing urea from imported natural gas ($9/MMbtu) is more than Rs. 20,000/ton. However, as domestic natural gas is priced lower than imported LNG, the cost of producing urea is lower. But how much it would be lower to landed price of imported urea depends on international prices. The Union Government covers the difference with subsidy (Lok Sabha, 2017). With a large urea subsidy bill, it imposes a large outgo of revenue for the Government of India. In the year 2019–20 a sum of Rs 57,000 crore was budgeted (Annual Report, Department of Fertilisers, 2019–20). The total subsidy payable was, however, much higher and arrears have also been mounting. The price of imported urea has been increasing and in May 2021 it, was at $365/ton which is much higher than $250/ton that had prevailed in the last two to three years.

The policy for subsidising urea manufacturers was earlier called Retention Price Scheme until 2003, and thereafter was renamed as the New Pricing Scheme. Plants of different vintage and with different energy consumption norms have been grouped and allowed varying price build-up (GOI, 2018d). There has also been a concern of differences in input prices with older plants getting domestic natural gas which comes at a lower price, while several new plants are consuming RLNG. In order to provide gas at uniform prices so that there is a level playing field for all, in 2015 the government approved a policy of 'pooled' pricing of gas (Economic Times, 2015). Under a similar dispensation, even the upcoming capacities in the public sector based on RLNG (via revamp and expansion) are being given the necessary purchase assurances, albeit their urea will be higher priced.

Naphtha is an alternate feedstock to natural gas. Indian urea plants were earlier based on naphtha, particularly since the nineties when refinery expansions took place and the prospect of easy availability of naphtha increased. But, the government reversed the decision in early 2000s when large natural gas discoveries were reported, particularly in the Krishna Godavari Basin. As naphtha prices were ultimately dependent on speculative crude prices, it was decided that domestic natural gas price would be a safer option, also because the PSCs provided for a government role in price fixation of natural gas. This was also a trigger for fixing a low price of gas under the PSCs. As mentioned earlier, this anomaly is now being set right to incentivise gas production. Hence, no new naphtha-based urea plant are being envisaged any longer. The existing three naphtha-based plants with a capacity of 1.5 MT/year each were directed to convert over time and are currently nearing completion of conversion to natural gas. With the above policy decision and conversion of the entire Indian fleet of naphtha-based urea plants, the question of market competitiveness with naphtha as a feedstock is no longer germane. In any case, naphtha-based urea manufacture has been more expensive than that from gas (Gulati and Banerjee, 2019). From market survey it is found that cost of manufacturing urea from naphtha at a prevailing price of naphtha in June, 2021 (between $670 and $700/MT) is nearly Rs 30,000/ton. Hence naphtha-based urea is virtually ruled out and even RLNG based urea would be cheaper. An emerging fuel is coal via the gasification route and a plant is now under implementation at Talcher in Odisha (PIB, 2019b). With recent decision of the government to extend a higher subsidy to this coal-based urea plant, it remains to be seen whether coal would now emerge as a preferred option in the long run. As full details of the costing of urea from the coal gasification process are not in public domain as yet, no comparative analysis can be offered. However, it is expected to be higher than natural gas-based urea typically somewhere in the range of Rs 24,000–25,000/ton, but lower than naphtha.

6.9 CONCLUSION

In this chapter, we conclude that differential pricing regimes for domestic and imported natural gas deepen the divide between them. With the two sources being near equal in their share of total supply (RLNG is marginally higher), this factor assumes greater significance for a discussion around competitiveness of natural gas in India. This distortion at the marketplace has been a major challenge for the policymakers, and they are gradually trying to align the two prices so that market priced supplies can find an increasing acceptance. The above move is being catalysed by two factors: rising share of new domestic supplies that have market-pricing provisions in their contracts, and second, softening in the price of long-term LNG contracts. The above trend is bound to help natural gas grow in volume because while increments to domestic production are probabilistic, imported natural gas supplies are available at market price. It is in this regard that the discussion in this chapter assumes an added relevance as to which gas demand sectors are really sensitive to prices. We saw earlier that in sectors where natural gas competes favourably with liquid fuels (transport, cooking, industrial sub-sectors), it is competitive even at market-determined price (or RLNG). However, when compared with solid fuels and some liquid fuels, imported natural gas loses out clearly. Of course, subsidies such as what exist for domestic cooking also lead to different outcomes.

The IEA's recent publication, India Energy Outlook 2021, supports the analysis presented in this chapter. It finds that natural gas competes well as a feedstock with competing fuels, and also in such sectors where the alternate fuels are liquid fuels. But, in power generation segment, it competes poorly. The above sectoral analysis has also found some support from the experts consulted for this book preparation. Within CGD, prices were considered to be a relevant factor in transport and cooking. However, in the commercial and industrial segments, most respondents felt that it will be environmental regulations and non-price factors that might ultimately drive natural gas consumption. Pricing was considered as a major factor in power, and few experts were confident of the likelihood of pricing reforms happening soon in this sector, without which the scope for natural gas-based power generation would be low. The above arrangement links price with other aspects of the energy economy, namely, clean energy policy, power sector pricing policy amongst others. It is notable that with a large renewable energy target earmarked in power, the ability of gas-based generation to ramp up and down quickly would have been very helpful, and may still drive demand for gas in power.

While there was a discussion on domestic gas pricing policy previously, there wasn't much clarity on how prices are actually determined for imported gas, namely LNG, in international markets. The latter is a complex subject and is linked to global demand and supply cues, as well price of oil. India is a smaller gas importer than the likes of China and Japan, and is a price taker. Suffice it to say that the gap between long-term price of crude and natural gas is increasing thus making the latter still more competitive. This offers a great opportunity to India which could theoretically substitute its large liquid fuel economy with that based on natural gas and thereby save billions of dollars. However, this is limited by the locking-ins into relevant infrastructure created over last several decades to receive, refine and deliver liquid fuels. There is merit in considering such a gas-based economy to replace the new demand for liquid fuels, which is probably already happening, catalysing a large ambition for CGD sector (discussed in the next chapter). On LNG price, what is also notable is that there are a large range of prices spread between long-term contract and spot LNG mechanisms. The real advantage of natural gas price being lower than liquid fuel can only be availed if, consumers struck long-term contracts. The comfortable position in upcoming capacities in regasification terminals does offer this opportunity.

The arbitrage between imported and domestic natural gas supply will always remain due to savings accruing in domestic gas supplies due to absence of liquefaction, ocean freight and regas charges. The government also has the option of protecting domestic sector by a suitable tariff wall. If, more domestic gas could be discovered and brought to the market, imported natural gas will face demand challenge. However, this does not seem to be the case, as new discoveries/supplies of natural gas are not happening in a significant volume. It does appear that urea price to the farmers will remain subsidised for the foreseeable future. This does put a real pressure on government's budget, and will perpetuate the policy of keeping the price of domestic natural gas low (albeit at a moderate discount to LNG prices).

BOX 6.1   WILL PRICE OF NATURAL GAS BE A RELEVANT FACTOR IN DEFINING ITS ROLE IN ENERGY TRANSITION?

For a long time now, developing countries including India have been negotiating with the West on seeking financial assistance for energy transition on the principles of common but differentiated responsibilities (CBDR). Without getting into this, it suffices to say that energy transition will come at a cost, both capital and revenue based. While solar and wind are cheaper sources of power over other fuels, the picture changes when the cost of balancing intermittency is added to it. Adoption of natural gas also faces a price challenge. Natural gas in India is of mainly two origins, wherein the imported supply being available at market price is more expensive than coal, the main source of power generation. This will definitely come in the way of its adoption as a bridge fuel to a clean energy future. Globally several measures have been taken to tax or price carbon emissions including via 'cap and trade' platforms so as to make the transition competitive. While India does tax fossil fuels quite high, which is a pseudo-carbon tax, it has not introduced carbon price and quotas thus far. Carbon taxation is relevant for this chapter as it might ultimately impact the economic viability of natural gas.

The Indian energy market is highly price sensitive. Nearly half of 26 GW of gas-based power generation capacity is stranded because it is unable to find a market for power based on LNG. These plants were set up with the hope of cheaper domestic gas availability which did not materialise. Examples of fuel choices driven by price consideration exist in many other demand sectors too. Even to address urban air quality concerns, the government drove CNG and PNG for transport and cooking only by supplying cheaper domestic gas. Therefore, in the changed circumstances post-COP 26, unless there is a positive discrimination by way of regulation or subsidy, etc., in favour of cleaner but more expensive fuels such as natural gas, the status quo may not change much. Regulatory measures including activism of NGT have been seen both in the industrial and commercial spaces. These may get further intensified and expectedly create demand for natural gas. In the domestic cooking sector, LPG has now got well entrenched especially in the rural areas under the Ujjwala (LPG Distribution scheme). As regards the urban areas, both PNG and CNG have also received a boost by interventions of policy and price support. In power generation, the government has outlined a renewable future. Hence, a mix of price and policy seem to be an effective combination that is helping dramatic growth of clean energy sources

Hence, more supply from domestic gas fields gives higher impetus to produce urea domestically, and thus eliminate imports. Similarly, in sectors like power generation and domestic cooking, higher production of domestically produced natural gas will drive demand in the long run.

In the end, suffice it to say that this chapter strongly brings out the need for a long-term energy pricing policy in preference over sub-sectoral fuel pricing policies, and holds the key to alignment of prices of different streams of natural gas. This ought to be the strongest driver of an integrated energy policy. While considering that with climate change/air quality imperatives requiring greater adoption of renewables, a market-determined pricing policy would help achieve the desired objective in an efficient manner, rather than multiple policies encouraging production, price-support, long-term purchase assurance, etc., for wind and solar power. Power supply from the latter would easily be able to compete with LPG in cooking, liquid fuels in transport, in manufacturing processes, too, if, all the fuels were market priced. The latter wouldn't come in the way of government's distribution objectives as DBT could deliver the subsidy without distorting the larger energy market. Should the country's energy policy incorporate carbon pricing, the clean energy agenda of the government could be implemented in an easier manner through markets, in place of multiple prices of fuels and taxation policies adopted in lieu of them. The main aim of an integrated energy policy of having a competitive economy cannot be met without adoption of market pricing in the complete energy sector.

NOTES

1 Downstream pricing policy refers to pricing of energy in transport, cooking, urea and other sectors.
2 See Sen (2015) for a detailed discussion on the 2014 policy. This is still WIP.
3 The price comparisons have been done as per 2018 prices. Due to the upheaval caused by Covid-19 in 2020 that has continued into 2021, the prices in the pandemic-affected period may not be truly representative for a discussion on competitiveness.
4 Delhi has a wider range of CNG vehicles in use than Gujarat. For conversion of natural gas volume to weight, a factor of multiplication by 1.3 is taken.
5 This study discusses the superiority of the levelised cost of electricity methodology and has compared it for projects based on Central Electricity Regulatory Commission (CERC) order.

7 Natural Gas Demand Scenarios for India

7.1 INTRODUCTION

Following the court intervention in the national capital, to promote clean air around the turn of the century, natural gas emerged as a serious energy choice. This established the credentials of natural gas as clean energy in comparison to the two other transport fuels—diesel and petrol. As a result of judicial activism, the world's largest public transport fleet conversion to CNG took place in Delhi. In this chapter, two demand scenarios for natural gas in 2030 have been generated. As mentioned earlier, the main aim of the study is to achieve a well-researched understanding of what role might natural gas play in India's energy mix in 2030, and not to 'estimate' its demand. A more convincing demand projection would require the use of modelling approaches, which is beyond the scope of this study. Simultaneously, without offering a quantitative estimate, merely saying that natural gas will play an 'important' or a 'minor' role would not be convincing. Therefore, in this chapter, underlying factors that impact natural gas demand have been discussed, and a bottom-up approach has been adopted to determine, what increments to present demand might be reasonably expected in the different natural gas-consuming sectors up to 2030. A brief methodology of the discussion followed in this chapter has been given in the following subsection. To start with, the shares of different energy sources in India's commercial PES during the last 24 years (since 1995) have been given in Table 7.1.

Natural gas was a part of India's energy mix even before 1995, and its share rose until 2010. It has, however, been falling since then, and even as recent as in 2020, it is at 6%, just equivalent to the 1995 level. To assess the growth in natural gas demand up to 2030, a base year of FY 2019 (also referred to as 2018–19) has been taken in this chapter. The Covid-19 pandemic impacted energy use across the world in 2019–20 that has continued into 2021. Hence, it is in the fitness of things to take 2019 data.

As was shown in Figure 5.1, imported gas now forms a larger market share than the domestic one.

7.2 PROJECTIONS OF EXPERT AGENCIES

A number of studies undertaken in the past by agencies such as Planning Commission, IEA and PNGRB are available that have projected future natural gas demand (Table 7.2). However, these reports suffer from the infirmity of

TABLE 7.1

Shares of Different Commercial Energy Sources in India's PES

	1995	2000	2005	2010	2015	2019
Oil	30%	34%	31%	29%	29%	30%
Natural gas	6%	7%	8%	10%	6%	6%
Coal	56%	52%	54%	54%	58%	55%
Nuclear	1%	1%	1%	1%	1%	1%
Hydro	7%	6%	5%	5%	4%	4%
New RE	0%	0%	1%	1%	2%	4%

Source: BP (2020).

TABLE 7.2

Overall Natural Gas Demand Projections by Different Agencies

	2022	2024	2025	2030
1. PNGRB Vision 2030 (MMSCMD)	517	571	598	746
Share in PES (%)				
2. Twelfth Plan Working Group (MMSCMD)	606		NA	
Share in PES (%)		NA		
3. IEA (India Energy Outlook)				
Stated Policies Scenario (MMSCMD)	NA	NA	259	340
Share in PES (%)	NA	NA	8	9
India Vision Case (MMSCMD)	NA	NA	NA	388
Share in PES (%)	NA	NA	NA	11
4. OIES (MMSCMD), Outlook 1	142	148	NA	
Share in PES (%)	NA			

Source: IEA (2021), pp. 221–2.
12th Plan Wkg Gr. Report on P&NG, Table 5.26, p. 48
PNGRB Vision, Tables 11, 12, p. 28
Sen (2017) Figure 20, p. 24

non-standard classification of certain sectors, and are not very useful for sectoral analysis. Indian energy data agencies classify natural gas in urea separately, and large industries are shown as separate consumers vis-à-vis smaller industries (located around cities) as served by CGD networks. IEA clubs the consumption in fertiliser manufacture within Industry. Hence, in different reports, there are different numbers mentioned regarding use of natural gas in India as feedstock versus fuel in industry. Due to the non-standard classification, only inputs have been taken/discussed from these reports. Thereafter, independent inferences have been drawn to estimate the demand and supply numbers for 2030 for the four main sub-sectors.

There are wide variances in demand projections of different agencies, across different timelines. For the year 2022, the projections of the erstwhile Planning Commission and PNGRB are four times higher than the projection of Oxford Institute for Energy Studies (OIES). Again, for 2030, the projections of PNGRB are nearly double than those of IEA's projections (Table 7.2). IEA's projections were published in 2021 itself. They are much higher for 2021 over OIES projections for 2020. No Planning Commission projection is, however, available for 2030. The variance is particularly large between the respective values of Indian government agencies and international ones. It is also in the above light that an incisive enquiry into the likely natural gas demand in the coming years becomes relevant. The main focus of this chapter is offering a detailed discussion on the factors that might determine demand for natural gas over medium term. The discussion on diversity and growth of natural gas in other countries within the earlier chapters converge in the findings herein. The analysis around price competitiveness is also included in this chapter. The methodology adopted in generating demand for natural gas scenarios for 2030 has been described below.

7.3   APPROACH

In Chapter 4, a number of factors and their likely impacts on natural gas demand were discussed. As stated earlier, a bottom-up analysis has been undertaken here by applying the above factors and others, too. Various policy tools that impinge on demand for a fuel such as administered pricing mechanism as prevalent in domestic gas, LPG and electricity, regulatory measures such as emission control and on use of certain fuels, timing and regularity of CGD bidding rounds and subsidy to renewables have been taken as levers. The discussion around these factors has been offered below, and is expected to add value for the readers, so that they may anticipate the impact of these factors on energy mix and particularly natural gas, the fuel of our principal interest.

7.3.1   UPPER AND LOWER LIMITS OF DEMAND PROJECTIONS

The analysis of comparative trends in diversity indicated that the Indian energy system was rather 'inflexible' in accommodating major shifts in respective shares of different energy sources. As there was a focus on self-sufficiency, it also unfolded a preference for coal. Further, our analysis of natural gas within the PES indicated that over the last several decades, most countries were able to reduce coal in their energy system, and either maintain or even enhance the share of natural gas during the study period. However, India was unable to enhance the share of natural gas, and while solar and wind technologies had not matured, and due to resettlement and other challenges as it became harder to increase hydropower capacity, India's energy mix remained coal-predominant. From learnings of the diversity analysis, it follows that any energy mix related projection for India must acknowledge the role of structural drivers. Accordingly, in this chapter, both structural drivers and fuel specific drivers have been kept in perspective, and both qualitative and quantitative methods have been used to estimate natural gas demand in 2030.

The uncertainties around domestic production of natural gas and RLNG supply infrastructure, call for a scenario-based analysis with upper and lower limits of both demand and supply. If, there is an increase in domestic production, it would also mean lesser reliance on LNG import infrastructure, and the supply numbers will have greater certainty. It is notable that domestic resources are 'given' for any nation, and cannot be 'manufactured as such'. On the other hand, imported supplies are flexible, but need a time lag. Therefore, for the purposes of this study, we take expected supply of natural gas from domestic and imported sources as the upper ceiling of likely supply in the short run (hence, of demand, too). As regards the lower limit of supply, this would be the availability of natural gas under all circumstances. In contrast, the lower limit of demand for natural gas would arise from bottom-up analysis. This has been explained later in this chapter when addressing each demand sub-sector. Various factors have been discussed in this chapter that might impinge on the growth in consuming sector itself—projections of urea demand, number of households (HH) specific domestic PNG connections, growth/PLF of natural gas-based power plants. Hence, an intensive application of different quantitative tools using the energy equivalence of different fuels with natural gas coupled with historical growth rates and likely growth in demand for service (energy delivery) from competing sources have been deployed.

Policy framework(s) have a major role to play in shaping the country's energy mix. These belong to the domain of clean air action—substitution of LPG in cooking by natural gas, and replacement of liquid fuels in transport by CNG, and even RLNG. If, the above policies are effectively implemented, then natural gas demand would increase. IEA's energy demand projections are under three possible scenarios. With growth in demand hinging on government policy and other factors, in this study, natural gas demand has been generated under two scenarios, one in the default case which may be akin to business-as-usual (BAU), wherein the current policies are not seriously implemented. And in the alternate ambitious scenario, the intended measures are realised in full. We may call the former as Lower Demand Scenario (LDS) and the latter as Higher Demand Scenario (HDS).

7.3.2 BOTTOM-UP APPROACH

Different factors impinge on natural gas demand in different sub-sectors. While pricing is a common factor and high natural gas prices have held back its share in many sub-sectors, but let us say even if, prices were competitive, demand may still not grow owing to a number of reasons. These mainly include entry barriers, air quality concerns, security of supply, consumer choice and existing government policy, etc. The above differing drivers eminently call for a sub-sectorial analysis or bottom-up approach. In this chapter, natural gas demand has been estimated within the four main consuming sub-sectors—CGD, Urea manufacture, Industry and Power—by applying these drivers (including price) and other 'concerns' as being relevant. As the existing studies including the one undertaken by OIES have largely been 'top-down' without much granularity, estimation of natural gas demand by various sectors is a major research outcome of this book. Even in the respective studies of all the four agencies already referred to in Table 7.2, the demand estimation in several sectors such as urban transport/cooking/urea are devoid of the workings or granular numbers, such as number of consumers or gas consumption per consumer, as the case may be.

7.3.3 ROLE OF PRICES IN GENERATING DEMAND SCENARIOS

In this study, price has not been taken as the sole trigger, and the role of prices has been discussed in tandem with non-price factors too. Another similarly placed large energy consumer, China, where attempts are being made to enhance the role of natural gas, there are similar challenge of price and non-price factors in making such energy choices. In a study of China, Wang et al. (2018) who have argued strongly in favour of natural gas in the Chinese economy have mentioned that over last three decades industry and power segments have been the major consumers of natural gas. This was made easy by moderate but steady growth of natural gas network across the country and use of natural gas grew in industrial processes, power generation and other domestic uses. Between 2009 and 2015 natural gas utilisation in China increased significantly (around 14% per annum), which was mainly driven by the power sector (18%) followed by transport (17.4%) and industry (15%). Interestingly, the authors argued that the price of natural gas in China has not negatively impacted its use much in various sectors including power, transportation, CGD, except industrial fuel and chemical gas use. Hence, non-price factors are important, and for India, this has been studied here in some detail.

Pricing has been carefully examined, as already seen in the previous chapter, wherein the sensitivity of demand to price has been brought out. In some areas such as power generation, coal has a clear price advantage over other fuels, particularly natural gas. Similarly, owing to liquid fuels (derived from crude oil) being priced higher than natural gas on a calorific parity basis, the latter has now become market competitive.[1] It is notable that liquid petroleum products are largely market priced (except for LPG and kerosene) and their demand is not a function of as to how much of it is produced in India—imported and domestically produced crude being priced almost the same. But, for domestic natural gas production as mentioned in earlier sections, the situation so far has been different. For those sectors that are prioritised for receiving domestic natural gas, a separate discussion exists below. As noted earlier, the impact of Covid-19 on global energy supply and prices has rendered 2020–21 numbers unreliable for analysis. Therefore, in this study, the price competitiveness between natural gas and competing fuels has been taken at the prices as prevailed in 2018–19, and demand estimations have been made assuming the arbitrage between competing fuels to remain the same (the level of difference may change) until the end of the study period (2030).

7.3.4 Recognition of Air Quality Concerns

Local air quality concerns are yet another factor that impinges on natural gas demand across consuming sectors. This factor also works in combination with other factors, such as technological feasibility to switch to different fuels, ability to pass on higher fuel price to customers and availability of infra to deliver the new fuels. Lately, both the courts and environment regulators such as NGT have been coming down harshly on polluting industries, requiring them to switch to cleaner fuels including natural gas, wherever it is available. This is especially the case in urban areas served by CGD networks where natural gas is available and the air quality concerns are equally grave. The recent ban on pet coke in several city limits is one such regulatory direction. Central Pollution Control Board (CPCB) has directed industries in National Capital Region (NCR) of Delhi to shift to natural gas wherever, it is available regardless of it being high-priced (HT, 2019).

7.3.5 Impact of Recent Upsurge in Clean Energy

The recent impetus in favour of renewables and clean energy, in general, and associated circumstances were briefly introduced in Chapter 4. But, in the current chapter while generating demand scenarios for natural gas, a careful examination of impact of these trends has been undertaken. The discussion around renewables is mainly focused on 'renewable electricity'. But, the analysis herein is not limited to renewable power related announcement of the Government under the 175 GW renewable power programme for 2022, which mainly focusses on 160 GW for solar/wind power, including 15 GW of small hydro and biomass. A yet higher ambition of 500 GW renewable capacity has been projected by the Government for 2030. It also goes on to discuss the impact of the roll-out of clean fuels including natural gas across end-uses such as cooking and transport fuels in urban areas, while phasing out of polluting solid fuels in industries and enforcing of tighter emission norms for thermal power projects (TPPs).

7.3.6 Demand Classification by Domestic and Imported Supplies

As a value-added outcome of this research, it has also been attempted to divide the natural gas demand into domestically produced and imported supplies. This builds up on the current priority policy for supply of domestic gas to certain sectors. Owing to the reason put forth here, the demand estimated to be met by domestic natural gas will not be impacted even if, the domestic supply was not realised—RLNG would make up the deficit. As the government has already announced that the new natural gas coming from freshly approved projects would be priced on market basis (as per prescribed formulae), the present gap between imported gas and domestic gas may not be much. There is already a policy move to migrate even the existing domestic supplies to market-determined pricing. Hence, the demand classification into domestic and imported natural gas may not matter much on price as a pivotal factor for demand. It is, nevertheless, worthwhile to estimate domestic gas demand within various sectors due to the following reason. Firstly, the existing allocation to priority sectors is expected to remain intact and has to be accepted as a non-market-based supply. It has been assumed that even new supplies would follow the existing top priority for CGD for cooking and transport purposes. The bidders in the CGD bidding rounds have assumed this priority to continue. Therefore, in this particular study, the incremental domestic natural gas supplies have largely been assigned to these sub-sectors, and the numbers so estimated help an interested reader to see as to what might be the natural gas demand for these price-sensitive sub-sectors.

7.4 CONSULTATION WITH EXPERTS

In the previous chapter, consultation with subject-matter experts on supply side issues was briefly highlighted. Here, the demand-related views as ascertained from them have been briefly mentioned to support/challenge the estimates made by the author.

7.4.1 REASONS FOR HIGHER NATURAL GAS DEMAND

Natural gas enjoys a number of distinctive advantages—environmentally more sustainable than coal and oil, its transportation is easier than that of solid fuels and ease of storage/transport by reduction in volume via liquefying or compressing, etc. While investigating these drivers, out of three options given, all the experts appreciated the environmental benefits of natural gas use leading to its demand growth. On the other two drivers, under 50% of the respondents felt that electric mobility might adversely impact the growth of natural gas demand in the country. Further, as regards gas-based power generation, again only 50% of the respondents supported that it could drive natural gas demand. (Figure 7.1).

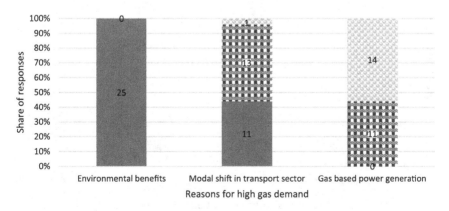

FIGURE 7.1 Reasons for higher natural gas demand.

7.4.2 SECTORAL DRIVERS OF THE NATURAL GAS DEMAND IN INDIA

Which sector might lead the growth in natural gas demand is a key question in this study? The expert consultation revealed that CGD is considered as the major driver for gas demand in India, followed by Industries. Fertilizers and Power might be the least demand generators for natural gas. Incidentally only about 10% of them felt that Power would be the number one driver for a surge in gas demand (Figure 7.2).

With a large dependence of the natural gas growth story riding on various commitments received in the CGD bidding rounds, it is important that the successful bidders fulfil their contractual commitments. Moderate to high number of respondents were confident that they will be honoured. This aspect has to be acknowledged as a policy recommendation for a close monitoring of achievement of milestones in the CGD contracts.

7.4.3 IMPETUS TO NATURAL GAS IN CGD

The experts generally agreed that the bidding rounds would have a positive impact on spurring future natural gas demand (Figure 7.3). Nearly 50% of the respondents (out of a total of 24) are cautiously optimistic about the demand growth actual happening due to commissioning up of city gas projects in urban areas. Around 30% of the respondents were just optimistic, while a mere 1% were highly optimistic (gave 10 out of 10 marks) about the spread of natural gas distribution licenses leading to increased natural gas demand.

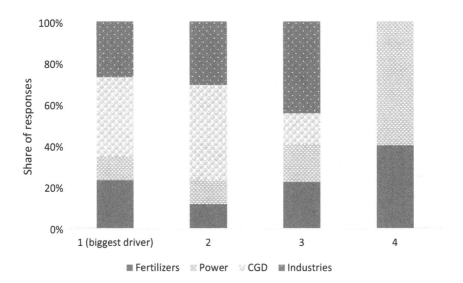

FIGURE 7.2 Sectoral drivers of natural gas demand in the market (by share of respondents). Note 1: Most important factor, 4: Least important factor.

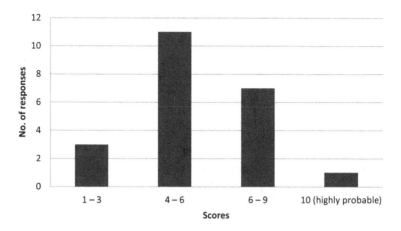

FIGURE 7.3 Impact of ninth and tenth round CGD contracts on natural gas demand. Note 1: Least optimistic, 10: Full optimism.

7.4.4 Natural Gas in Power

While natural gas was not found by experts to be the preferred fuel in power (it was ranked the last), yet simultaneously, it was considered that natural gas-based generation would not be without its due impact on overall natural gas demand in power sector. Accordingly, in the section on power sector later in this chapter, the HDS has been developed around this emerging possibility. Coal (and not renewables) was acknowledged as the main challenger to natural gas in power. To a question as to whether tight thermal emission norms might mitigate the negativity around coal and promote natural gas, it lacked support from many.

7.4.5 Urea Sector as a Driver of Demand for Natural Gas

Urea sector was not considered to be a major driver of natural gas demand— placed at the third place behind CGD and Industry, just above power. The national aim of becoming self-sufficient in urea was overwhelmingly stated to be the main driver of domestic production of urea. This aspect has been adopted as a major factor in building the gas demand scenario for 2030. On the issue of as to whether urea demand might rise in future, majority of the respondents answered that the growth rate might actually reduce to moderate level from existing one in future. Coal gasification may be a source of raw feedstock for urea manufacture, and the success of this emerging technology, may further diminish the role of natural gas in urea manufacture.

7.4.6 Driver for RLNG Demand

For RLNG, Industry was affirmed by all to be the most promising demand sub-sector. In this chapter, as guided by the consultation, RLNG has been allocated to meet the growth in natural gas demand within industrial sector.

7.4.7 ADVANTAGEOUS OVER OTHER FOSSIL FUELS

Environmental benefits were acknowledged by all as the major advantage enjoyed by natural gas over other fossil fuels. This is likely to work in its favour in Industries, too, especially due to regulatory action on emissions. Liquid fuel was supported by all as the most likely one to be replaced by Industries, should natural gas become available. This has also been confirmed in the current research especially in refining and other Industries.

7.5   NATURAL GAS DEMAND IN CITY GAS DISTRIBUTION (CGD) SECTOR

7.5.1 BACKGROUND

Indian cities face severe air quality concerns. With 15 of the top 20 cities in the world having the poorest air quality, natural gas is expected to cut down ambient emissions in urban areas by substituting polluting fuels both in cooking and transport (The Hindu, 2019b). Within the urban areas there are four main natural gas-consuming sub-sectors: cooking, transport, commercial (which include hotels/restaurants), and small industries located within and close to urban areas. The price competitiveness of natural gas and its lower emission levels make it favourable for adoption in urban areas.[2] While acknowledging the above prospect, Indian policy makers have created a favourable environment for adoption of domestic natural gas in the CGD sector.[3] The large potential in the latter is evident from the fact that in the past decade, total natural gas consumption in the country rose 1.5 times (from 103 MMSCMD in 2008–09 to 147 MMSCMD in 2018–19). However, natural gas consumption in the CGD sector grew 2.5 times (from 10 to 25 MMSCMD) during the same period.

Other than for sale via CGD networks, no license is required for marketing of natural gas. The authorisation to sell it within the limits of districts/areas, which is called geographical area (GA), has to be won through an auction process as conducted by the PNGRB. Until December 2018, the Board had conducted nine bidding rounds. In the ninth round, it awarded rights to entities to set up networks in 86 new GAs by 2028, over and above existing networks in 92 areas. With commitments obtained under the tenth bidding round, expectedly that by 2028, 53% of the country's area and 70% of the country's population will get access to CGD networks (Annual Report, MoPNG, 2021). The above positives signify availability of piped natural gas networks on a geographical basis, but household connectivity would actually depend on consumer preference. Evidently, LPG has a near complete penetration in domestic cooking. Although the potential for gas utilisation in the CGD sector has been high, when compared with all energy used in urban areas, the existing share of natural gas is modest and could have been higher. Sen (2015) highlights the role of related infrastructure, the limited presence of which has hampered the growth of natural gas in CGD.

In this section, natural gas demand for the four sub-sectors within CGD in 2030 has been estimated. As regards cooking (PNG) and transport (CNG) sub-sectors, the estimations are based on commitments received in the ninth bidding round for PNG households specific connections and number of CNG stations committed to be set up (the tenth bidding round has also been concluded, but the commitments herein are based on ninth bidding round only), respectively. As regards the other two sub-sectors (commercial and urban industries), where creation of specific delivery infra like CNG stations and pipeline connectivity to residential areas is not required, no commitments for sale volume, etc., were sought from the bidders. Further, these sub-sectors do not get preferential domestic natural gas supply (which is lowly priced), and their demand is market-based, which has been extrapolated using other assumptions as explained below. In the next subsection, factors upon which the demand might depend and their likely impacts have been discussed.

7.5.2   FACTORS DRIVING NATURAL GAS DEMAND IN CGD SECTOR

The growth of CGD sector in India was first triggered by court orders, especially in Delhi (PIB, 2001). This led to a policy push for use of natural gas in other select cities, regardless of considerations such as consumer preference or domestic availability of this fuel. However, the pace generally remained slow and by 2015—within a decade of its establishment—PNGRB could only realise construction of CGD networks in 67 cities. However, lately the pace has picked up in the last three to four years with frequent rounds of offer of GAs for setting up CGD networks. The ninth round offered improved bidding terms which attracted a good response from interested parties (LiveMint, 2018). Even the 10th round has been successful. As government companies are not entirely led by considerations of commerciality, earlier they would win bids over private bidders by offering generous terms. In the new terms, tariff floors were set to obviate unviable bids and more weightage in award was given to infrastructure creation. Moreover, in the initial years this sector was almost entirely dependent on domestic natural gas which had limited availability, and also due to lower priority accorded to CGD earlier in the gas utilisation policy.[4] The policy directions and factors related to this are discussed in detail below:

7.5.2.1   Slow award of CGD Authorisations

The pace of bidding rounds and awards made (between 2006 and 2016) were slow, with the result that the Board (PNGRB) could only bid out right through eight bidding rounds carried out in 97 cities, whereas in the ninth round 86 GAs have been given just in one round. The actual setting up of networks has been even slower than the number of GAs awarded. Coupled by dominance of PSUs, the number of players in this business has remained more or less limited.

7.5.2.2   Poor Availability of Domestic Gas

While availability of domestic gas is common across demand sectors, it has played a major role in CGD as two sub-sectors depend on domestic natural gas (at administered price) entirely. Due to poor availability of domestic gas (average annual supply of 33 BCM/year), the distributors had to depend on the more expensive RLNG, for which there isn't much demand. Moreover, the Government has ordered that domestic natural gas allocations could only be used for cooking and transport, which further dampened the scope for demand growth in commercial and industrial sub-sectors who were left behind to source RLNG. There is no dearth of demand for domestic gas as it is cheap, and even the price of PNG and CNG had been kept lower than the competing fuels.[5] With such constraints in domestic natural gas availability, expansion in networks was largely restrained.

7.5.2.3   Competition from Cheaper Fuels

Cheaper fuels have had a varying impact across demand sectors, and have been discussed in different sections of this chapter. Within CGD, unlike the household and transport sub-sectors, in commercial and industrial sub-sectors, the demand is met by RLNG which is priced on a market basis. This has resulted in its demand linked to its price competitiveness relative to other fuels, where subsidies have prevailed such as diesel, and power and coal where again some sort of subsidy has been there for long. It is only after the recent petroleum pricing reforms that have removed diesel subsidy, can it now be expected that RLNG demand may finally receive a boost especially for an industrial use. However, coal continues to sell mostly at administered prices fixed by Coal India Ltd. It is notable that coal price for power sector was last raised in January, 2018.

7.5.2.4   Resistance from Liquid Fuel Players

Penetration of a new substitute fuel like natural gas faces a challenge from the well-entrenched large liquid fuel companies in energy sector. Huge investments are locked into refineries, pipelines, storages, LPG bottling plants and retail outlets. Unsurprisingly though, no major Oil Marketing Company (OMC) has made such big investments in natural gas business, and GAIL, the dedicated gas transport company, continues to be the only PSU in this business (Petronet LNG Ltd. is merely an LNG terminal owner/operator). Consequently, investment in CGD business has been subdued and CNG retail outlets are scarce, often leading to large queues of vehicles waiting to fill gas from these outlets.

7.5.2.5   Absence of a Coherent Energy Policy
Favouring Natural Gas in Urban Areas

A comprehensive air quality strategy that places premium on natural gas as a clean fuel is largely missing in the country. It is only when tribunals/courts mandate a sudden shift, does natural gas get impetus. There are several demand areas where there is scope for natural gas to replace polluting fuels. The air pollution in the cities due to high consumption of diesel and petrol can be genuinely reduced if, vehicles convert to CNG, as has been seen in the case of Delhi (Jain, 2018). Similarly, coal and wood used for cooking in the hotels/dhabas, and coal and diesel in small industries in and around urban areas could be replaced with PNG. Now that the government has launched the National Clean Air Programme

(NCAP) in 102 cities that have been identified on the basis of high levels of ambient air pollution, natural gas may get the much desired push (PIB, 2019a).

7.5.3 Natural Gas Demand in CGD Sub-Sectors in 2030

Unlike sale of natural gas to de-licensed sectors like urea and power plants, the case of CGD is different. For CGD to grow, there needs to be a natural gas distribution network, which is promoted by the PNGRB through a bidding process. The investor is incentivised by giving a monopoly period and after the lapse of this period, a regulated entry of gas providers while preserving the monopoly in the distribution pipelines is ensured. The government assists the operator in connecting households (including high rise residential apartments), getting sites for CNG stations, and actively promotes the adoption of natural gas on a mass scale in urban areas. There are four traditional sub-sectors in CGD areal limits—transport, cooking, commercial enterprises and small industries that abound the urban areas. The PNGRB has obtained commitments from successful bidders for award of licenses as to how many households would they actually connect for provision of PNG, and the number of CNG dispensing stations would they be setting up within the defined timelines. Natural gas demand estimation in these two CGD sub-sectors has been tabulated in Table 7.3 based on the commitments received in the ninth bidding round (until 2028), as well as pro-rated expansion of GAs during 2028–30 (as the timeline for this study is 2030), and growth of natural gas consumers in existing GAs as they existed in 2018.

From Table 7.3, it is evident that at present, numbers of CNG stations and PNG connections are insignificant, and there is a vast scope for this clean fuel to grow. While the country's population having access to CGD networks was claimed to be 20% (260 million people or 52 million households @ 5 persons per HH), domestic PNG connections are merely 4.26 million. It is notable that in this study

---

TABLE 7.3
Projected CGD Access (2030)

	GAs	CNG Stations	Domestic	Population with Access to CGD[c]
1. Existing (2018)	97[a]	1424	4.26 million	20%
2. Growth in existing GAs	97[a]	2831	19.87 million	20%
3. 9th Round[d]	86	4346	21.04 million	30%
4. Growth during 2028–30[b]	16	868	4.20 million	6%
Total	199	9469	49.36 million	56%

[a] including 5 sub-judice.
[b] Prorated increase.
[c] percentage as per ET, 2018a).
[d] ET, 2018b; PNGRB, 2018.

we take a section of the population to be covered if there is availability of a CGD licensee in a close proximity. But, for this availability to convert to actual connection depends on consumer choice as well as efforts made on the part of the CGD licensee. Looking at the low connections despite coverage (even at 20% penetration of CGD), large scope stills exists for growth of this convenient fuel even in existing GAs. The estimation of demand and methodology used for calculating the same has been discussed below.

7.5.3.1 Transport

Natural gas is an attractive option for the transport sector because of its price competitiveness relative to petrol and diesel. It may be recalled that the cheap APM priced gas is reserved for transport and cooking sub-sectors alone. Consequently, the overall growth in CNG sales has risen by approximately 10% per year from 2.24 BCM in 2013–14 to 3.47 BCM in 2017–18 (Table 7.4).[6] This growth was supported by a more than doubling in CNG stations from 674 in 2013–14 to 1,424 by April 2018 (CAGR—16%). Of these stations, 82% were in Delhi, Mumbai and Gujarat (ET, 2018a). It is assumed that growth in CNG stations within the existing GAs will also continue in these mature markets, albeit at an assumed muted growth rate of 5% per annum. This yields a total of 4255 CNG stations in existing GAs by 2030. Successful bidders of the ninth bidding round in 2018 had committed to set up 4346 CNG stations in new GAs by 2028 (PNGRB, 2018). As the timeline of this study is 2030, the number of CNG stations is estimated further by two years (2028–30), by taking a simple annual average from 4,346 CNG stations in ten years period, i.e. 2018–28 (at the rate of 434 new stations/year). By projecting the above figures up to 2,030 yields an additional 868 stations for the period 2028–30. Adding up all the four numbers (existing, growth in existing GAs, in new GAs—up to 2028 and between 2028 and 2030) above yields a total of 9,469 stations in 2030. In IEA's India Energy Outlook, 2021 a total of 8,190 CNG stations have been stated to be planned in addition to 1,730 existing stations.

Sale per station is obtained by dividing the yearly sales of CNG with the number of CNG stations, as shown in column 4 of Table 7.4, i.e. for the year 2017–18 (CNG sale of 2,638 TMT), we derive a per station sale of 1.85 TMT (total CNG sales in 2017–18/number of stations 2017–18). In the LDS, it is assumed that sale per station of 1.85 TMT in 2017–18 remains unchanged in 2030. To estimate the demand in 2030 for these stations, the average CNG sale per station is multiplied with the number of stations projected for 2030. This yields a natural gas demand of 23 BCM in 2030. The sales of 2017–18 may be low because new stations set up recently may not be truly representative of demand, because there will be a lag in growth of CNG fleet after the setting up of new stations. Hence, a longer-term average including both mature and new markets may be a more realistic number. From Table 7.4 we can also calculate a five-year average sale per station (2013–18) at 2.13 TMT/year. The average so derived may be taken to estimate demand under the HDS. In the latter case, the total demand for CNG in 2030 is likely to be 26.53 BCM.

The above estimate may be subjected to a test as to how the estimated CNG sales in 2030 compare with those of liquid transport fuel. In 2017–18, MS (Petrol)

TABLE 7.4
Projected annual consumption of CNG in 2030 (domestic gas)

Year End	CNG Stations	CNG Sales in TMT	in BCM	Sale/Station in TMT	Average/Station in TMT
2013–14	674	1,928	2.24	2.86	2.13 (Average sale
2014–15	1,009	2,037	2.68	2.02	during 2013–18)
2015–16	1,081	2,155	2.83	1.99	
2016–17	1,233	2,365	3.11	1.92	
2017–18	1,424	2,638	3.47	1.85	
2029–30	4,255[a]	NA	NA	NA	NA
	5,214[b]	NA	NA	NA	NA
Total (high scenario)	9,469	20,169	26.53		2.13 (Average sale of 2013–18 is taken)
Total (low scenario)	9,469	17,518	23		1.85 (Sale/station in 2017–18 is taken)

Source: PPAC (2018b).
[a] In existing GAs estimated @5% p.a over 2018.
[b] Ninth bidding round (2028) and pro-rated 2028–30.
Note: The two rows relating to 'Total' indicate the working of demand estimation for CNG stations in existing and new GAs in 2029–30 under two scenarios of sale of CNG per station.

and HSD sales figures were 26.2 and 81.1 MT, respectively. It was estimated by the government that all of petrol, and 70% of HSD sales (56 MT) is consumed in the transport sector (PPAC, 2019). Hence, the transport sector consumed 26.2 MT of petrol and 56 MT of diesel (total of 82 MT) in 2017–18. The estimated natural gas demand in the HDS (2030) of 26.53 BCM in 2030, is in energy equivalence terms a mere one-third of the present liquid fuel consumption. Looking to the nearly 5% annual growth in liquid fuel consumption as experienced in the past decade (2009–19), the above derived CNG demand leaves a large scope for further adoption of natural gas, and is quite achievable in 2030 (PPAC, 2019).

The above demand growth has been estimated on an underlying assumption that the allocation of cheaper domestic natural gas to the transport and domestic cooking end-uses would continue. However, even if, RLNG were used, due to price advantage enjoyed by natural gas over liquid fuels, it would still be competitive (discussed later).

7.5.3.2 Domestic Cooking
PNG is a cleaner, cheaper and more convenient cooking option than LPG (ERG, 2017, pp. 1–15). The government has declared that with the spread of CGD, it would substitute LPG in urban areas with PNG. The share of PNG sales (cooking) in total natural gas sales in CGD sector is rising and has grown rapidly from 16% in 2015 to 22% in 2017. The number of PNG connections rose by one-third during

the same time, nearly 17% per annum. It is likely that with extension in pipelines within the cities, the present growth rate in PNG connections in existing GAs may continue. In Table 7.5, it is brought out that in 2017 with the reach of CGD limited to 20% of present population (260 million against a total population of 1.3 billion), the number of PNG connections is merely 4.26 million or 9% out of a total of 52 million families. The growth in existing GAs has been assumed at a rate of 15% per annum or slightly lesser than 17% seen in the last two years (there will be a decline as more and more households get connected), reaching a total of 24.13 million connections in 2030. This is feasible as even at the present level of population served by CGD networks (52 million), this would translate into less than 50% of total families in the coverage area.

The future demand of PNG can be estimated by using the equivalence of natural gas in calorific value terms with LPG, as the default cooking fuel. Based on average consumption of LPG at 11 LPG cylinders (14.2 kg each), a calorific equivalence of roughly 186 SCM/year of PNG (GOI, 2018b) is derived.[7] As this is the bare minimum fuel needed for cooking, this could form the basis for determining the total PNG demand in the LDS scenario in 2030. In the HDS scenario, an average of the actual consumption of PNG per domestic connection in the past three years (for which data is available) has been taken, which amounts to 261 SCM/year (Table 7.5), nearly one-and-a-half time the energy equivalence of 11 cylinders of LPG, and is very much on the higher side. This number has been derived from PPAC data and a possible reason for the exaggerated estimation may

---

TABLE 7.5

Projected annual consumption of PNG in cooking in 2030 (domestic gas)

Year	Progressive PNG Connections (million)	Total PNG Sales (BCM)	PNG Sale/ Connection (SCM)	Avg. PNG/HH (SCM)
2013–14	2.6	NA	NA	NA
2014–15	2.87	NA	NA	NA
2015–16	3.16	0.57	180	261
2016–17	3.6	1.17	325	
2017–18	4.26	1.19	279	
2029–30^	24.13	NA	NA	NA
2029–30*	25.24	NA	NA	NA
Total (High Scenario)	49.37	12.88	261	261
Total (Low scenario)	49.37	9.4	186	186 (calorific equivalence of 11 LPG cylinders)

^in existing GAs projected @15% p.a over 2018.
*9th bidding round (2028) and pro-rated 2028–30.
Source: PPAC (2018b).

be inclusion of non-cooking or commercial usage of PNG in hotels/restaurant. The inefficiency in combustion of natural gas in retrofitted LPG stove is also a contributory reason. Therefore, the higher demand estimate may need to be seen in the above light.

Under the ninth bidding round, a commitment of adding 21.04 million domestic connections during the period 2018–28 has been made. For the next two years (2028–30), this can be pro-rated (as has been done for CNG demand) as an increase at the rate of 2.1 million/year, could yield an additional 4.2 million connections. Therefore, including the existing 24.13 million connections in existing GAs, Table 7.5 projects the domestic PNG connections in 2030 at 49.37 million (in India Energy Outlook, 2021, IEA has projected 42 million PNG connections over the existing 5 million connections). In the LDS scenario, at the rate of 186 SCM/year, a total PNG demand of 9.4 BCM (in 2030) can be expected for domestic cooking. In HDS scenario, at an average household consumption of 261 SCM/year, PNG demand is expected to be 12.88 BCM (2030).

7.5.3.3 Commercial and Industrial Demand

There has been a steady growth in natural gas demand by commercial and small industrial entities served by CGD networks. This consumer category is dependent on RLNG. These commercial and industrial units are of different types that exist in urban areas and cannot be classified by their end-product manufacture. Although these units find it attractive to use cheaper alternate fuels (such as pet coke, fuel oil and LDO) over the expensive market-priced RLNG, but due to the Supreme Court and NGT orders that have placed curbs in usage of these polluting fuels (in select urban areas including NCR region of Delhi), the demand for natural gas in these sub-sectors has been rising (CRISIL, 2019). In the post-ninth bidding round period with expansion in the coverage of CGD, and enhanced court activism, it is expected that the demand of natural gas for these sectors will become stronger. One aspect to be borne in mind is that the net returns on sale of natural gas to the CGD operator, are different between the two types of gas (domestic and RLNG). On the basis of past trend of sale of domestic gas versus RLNG, a healthy mix of the two streams in a certain ratio has been observed in the CGD business of existing operators (discussed later). To estimate the demand in these sub-sectors of CGD in 2030, we assume that the historical ratio of natural gas sale in CGD areas between domestic (cooking and transport end uses) and RLNG (commercial and industrial) sale, will be maintained in future as well at least up to 2030. This is a reasonable assumption as both the categories of gas sales are likely to rise due to commitments in bidding rounds, and regulatory action, respectively.

As may be seen in Table 7.6, the overall share of natural gas consumed in non-transport and non-domestic cooking gas end-uses in CGD, i.e. the sectors that depend on RLNG, has been approximately 43% (simple average of sales over four years, 2015–19), and domestic natural gas related sales at 57% (PPAC, 2018b). The above share may be skewed at local levels and could favour domestic gas share in metros due to court mandated shift to CNG, especially for public transport vehicles.[8] Even the PPAC data shows that on an all-India basis, share of CNG sales

TABLE 7.6

Projected demand for natural gas in commercial/industrial sectors in 2030 (BCM/yr)

	2015–16	2016–17	2017–18	2018–19	2029–30* HIGH	2029–30* LOW
CGD Sale	6.15	7.28	8.54	8.95	70.31	56.1
RLNG	2.75	3	3.88	4.05	31	23.7
% of RLNG in CGD	45%	41%	45%	45%	43%	43%
Domestic	3.4	4.28	4.66	4.9	39.31	32.4
% of Domestic in CGD	55%	59%	55%	55%	57%	57%

*As per trend, 43:57 for RLNG/Domestic gas.
Source: PPAC (2018b).

is lower as a percentage contribution of overall CGD sales than in metros. The estimated domestic natural gas sales in CGD sector (CNG and PNG) in 2029–30 has already been presented in Tables 7.4 and 7.5 (26.53 BCM for transport and 12.88 BCM in cooking) a total of 39.31 BCM in 2029–30 in HDS scenario, and a total of 32.4 BCM in LDS. Due to commitments received for both the transport and cooking sub-sectors, there may be a slight rise in share of gas consumed in these sub-sectors (taken as domestic gas). Taking the above ratio between industrial/ commercial natural gas (RLNG) and domestic/transport gas sales in CGD (43:57), the gas demand for commercial and industrial sub-sectors (RLNG) is likely to be 31 BCM and 23.7 BCM in HDS and LDS, respectively (Table 7.6).

7.5.4 AGGREGATE NATURAL GAS DEMAND IN CGD SECTOR

The conclusion of the ninth and tenth CGD bidding rounds presents a positive outlook for future natural gas demand. The committed numbers for CNG stations and domestic PNG connections (ninth round) cover nearly 56% of India's population (the commitments under the tenth bidding round will take it up to 70% coverage). As natural gas is cheaper than crude oil on calorific parity basis, it is expected that it will be more competitive in sectors where it could substitute oil-based products, notably in cooking and transport sub-sectors. As far as natural gas demand in non-domestic segment is concerned, i.e. the commercial and small industries, the availability of infrastructure will generate options of switching to this cleaner fuel. Using the approach of bottom-up analysis, it is found that the total demand for CGD will be 70.31 BCM in HDS and 55.1 BCM in LDS, only about 20% lower. Figure 7.4 presents a consolidated picture of the estimated demand under both scenarios, further classified by domestic natural gas and RLNG (for commercial and industrial sub-sectors).

The analysis in this section reveals a much more positive picture for natural gas in CGD than what has been stated in literature. The PNGRB's 'Vision 2030'

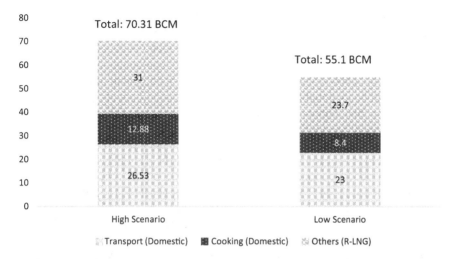

FIGURE 7.4 Projected natural gas demand in CGD sector in 2030 (BCM/year).

finalised in 2013 projected the demand to be 85.6 MMSCMD or 31 BCM in 2030 (PNGRB, 2013), which is significantly lower than even the LDS demand of 55.1 BCM in Figure 7.4. The reason for this could be that the Vision document was made public in 2013, five years before firm commitments were received under the large CGD bidding round as seen in the ninth round. Similarly, IEA's projections are also likely to be lesser because the PNG connections and CNG stations given in their India Energy Outlook, 2021 are both lesser than the numbers envisaged in this study. It is notable that the demand potential in 2030 could be even higher as with 56% geographical coverage of CGD networks after achievement of the commitments under ninth bidding round, PNG connections would be within the reach of 150 million families (56% of assumed population of 1.4 billion in 2030, and a HH comprising five persons). With the commitments received under the tenth bidding round, the coverage would even exceed 70% population coverage. However, the projections in this study assume only 49.36 million households availing of PNG. Based on the analysis in this section, the demand outlook for CGD sector looks quite positive. The proactive stance of the regulator in addition to according of first priority to CGD in domestic gas allocation and environmental triggers, can further boost this demand.

7.6 DEMAND FOR NATURAL GAS IN POWER SECTOR

7.6.1 BACKGROUND

Power sector is a major consumer of natural gas and in 2017, it accounted for 39% of all natural gas produced in the world (BP, 2019a). However, in India, due to poor availability of natural gas on one hand and large domestic coal reserves on the other, and other reasons discussed in this subsection, it is coal-based power that accounts for the highest share in power generation—in 2017–18 it amounted to 76%—while natural gas-based power was a mere 3.8% (GOI, 2019a) and (Lok Sabha, 2019). Thus, what might be the role of natural gas in power sector in the coming decades, there is limited certainty. India's per capita electricity consumption is still small at only about 1181 kWh/year (2018–19) (GOI, 2019b). With growth in GDP, demand for power can be expected to rise, pushing up generation from all types of power sources. Since 2011, natural gas-based power plants have faced shortage of domestic gas leading to falling PLFs and stranded capacities (GOI, 2019b).[9] Declining domestic production has resulted in 6 GW out of a total of 25 GW gas-based generation capacity not receiving any allocation of domestic natural gas, and stranding of more than half the capacity (14,305 MW) (GOI, 2019b). After the announcement of a target for setting up 175 GW of renewable power generation capacity by 2022, there was a rise in expectation that gas-based power may be required to address balancing and peaking requirements.[10] However, studies undertaken by the Ministry of Power suggest different kinds of interventions.

A quick background of Indian electricity and fuel markets is desirable to understand the domestic dynamics of the regulatory set-up, especially as this sector works in a highly regulated regime. In the electricity markets, around 92% of the total power sold in the country is via power purchase agreements (PPAs) and the rest is sold through short-term power instruments at power exchanges (RBI, 2019). The Electricity Act of 2003 provides for power to be bought by distribution companies only through competitive bids. In the bidding process, expensive power like RLNG-based power does not find any buyers. In the fuel markets, domestically produced fuels such as coal and natural gas have been priced administratively. Coal is largely produced by state-owned companies that provide it to power producers at administered price, which is lower than the price of imported coal on calorific-parity basis. It is not uncommon for countries with large domestic coal production and poor natural gas production to price coal cheaply (Rybak, 2019).

In India, domestic gas has been priced at a discount to imported gas, but the power sector gets a small part of the total domestic supplies. The future domestic gas supplies coming at market-determined price will further work to the disadvantage of gas-based power. In addition to price and availability disadvantages, natural gas suffers from other structural challenges in power sector. PPAs of coal-based power work well with India's electricity market. This is because there is only a marginal yearly increase in the administered coal price and under the provisions of PPAs, distribution companies are able to pass on these minor changes in coal-based tariffs forward to consumers. On the other hand, the price of imported LNG prices is market-linked and highly variable without the provision of 'pass-through', which works against gas-based power. Resultantly, PPAs for gas-based power could be signed only for a small capacity. These are the main reasons which deter scaling up of RLNG-based power.

Domestic natural gas production peaked in 2010, and then kept falling every year until 2017 (MoPNG, 2017).[11] However, gas-based power generation capacity has continued to grow regardless of trends available in domestic gas production. Figure 7.5 presents the growth in gas-based generation capacity for four five-year

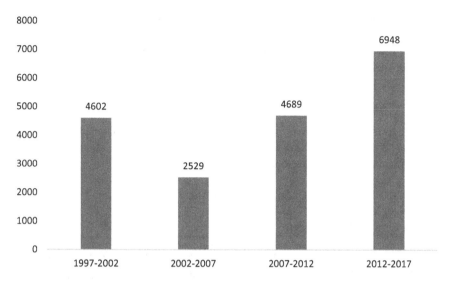

FIGURE 7.5   Growth in natural gas-based generation capacity (MW).
Note: Marginal additions after 2017. (GOI, 2019b).

TABLE 7.7

Average daily consumption of natural gas in power sector (MMSCMD)

	Gas in Power				Generation (in TWh)	
Year	Domestic Gas	LNG	Total	LNG (all sectors)	Gas-based	All sources (renewables not included)
2014–15	25.2	0	25.2	51	40	1049
2015–16	28.26	9.13	37.39	59	47.3	1108
2016–17	29.59	6.6	36.19	68	48.4	1160
2017–18	22	7.24	29.24	75	49	1206
2018–19	25	8	33	79	50	1249

Source: CEA, 2018b; 2018a; GOI, 2020; PPAC, n.d.

time cohorts from 1997 to 2017 (confirming to the five-year plan cycles). Thus, it can be seen that there was no correlation between domestic natural gas production and growth in gas-based capacity, and stress in gas-based power only increased.

Table 7.7 further indicates that consumption of natural gas in power sector has remained nearly static, while power generated from all sources increased barring a lone exception of power from gas-based power generation. Figure 7.5 and Table 7.7 together indicate that upcoming capacities did not uptake additional volumes of RLNG, and these did not even receive higher domestic natural gas supplies. This shows that as capacities were rising, there was a corresponding fall in PLF. The share of RLNG in total natural gas consumption in power sector was static at about 30%. Table 7.7 shows that during that period (2014–19), total LNG supply grew from 51 to 79 MMSCMD, thus implying that RLNG supplies were not a constraint.

7.6.2 PROJECTIONS OF DIFFERENT AGENCIES

A number of agencies have projected natural gas-based power capacities and natural gas demand in future, as shown in Table 7.8. Projections contained in three government documents have been examined:

a. 12th Plan Working Group Report (2012–17)
b. National Electricity Plan (NEP) and
c. Vision 2030 of PNGRB.

The 12th Plan Working Group Report on Petroleum and Natural Gas sector prepared in 2011, is largely pessimistic about availability of domestic natural gas, and perhaps due to price competitiveness, it did not envisage any substantial growth in gas-based capacity (RLNG-based plants was ruled out and not considered at all). It thus projected a growth of mere 1,086 MW during 2012–17, but another 12 GW was expected if, additional domestic natural gas became available. As given in Figure 7.5, actual growth recorded was 6,948 MW) While the Report contained projections for coal and lignite capacities for the next five years (2017–22), but due to above reasons, it did not anticipate any natural gas-based units for this period (GOI, 2012a).

TABLE 7.8

Projections of natural gas-based capacity (MW) and natural gas demand (MMSCMD) by different agencies

		2016–17			
	Capacity	Low	High	2022	2030
1	Vision 2030 of PNGRB (MW)	42917	42917	62917	94917
	Gas Demand	159	199	234	354
		(75% PLF)	(90% PLF)	(75% PLF)	(75% PLF)
2	NEP (base year is 2016–17)	25330	25330	25735	NA
				(same in 2027)	
	^Gas Demand at 90% PLF	123	123	125	NA
3	12th Plan Working Group*	31786	43786	307	NA
	Gas Demand	225		NA	NA

^not a NEP projection, but normative requirement for projected capacity
*as on 31st March 2011 with existing 17.7 GW capacity
Source: PNGRB, 2013; CEA, 2018a; GOI, 2012a.

The PNGRB Vision 2030 document, submitted in 2013, had assumed a robust growth in natural gas-based capacity from mere 18,381 MW in 2012 to 42,917 MW in 2016–17, and natural gas demand of 199 MMSCMD at 90% PLF and 159 MMSCMD at 70%–75% PLF (PNGRB, 2013).[12] It is surprising that while this document was finalised at around the same time when the 12th five year plan was prepared (2013), but the projections of these two government documents are wide apart. For the period beyond 2017 up to 2030, it has assumed a fresh addition of 20 GW (@4,000 MW/year) with fresh natural gas demand of 75 MMSCMD at 75% PLF (base of 2017), every five years. This leads to a projected capacity of 94,917 MW and aggregate natural gas demand of 354 MMSCMD in 2030.

In comparison to the two reports mentioned above, the most recent projections are of NEP that was released in 2018, and it projects a much smaller growth than those available from the first two reports (the next NEP is still in the making). A fresh addition of merely 406 MW has been noted for the period 2017–22 and this too was marked only for balancing power from variable renewables. For 2022, the normative natural gas demand for the existing gas-based power capacity is 125 MMSCMD. However, the NEP does not even envisage a need for the latter, as it projects a much smaller gas-based generation to suffice balancing requirement for 175 GW renewables targeted for the same year.

From the discussion above, it is evident that NEP and 12th Plan projections are based on power generation based only on domestic gas, while PNGRB Vision 2030 looks at imported supplies (RLNG), too. This distinction is understandable as the latter document was prepared by the PNGRB. It was addressing the need for natural gas-related infra (pipelines, etc.) for an optimistic scenario, where even RLNG for power may also need transportation and while the others were looking at the bare minimum natural gas that might go into power generation. It is notable that both 12th Plan and PNGRB's Gas Vision 2030 are now nearly a decade old projections.

7.6.3   FACTORS THAT COULD DRIVE NATURAL GAS DEMAND IN POWER SECTOR

A set of complex factors impact gas-based generation. Some important ones from the point of this study were examined below to provide further insights.

7.6.3.1   Growing Electricity Demand

A rising demand for electricity may need supplies from all possible sources. Given that at present, India has a low per capita electricity consumption, one can expect a robust increase in future. However, growth rate over the last two decades has only been moderate—about 5% per annum as per CEA's 19th Electricity Power Survey (EPS). (The 20th EPS is expected later in 2022.) According to the latter, going forward from 2017 into the period 2017–22, the electrical energy demand is expected to grow at a CAGR of 6.18% and reach 1,566 BU (CEA, 2015). For 2027, the projection is of 2,047 BU, at 5.51% CAGR over the demand in 2022. Looking to the low base of power demand, the above growth seems to be feasible for the next decade or so. For 2031–32, the projected demand is 2,192 BU.

The NEP contains the power generation scenario for 2027 so as to meet the electricity demand as estimated in the 19th EPS. It has projected that power plants based on different sources that were under construction in 2017, would be sufficient to meet demand in 2022, and for 2027, further demand may be met by achieving higher PLF from within the same capacity. Even in the 'alternate demand scenario', during 2022–27, a fresh capacity addition of 46,420 MW from non-gas-based conventional sources has been projected to meet peaking demand, with no role left for gas-based generation (GOI, 2018c). Hence the NEP does not see a balancing role for natural gas-based power at all even in the higher electricity demand growth scenario.

7.6.3.2   Availability of Domestic Natural Gas

Presently the share of domestic gas relative to RLNG is higher in power sector, and with static domestic gas production, the domestic supply has remained unchanged for several years now (Table 7.7). The share of RLNG in power has been just a quarter of total RLNG sales (average supply of 8 MMSCMD out of a total RLNG sale of 33.5 MMSCMD in 2018–19). In the non-power sectors on the other hand, the share of RLNG is higher. The above figures testify to the price sensitivity of power market. It also underlines the need for reforms in power sector pricing so as to usher in the much-needed generation from market priced fuels. Regarding future natural gas production, as discussed earlier, the prospects of domestic gas production are not bright, but sufficient imported supplies are likely to mature.

7.6.3.3   Decarbonisation of the Power Sector

India had made two major commitments at the COP 21 held at Paris in 2018. It declared its intention to achieve a renewable energy capacity of 175 GW by 2022, and reduce its emission intensity by 33%–35% over 2005 by 2030. The above is leading the electricity sector to transition in favour of clean power that might eventually go against all fossil sources including natural gas. Earlier India had a large hydropower capacity that resulted in share of clean energy being moderately high amongst the leading energy consumers. However, as the pace of electricity demand grew faster than growth in new hydro capacity, the share of latter also fell in relative terms. This has happened in other countries, too, especially where hydropower comprised the bulk of clean power (Mondal et al., 2019). The calls for decarbonisation extending into the power sector (basically impacting coal) along with phase-out of nuclear power in some countries in the post-Fukushima era is likely to boost the natural gas-based power (Hauser et al., 2019).

7.6.3.4   Price of Natural Gas

The price of natural gas will be a critical factor as energy charges form the bulk of power price. The pricing aspects have been discussed in detail within the previous chapter and difference between domestically produced and imported supply has been brought out in some detail. The role of domestic production becomes still more relevant and has been discussed above.

7.6.3.5 Stricter Power Sector Emission Norms

Nearly three-fourths of India's electricity generation is coal-based. In 2015, the Ministry of Environment, Forest & Climate Change (MoEFCC) further tightened the emission norms for TPPs, presented in Table 7.9. These norms were to become effective by 2017, however, on a representation by Ministry of Power the timelines were relaxed and will now become effective by 2022 (CPCB, 2018). In a recent development, these are expected to be further delayed. To implement these norms, coal-based power plants will require emission control equipment thus raising cost of their power. This might enhance the market competitiveness of natural gas vis-à-vis coal-based power. There are some research estimates available that assess the impact of this cost hike on power cost. Brookings (2017) found that the cost may go up by 6% on an assumed cost of Rs 4/kWh for coal-based power (Tongia and Seligsohn, 2017). CSTEP has estimated the impact of these installations on plants operating at lower PLFs to be significant—it could mean a tariff hike of INR 1/kWh or more, a cost increase of over 30% (CSTEP, 2018). For this reason, one may expect price competitiveness of natural gas-based power to increase relative to coal based power. There is a strong possibility that coal-based power will continue to be cheaper than gas-based power, and hence more attractive. Similarly, there is also possibility that with strict emission norms in place, coal-based power will become more environmentally acceptable. A detailed discussion on the future market dynamics is beyond the scope of this section.

7.6.3.6 Natural Gas for Balancing Variable Power

India has committed to achieve 175 GW renewable energy capacity by 2022. Achievement of this target can transform India's electricity system. As in March 2019, there was an installed capacity of 81 GW of renewables (GOI, n.d.).

TABLE 7.9
Emission norms for thermal power plants

		Year of Installation of TPPs		
	Existing Standards	Before 2003	2004–16	Post 1.1.2017
Sulphur Dioxide	No standard	600 mg/Nm^3 for <500 MW, and for others 200 mg/Nm^3		100 mg/Nm^3
NOx	No standard	600 mg/Nm^3	300 mg/Nm^3	Do
Mercury	No standard	0.03 mg/Nm^3 (>=500 MW)	0.03 mg/Nm^3	0.03 mg/Nm^3
PM	150–350 mg/Nm^3	100 mg/Nm^3	50 mg/Nm^3	30 mg/Nm^3

Source: Adapted by author from Tongia and Seligsohn (2017).

Although there is some uncertainty whether the renewables target can be met, government agencies are planning generation and dispatch on the premise that this capacity will indeed be realised. Simultaneously, solar and wind technologies are becoming increasingly attractive with falling cost. Solar and wind costs have fallen by 60% and 40%, respectively during 2014–18, thus making them as competitive as coal. There are visible concerns that a relentless pursuit of the renewable target may lead to overcapacity in generation, and the PLF of thermal capacity will fall and end up with scope for more generation should the demand rise in coming years. On the other hand, the power supply from renewables is unlikely to face challenge from this concern because renewables are tied with government backed purchase guarantees, and will get despatched regardless of price.[13] Ministry of Power identifies variability and uncertainty of generation as a challenge from renewables-based power. In 2018 an Expert Committee of Government of India estimated that 175 GW renewable capacity (in 2022) will require maximum positive ramping requirement of 400 MW/minute which can be achieved with the existing flexible sources of generation such as natural gas- and hydro-based power plants (CEA, 2018b).[14] They stated the same for the period 2026–27 for projected 275 GW of renewable capacity (an addition of 100,000 MW between 2022 and 2027) (CEA, 2018b). In more recent reports, it appears that even coal-based TPPs can provide flexible power, albeit at a higher cost.

For the above-mentioned reasons, NEP does not propose any additional flexible capacity such as natural gas-based option in 2022 and 2027. Some experts argue that with renewable cost reductions and fast moving advancements in battery storage, the use of natural gas for backing intermittent renewables may be less (Stern, 2017). Based on this, it can be inferred that natural gas-based capacity will remain static at 25,735 MW in 2027 same as that in the previous period, and this would be 4% of the total capacity and along with diesel gensets, constitute 3.8% of total power generated (Stern, 2017). At 90% PLF, the above gas-based capacity would generate 185 BU, accounting for nearly 9% of total demand of 2047 BU in 2027 and consume nearly 45 BCM of gas (Stern, 2017). However, if, the above capacity was not harnessed to meet the normal power demand, and used only for balancing renewable energy, the NEP has estimated a mere 16 BCM of gas demand (CEA, 2018a) NEP. POSOCO came up with similar results and even suggested a small curtailment in natural gas-based generation even while balancing 175 GW of renewables (USAID, n.d.) at the same time. Various studies have found that balancing of variable renewable power can be addressed up to moderate levels (30% or so) through better visualisation tools in solar/wind generation (Bloom et al., 2016).

7.6.4 Demand Projection for Natural Gas in Power

Based on the discussions above, the natural gas demand from power sector for the year 2030 has been estimated. The electricity demand has been taken from the authoritative projections of the government as contained in the prior discussed 19th EPS. There is no other agency that does such an intensive electricity demand survey. Therefore, we may accept the 19th EPS projections in toto. While the

TABLE 7.10

Estimations of gas demand in power in 2030 (BCM/year)

		2022	2027	Growth Rate 2022–27	2030
Total Power Demand (NEP)	in BU	1566	2047	CAGR 5.51%	2342^
Gas-based Capacity (NEP)	in GW	25.7	25.7	No growth	29.8^
Scenario 2: HDS, capacity of 29.8 GW (2030), 90% PLF and 90% availability					
Gas-based generation	in BU	185	185	no growth	214
Gas Demand (at 90% PLF)	in BCM	39	39	no growth	45
Scenario 1: LDS, static capacity at 25.7 GW (2030), 37% PLF and 90% availability					
Gas based generation	in BU	76	76	no growth	76
Gas Demand (only to meet balancing requirement)	in BCM	16	16	no growth	16

^extrapolated at the growth rate of 5.51% between 2027–30 for Scenario 2.

Note 1: 19th EPS numbers for 2031–32 are lower.

Note 2: (PRAYAS, n.d.) C-1.

Source: (GOI, 2018c) and (PRAYAS, n.d.).

latter gives numbers for 2027, the terminal year of the enquiry under this study is 2030. For 2027–30 numbers, it is proposed to apply the same CAGR that was applied in NEP for the period 2022–27. This yields an electricity demand of 2,342 BU in 2030 (Table 7.10).

While calculating natural gas demand in power, the role of two levers is manifested—projected gas-based power generation capacity and likely PLF. In LDS scenario, the present gas-based capacity (25.7 GW) is kept static until 2027 based on the discussion in subsection 6.6.2 (a minor 406 MW capacity addition is envisaged). The NEP assumes a PLF of 37% (only to meet balancing requirement for renewables). The above two assumptions generate a natural gas demand of 16 BCM in 2027 (CEA, 2018b). This exceeds present supply of 12 BCM/year. In the LDS, going beyond 2027–2030, it is again assumed that there will be no addition to gas-based generation, and as such no change in natural gas demand for power generation (16 BCM).

In HDS scenario, until 2027, the present capacity has been kept static but while going beyond 2027 until 2030, both gas-based capacities and PLFs are assumed to rise. A 5.51% CAGR has been applied to gas-based capacity—the same rate as applied in the EPS for power demand to rise during 2022–27. This yields a capacity of 29.8 GW in 2030. Further, a 90% PLF is taken, with a net saleable power generation of 214 BU, thus generating a gas demand of 45 BCM in 2030 (Table 6.18).[15] It will mark a major hike from the present generation of nearly 50 BU in 2017–18 (Lok Sabha, 2019).

The estimations in Table 7.10 may be vetted by applying various other considerations. In NEP, the PLF of thermal plants has been envisaged at 60%–61% in

2026–27 (P.5.21). With low PLFs, there is an overhang of excess power capacity, exacerbated by addition of renewables (further 100 GW between 2022 and 2027). This leaves scope for obtaining more power from thermal plants by raising the PLF that can even go up to 90%. Secondly, the pricing of coal is likely to remain administratively determined especially for the production of CIL. However, new coal available from commercially allotted coal blocks may be at market-determined prices. On the other hand, even the domestic natural gas is now to be priced at market prices. In the light of sufficient coal capacity at cheaper prices, there is a little chance of natural gas making a mark in power sector. The existing gas-based power generation capacity is working at near 25%–30% PLF, which has been estimated to achieve 90% in HDS. This itself will be a large gas-based power supply.

7.6.5 Aggregate Natural Gas Demand in Power Sector

Power sector offers a complex scenario with a number of factors having a role on what might be the level of gas-based generation. In a HDS, at a PLF of 90% PLF, 45 BCM will be needed by gas power plants in 2030. If only a minor role of gas is assumed—just enough to balance variable renewable electricity—then merely 16 BCM of gas may be needed. The latter is under LDS scenario. In light of insufficient availability of domestic gas and plentiful availability of coal- and renewable-based electricity at more competitive prices than RLNG-based power, it follows that natural gas has a limited role in this sector.

7.7 NATURAL GAS DEMAND FOR UREA PRODUCTION

7.7.1 Background

India is a major producer of food grains and also consumes a large quantity of fertilizers, in fact the second largest in the world (UNFCCC, 2018) (FAI, 2018). To meet the large domestic demand, India supplements its domestic fertilizer production with imports. Urea based fertilizers are the most widely used in India. Here the fertilizers sector (urea manufacture has an overwhelming larger share) along with other industries are the top two consuming sectors of natural gas, and are collectively taken as anchor consumers. The twin concerns of insufficient domestic gas production and increasing (urea manufacture has the overwhelming larger share) gas demand as feedstock in urea production, resulted in firming up of a policy debate on whether to import urea or import gas (RLNG) directly so as to manufacture urea domestically. The issue was addressed only recently when the government decided to encourage domestic manufacturing of urea by using RLNG. Consequently, old urea plants that were lying closed for some time have been taken up for revival and expansion too.

In the absence of new greenfield plants in the past, urea manufacturers have been producing as much as they can, and even achieving above 100% capacity utilisation. Against an installed capacity of 20.75 MT, the production in 2018–19 was 24 MT. In recent years, the capacity has been reassessed and raised accordingly.

These plants belong to different vintage and the recent plants have a higher fuel efficiency. As government is the procurer of full urea production, these plants are supported by a regime, wherein they are given a urea purchase price as per energy-consumption norms. In the light of insufficient availability of domestic gas, several policy interventions have been made by the government to enhance local urea production both with domestic and imported gas. The provision of domestic gas to the plants at administered price is an input subsidy, and then the urea is also priced at a discount, which is an output subsidy. The application of both input and output subsidy has resulted in a complex scenario, where the demand for urea gets inflated due to low price. In the light of the above policy-driven scenario, estimating demand for urea, and of natural gas as feedstock for urea manufacture is not that easy. This is subject to decisions of the government that is in office.

At the heart of the debate on whether India should manufacture or import urea has been the issue of price competitiveness of imported urea versus cost of producing urea with imported gas (Jain, 2011).[16] India has traditionally imported nearly a quarter of its total urea sales. In light of the above, self-sufficiency in urea manufacturing was sought earlier on grounds of food security and protection from speculative prices of imported urea. The latter depends on global demand–supply situation of urea and gas prices. The discovery of large gas fields in India's KG Basin in the first decade of 2000, brought forth the promise of additional domestic supplies. This led the government to encourage urea manufacturers to switch to natural gas from naphtha as feedstock in urea manufacture. Presently, out of 30 urea plants, 27 are gas-based (GOI, 2018d). However, over time it became clear that the new gas fields resulted only in a temporary spike in production. Resultantly, in the year 2018–19, against a natural gas demand for urea manufacture of nearly 40 MMSCMD, the domestic supply was only about 17 MMSCMD and the gap was met by LNG imports. Figure 7.6 gives a snapshot of natural gas supply position (by source) for

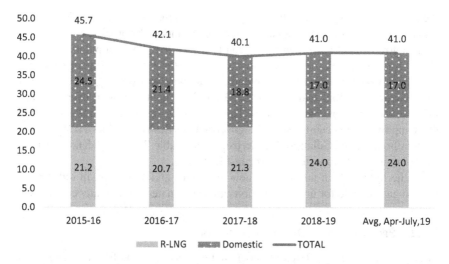

FIGURE 7.6   Gas supply (by source) to fertilisers sector (MMSCMD). (PPAC, 2020).

TABLE 7.11

Production/import/sale of urea (MT/year)

	Production	Import	Total	Sale
2012–13	22.6	8.0	30.6	30.2
2013–14	22.7	7.1	29.8	30.5
2014–15	22.6	8.8	31.4	30.9
2015–16	24.5	8.5	33.0	32.0
2016–17	24.2	5.5	29.7	29.6
2017–18	24.0	5.9	29.9	29.9
2018–19	24.0	7.5	31.5	32.0
2019–20	24.4	9.1	33.5	33.7

Source: GOI (2017a), Annual Report of Department of Fertilizers (2021).

TABLE 7.12

Urea and natural gas demand projections by different agencies

		Natural Gas (MMSCMD)		Urea (MT)
PNGRB	2022–23^	110	NA	NA
12th Plan	2016–17	72.39	2024–25	38
OIES	2024–25	66*	2024–25	38

^steady up to 2030. . .
*most likely scenario.

the period 2015–16 to July 2019. It can thus be seen that post-2017, RLNG meets a greater share of natural gas demand of fertiliser plants than domestic gas.

The government has taken a decision to revive five old urea plants that were shut, to add to the domestic capacity (GOI, 2019b). Bold investment decisions have been taken in approving new natural gas pipelines (by a grant of subsidy for their construction) and signing LNG purchase contracts with overseas suppliers to meet their gas requirement. This is a major step towards raising RLNG consumption, and is catalysed by the government's desire to achieve self-reliance in urea production (Gulati and Banerjee, 2019). Table 7.11 gives details of urea manufactured and imported over the last few years.

In the light of firm decision on new capacities and expansion in older ones, natural gas demand for urea production can be estimated with greater confidence.

7.7.2 PROJECTIONS OF DIFFERENT AGENCIES

Several agencies have offered urea demand scenarios for the future (Table 7.12). The 2030 Vision Document of PNGRB has not offered a urea demand number and has instead offered natural gas demand projection for urea manufacture in 2030 (PNGRB, 2013). It took a starting demand in 2012–13 of 59.86 MMSCMD, which seems to be high as the actual consumption even five years later (2017–18), has been much lower at 40 MMSCMD (Figure 7.6). Using the above base figures, it projects a demand of 110 MMSCMD in 2022–23. Thereafter, until 2030 no further gas addition has been envisaged.

The Working Group Report for Fertilizer sector for the 12th five year plan projected the demand for urea to be 33.75 MT in 2017–18, and a further rise to 36.81 and 38 MT by 2021–22 and 2024–25, respectively (GOI, 2012b). This was estimated by applying a CAGR of 2% to urea demand (higher than 1% CAGR that has actually been experienced).[17] It is notable that the actual urea demand experienced even in 2019–20 was much lower (Table 7.11). However, even to meet the above growth in urea demand, no addition to natural gas demand was projected as it was assumed that going further after 2014–15, no new urea plant might come up during the 13th Plan (2017–22). A third projection has been offered by OIES, wherein three scenarios of domestic urea manufacturing were taken for 2024, with a wide variance in natural gas demand ranging between 14 BCM (38 MMSCMD) and 42 BCM (115 MMSCMD)—the latter being 'high case' of self-sufficiency in urea at 38 MTPA production (Sen, 2017).[18] The government's decision in 2017 to revamp already shut urea manufacturing capacities leading to fresh demand for RLNG has superseded the above three projections.

7.7.3 Factors Driving Natural Gas Demand in Urea Sector

In determining likely gas demand for manufacture of urea until 2030, there are three major drivers—urea retail price (impacted by subsidy policy), urea demand and domestic urea manufacturing capacity. There are other factors, too, that impinge on these three main factors. All of them are discussed below.

7.7.3.1 Urea Demand

A large tract of land is cultivated in India without any use of chemical fertilisers. On the other hand, India's growing population needs large food supplies. In BAU scenario, the consumption of fertilizer in India being low on a per acre basis, might rise significantly. The low crop response ratio across major crops suggests that Indian agriculture needs higher nutrient input (Parikh et al., 2009). However, rationalisation of existing nutrient use via a number of measures to achieve nutrient balance, might moderate the growth in urea demand. Due to large subsidy burden, and demand being high due to market imperfections, the consumption of nitrogenous fertilizers such as urea have been 'controlled' by limiting supply. Only authorised suppliers are allowed to market urea and need to get registered for subsidy purpose. This has created a fair distinction between 'demand' and 'consumption' and demand is high while consumption is lesser. The government has adopted a series of measures to encourage a balanced use of fertilizers that has started to deliver results (discussed later). The yearly CAGR in urea consumption (demand) between 2011 and 2018 has been quite low, only about 1% (demand has in fact fallen after 2015–16 only to rise marginally in 2019–20) (Table 7.11). Other than large subsidy incidence, urea is also responsible for environmental impacts—by ammonia release to atmosphere, and leaching of nitrogen into the soil through water absorption. Hence, several countries including India are taking various measures to curb urea use in line with government policy to curb its consumption. In the near future, the growth in demand for urea is likely to be constrained by the subsidised volumes that are supplied. As regards this study, we only assess natural gas demand for urea manufacture. It is assumed that in the LDS scenario, no new urea manufacturing capacity will come up beyond what is already announced and the one which will be ready by 2022. With the new capacities and brownfield expansion, it has already been estimated that in 2021–22 a domestic production of 31.76 MT is likely to be achieved. In the HDS scenario, we may assume that the entire urea demand in 2030 will be met by domestic manufacture for which natural gas demand needs to be estimated. In 2019–20, a total of 33.7 MT of urea was supplied which included 2 MT from Oman and rest being from other imports (Table 7.11). In this decade (2010–11 to 2019–20), urea demand has risen at a CAGR of 1%. It is assumed that in the next decade (2020–30), due to a new scenario of self-sufficiency and higher domestic availability, urea demand may grow at a higher CAGR of 2%, and rise to 37 MT in 2030.

7.7.3.2   Domestic Manufacturing Capacity

Due to uncertainty both in the pricing and subsidy regimes, private sector has been reluctant in setting up new urea plants (Lok Sabha, 2018). This could also be seen from Table 7.11, which shows nearly no change having occurred in domestic production for almost a decade. Resultantly, as demand for urea has been increasing, imports have been inevitable year after year (fallen after 2015–16, and risen again to achieve a new peak in 2019–20). The five urea projects that have been approved and are currently under construction, have a capacity of 6.42 MT/year each, along with one brownfield expansion with a capacity of 1.34 MT/year, likely to be commissioned by 2022 (a total of 7.76 MT of additional capacity). It may be added that India receives urea imports of 2 MT/year from a JV between Indian and Omani companies, which is likely to continue under the existing long-term arrangement. Within the present overall domestic production of 24 MT/year, nearly 1.5 MT of urea is produced in three plants with naphtha as feedstock. Their ongoing conversion to natural gas would result in an additional gas demand (without making a difference to urea supply).

7.7.3.3   Retail Price of Urea

Urea prices are subsidised and their low price is the major reason for high demand. While urea prices are stable, other soil nutrients are under the regime of fixed subsidy thus leading to rising prices. The ideal ratio of the three nutrients—nitrogen (supplied by urea), phosphorus and potash (N, P, K)—that ought to be 4:2:1 has skewed disproportionately in favour of nitrogen to 7:2.7:1 due to the price attractiveness of nitrogen bearing urea (Chander, 2019). Had the price been cost-reflective, some urea demand would have evaporated for sure. In the study by

Parikh et al. (2009) it was found that urea demand is price sensitive and might lie between 40 and 52 MT (requiring 24–30 BCM of natural gas) in 2025 at varying urea prices (Rs. 4,830/MT–11,250 MT) (Parikh et al., 2009). This brings in the role of government in making 'supply' equal to 'demand' through price and supply interventions. The retail price of urea has not been altered for a long time now, and has been steady at Rs 5,360/ton since 2010 (Lok Sabha, 2017). Since there is no long-term farm input including urea pricing policy in the country at present, for the purpose of this study, it is assumed that the price attractiveness of urea is unlikely to change, and its demand as such may remain buoyant.

7.7.3.4 Price of LNG

The Gulf Region including Russia, Iran and Oman has been amongst the major urea producers and exporters of urea to India due to abundant availability of feedstock (natural gas) (GPCA, 2017). However, market price of their urea supplies is marked to prevailing price of LNG in international markets, amongst other factors. As a urea and natural gas deficit country, India has a compulsive option of importing urea or LNG, with both these prices moving in tandem.[19] One major reason for poor growth in capacity of domestic urea manufacturing has been high LNG prices and its volatility. Successive governments have hesitated in committing to promote domestic manufacturing of urea based on imported gas, especially as the movement in the prices of the two commodities cannot be correctly predicted (Jain, 2011). As the government has removed this dilemma, therefore, the question of whether LNG price may be high and yield higher price than imported urea is no longer germane.[20] It is notable that the share of cheaper domestic natural gas in urea manufacture has been falling, which has resulted in rising cost of domestic manufacture. The present system of LNG pricing comprises of long-term supply contracts with market-linked price factors, which makes the long-term price of LNG as uncertain.

7.7.3.5 Imported Urea Price

Insofar as the new capacities are concerned, their output has an assured offtake, without any dependence on price of imported gas or international price of urea. It is for urea imports, if any, due to deficit in meeting demand, for which the price of imported urea has an immediate relevance. With the likely urea demand in 2022 to be met by domestic production, it is for the new urea demand in coming years that the price of imported urea is a decision factor on whether to expand domestic capacity. The soft natural gas price in gas exporting countries, makes their cost of urea manufacturing lower than what it costs to manufacture urea from imported RLNG in India. A decision to expand urea capacity further in India, implies an additional natural gas demand from these plants. If, long-term gas supplies were available on soft terms, it may encourage further expansion in domestic manufacturing capacity. Within these two factors—international price of urea and price of RLNG—it is uncertain as to how the economics of importing urea versus manufacturing it domestically (based on RLNG) might play out in future.

7.7.4 Aggregate Demand for Natural Gas for Urea Manufacture

As discussed earlier, the government intends to reduce superfluous urea demand, for which a number of measures such as resorting to 100% 'neem' coating and reducing the weight of urea bag by 5 kg per bag to 45 kg have been seen along with limiting imports to subdued availability. The LDS demand for urea production has been taken up in the first scenario. The gas demand working for both the scenarios has been tabulated in Table 7.13. For the four new 5.14 MT gas-based capacities underway (the Talcher unit of 1.28 MT/year is based on coal), including 2.1 MMSCMD for brownfield expansion of 1.34 MT, an additional gas demand of 12.3 MMSCMD of gas is posed by 2021–22 (Business Standard, 2018). Further, gas demand of 4.2 MMSCMD is likely for the three urea plants to be converted from naphtha to gas. This leads to an additional gas demand of 16.4 MMSCMD in 2022 (The Indian Express, 2019). When added to the existing gas demand of 40 MMSCMD in 2018, a total demand of 56.5 MMSCMD (20 BCM) in 2022 is to be realised in urea sector for manufacture of 31.76 MT (Table 7.13). In the LDS, firm urea production outlook in 2022 and thereafter no new urea plant until 2030 has been envisaged. Assuming that five new plants (including the Talcher unit) and one brownfield expansion capacity will come up with a capacity of 7.76 MT by 2021–22, this will also substitute the current annual imports of nearly 6 MT (excepting 2 MT/year coming from the Oman JV). With no further capacity expected to come up until 2030, the above demand is likely to remain more or less unchanged in the LDS scenario in 2030.

In the HDS scenario, the analysis assumes that the policy makers might desire to achieve self-sufficiency in domestic manufacturing to meet the enhanced urea demand that may come up during 2022–30. Therefore, in this scenario, another 5.24 MT of urea capacity has a definite scope to come up domestically much beyond the capacity envisaged in 2022, possibly leading up to 37 MT of urea manufacture in 2030. With the pro-rated gas demand to produce the above hike in urea demand, an additional 7.8 MMSCMD natural gas may be required. In

---

TABLE 7.13

Estimated natural gas demand for urea manufacture in 2030 (MMSCMD)

	Urea Production (in MT)	Gas Demand
Current urea plants (2019–20)	24	40
Conversion of 3 naphtha-based plants (2022)	Already Included in above	4.2
For 5 new and 1 brownfield plant (2022)	7.76	12.3
LDS (2030)	31.76	56.5
Add For rise in urea demand (2022–30)	5.24	7.8
HDS (2030)	37	64.3

Source: GOI (2017d) and own calculations.

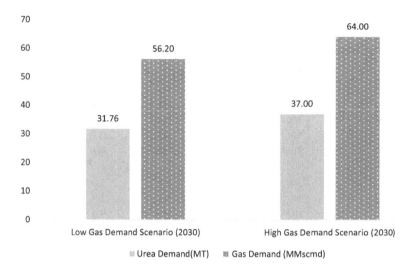

FIGURE 7.7 Estimated urea and natural gas demand in 2030.

Table 7.13, the total gas demand in the HDS scenario has been estimated at 64 MMSCMD.

The gas and urea demand estimations for 2030 in the two scenarios have been graphically presented in Figure 7.7.

7.8 NATURAL GAS DEMAND IN INDUSTRY

7.8.1 BACKGROUND

Industries (even after excluding urea manufacturing units) are the largest consumer of natural gas, and nearly one-third of India's natural gas demand comes from them. What is of great significance is that as this sector works on commercial terms and is not regulated under any price control mechanism, it is able to consume market-priced gas and accounts for more than half of all the LNG sold in India. What also follows is that this demand is price sensitive and could vary if, the market-determined LNG prices were to shift significantly (even the demand from small industries served by CGD networks is price sensitive). Within the broad category of Industries come refineries, petrochemicals and steel as being the largest single consumers, in that order. The smaller industries in the close vicinity of urban areas are served by CGD networks and figure in the earlier discussion. It is notable that several industries consume natural gas both as fuel and feedstock (e.g. petrochemicals), however, most of them use it as a fuel. Even though industries are largely dependent on LNG to meet their natural gas demand, however, in spite of sharp decline in LNG prices since 2014 (when crude price decline began), industrial demand for natural gas has still not grown robustly in India. As per data available from different sources, its consumption in Industries has moderately

TABLE 7.14

Past trend of natural gas supply in industry sector (MMSCMD)

	2015–16	2016–17	2017–18	2018–19	2019–20
RLNG					
Refinery	NA	NA	NA	16.0	18.0
Petrochemical	NA	NA	NA	7.0	9.0
Others	31.6	34.1	34.0	11.0	9.0
Subtotal	31.6	34.1	34.0	34.0	36.0
DOMESTIC					
Refinery	NA	NA	NA	3.0	3.0
Petrochemical	NA	NA	NA	2.0	1.0
Others	10.6	10.9	13.5	9.0	10.0
Subtotal	10.6	10.9	13.5	14.0	14.0
TOTAL	42.3	45.0	47.5	48.0	50.0
Total Gas to all sectors	136.6	138.7	143.1	147.0	153.0
Share of Industry in Total Gas	31%	33%	33%	33%	33%

risen from 42 MMSCMD in 2015–16 (total consumption 136 MMSCMD) to 50 MMSCMD in 2019–20 (total consumption 153 MMSCMD), with LNG comprising nearly three-fourths of the same in both these years (Table 7.14). As data of natural gas consumption by source—domestic or LNG—in different end uses is not available in detail, especially for the pre-2015 period, knowledge of the past experience is thus limited.[21]

7.8.2 THREE LARGE INDUSTRIES

The key drivers of natural gas demand in different industry types are varied and have been discussed elsewhere in this section. These industries are organised and consume large volumes of energy. On the other hand, there is a widely dispersed unorganised small-scale industrial sector such as that of brick-making, refractories which is again a large consumer as a group, but small consumer individually (also a large consumer of non-commercial energy). The large industries are more efficient in their energy consumption and also face tighter emission regulatory regime—factors that work in favour of natural gas uptake. Within this category, the largest distinctive demand comes from crude oil refining. With India's rising demand for liquid fuels, and natural gas being cheaper than oil on calorific parity basis, its demand (for heating/refining crude) is set to rise.[22] Next comes the petrochemical sector. India's per capita consumption of petrochemical products is much below the global average, spurring expansion in capacity of petrochemical plants, with natural gas as feedstock (IEA, 2021). Within the third major industry, i.e. iron and steel sector, there are three well identified technologies—blast furnace (coking coal dominant), sponge iron by Direct Reduction of Iron process or DRI (thermal coal and natural gas) and electric arc furnace. In the light of abundance of coal (and natural gas shortage), and economies of scale achieved by large integrated steel plants, this sector will see a small increase in gas demand and blast furnace technology is likely to prosper (IEA, 2021).

7.8.3 Natural Gas Demand Projections in Industries

As the outlook on domestic natural gas is still poor, it is LNG that might be the main driver, then Industries seem to be the main client of this gas source. While being consistent with the national aspiration to achieve 15% gas share in commercial PES by 2030, industrial uptake of natural gas might make this happen. However, the future projections of its consumption in industrial sector present a mixed picture. While the in-house projections of the Government such as 12th Plan projections (up to 2022) and the PNGRB Vision 2030 (up to 2030) are highly optimistic, two other studies undertaken by external organisations, namely, OIES and IEA expect only a moderate increase (Table 7.15). In the Stated Policy Scenario, IEA expects the share

TABLE 7.15

Natural gas demand projections in industry by different agencies (MMSCMD)

		2020	2022	2024	2030	2040
1	PNGRB Vision 2030$					
	Petchem/Refineries/Internal Consumption	75	82	90	119	NA
	Sponge Iron/Steel	10	10	11	14	
	Industrial	35	37	42	64	
	TOTAL	125	129	143	196	
2	12th Plan Working Group#					
	Petchem/Refineries/Internal Consumption	80	82	NA	NA	NA
	Sponge Iron/Steel	10	10			
	Industrial	35	37			
	TOTAL	125	129			
3	IEA (India Energy Outlook)*					
	Stated Policy Scenario	NA	NA	NA	159	277
	Indian Vision Case	NA	NA	NA	154	277
4	OIES^					
	Industry (share of manufacturing in GDP is 25%)	NA	60	NA	NA	NA
	TOTAL	NA	60	NA	NA	NA

• IEA (2021), includes urea, and all Industries. Not comparable as it is final consumption.
^ Sen (2017)
# MoPNG (2011)
$ PNGRB (2013)

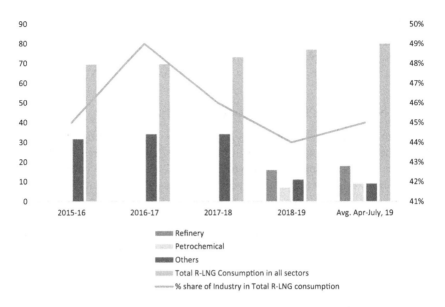

FIGURE 7.8   RLNG demand in industry sector by major Industries (MMSCMD) and by percentage in total natural gas supply (right vertical axis).

of natural gas in Industry to rise from 9% to 16% with coal continuing to hold a large share. However, available data on natural gas consumption by industries may have to be seen in the light of differences existing in categorisation of industries. At places, they are classified as miscellaneous, as in Figure 7.8. In some cases, even fertilisers and power, or even the smaller industries that are served by CGD networks get grouped under it. In this section, we are interested only in natural gas consumed by refineries, petrochemicals and other industries (not served by CGD).

7.8.4   WIDE VARIANCES IN DEMAND PROJECTIONS

The 12th Plan Working Group Report projected a moderate increase in natural gas demand in the large industries from 81 MMSCMD in 2012–13 to 129 MMSCMD in 2021–22 (MoPNG, 2011) (Table 7.15). Their projections are classified industry-wise. PNGRB's Vision 2030 is also an optimistic one and estimates natural gas demand to grow to 196 MMSCMD by 2030 (PNGRB, 2013) (Table 7.15). This document relies on 12th Plan until 2022, and makes its own estimates thereafter for 2030. IEA's projection is bullish on energy demand growth in the wider industrial sector, including that for natural gas. It projects the share of natural gas in Industry to rise from 6% in 2019 to 9%–12% (IEA, 2021). The above numbers are much lower than the projections of government agencies (IEA, 2021).[23] For 2030, its projections are smaller than the estimates in PNGRB's Vision, but they are recent projections (2021). The OIES study is of 2017 vintage and its projections are largely up to 2024 (Sen, 2017). It projects doubling of natural gas demand in Industries from 35 MMSCMD in 2015 to nearly 60 MMSCMD by 2022. It is notable that this is just half of what has been contained in 12th Plan, and PNGRB's Vision 2030. One notable aspect of the above projections is that while OIES study is based on actual past consumption, the government sources have taken unmet demand also into account.

The wide variances in future demand estimates for natural gas in Industries go to show as to how difficult it is to project demand for a market-priced fuel. Perhaps, future price of LNG being a major variable, and the existence of price controls in competing fuels such as coal (and electricity sector) makes the task all the more difficult. As regards classification of industries, this study follows the government classification as given in the 12th Plan and PNGRB Vision, 2030 (Table 7.15).

7.8.5 INDUSTRIES AS THE MAJOR DRIVER OF RLNG DEMAND

This category of consumers operates in free market and make fuel choices on the basis of sheer competitiveness. Some form of subsidy regime prevails in end-products of the other demand sectors—urea, cooking and power. Therefore, industries are the best placed to drive the demand of market-priced RLNG, or even new natural gas that might come from domestic fields at market prices. While there may be some technological process barriers present to sizeable adoption of a particular fuel, especially where feedstocks are involved (petrochemicals and steel making), industries usually have more fuel choices.

7.8.6 FACTORS DRIVING GAS DEMAND IN INDUSTRIES SECTOR

One approach to project future natural gas demand may be to apply the rate of historical increase in gas consumption by industry. However, this task is rendered difficult due to lack of dis-aggregated data. The government data sources— Ministry of Petroleum & Natural Gas and its arm, Petroleum Policy and Analysis Cell—offer detailed end-use information of RLNG, or even consumption data by industry for the period only after 2015 (Table 7.14). Further, as already discussed the classification of 'Industries' varies across different agencies. In the later discussion, a bottom-up analysis of natural gas demand in major industries has been undertaken. In order to discuss the above, it is useful to identify the structural factors that commonly relate to natural gas demand across industries. Several of the salient ones have been discussed below.

7.8.6.1 Price Competitiveness

Unlike the other sectors, natural gas faces stiff competition from a range of fuels— coal, liquid fuels, pet coke, biomass, etc. In other sectors such a competition is largely with liquid fuels. Competitiveness of natural gas impacts its demand as a feedstock separately as that from fuel. In both these end-uses, wherever the process has been dependent on oil-based products such as naphtha (feedstock in urea manufacture) and diesel (fuel in power generation), it is expected that switching to natural gas will ultimately happen. Urea making and petrochemicals are good case specific examples. This has already been examined in Chapter 6. Further, the situation is different with coal. In a vast array of industries—both large and small—that have coal 'linkages' for direct supply from CIL or have won captive coal blocks for power generation, coal is expected to remain more competitive. While the former enjoy stable coal prices as determined in auctions for five years, the latter can produce coal for captive use at cost price itself. Only about 20% of the former's production is marked for sale at market price (Economic Times, 2019).

7.8.6.2   Tax Regime

A contributory cause behind poor competitiveness of natural gas in some end-uses is the taxation structure—the rate of tax and whether input credit can be availed in the tax on final product. States are imposing VAT on natural gas at a high rate, an example being Bihar that levies 20% (Economic Times, 2018). The non-inclusion of natural gas in the list of commodities on which GST is levied has worked to its sheer disadvantage, particularly because under the VAT regime States are completely free to determine the tax rate (Economic Times, 2018). Secondly, due to non-inclusion under the GST regime, input credit cannot be availed of. On the other hand, GST on coal can be accounted for to avail of input credit. At the same time, the relief given by many states to natural gas by imposing a lower rate of VAT, and in some cases, only to specified end-uses such as CNG/PNG, has helped their uptake as transport fuel, while the same is not available for use as a fuel in industries.[24]

7.8.6.3   Pricing Regime

As discussed earlier, domestically produced gas and RLNG face different price regimes. As per government's policy announcement, future domestic gas production is to be assessed on the basis of market prices, which again makes it unattractive as compared to administratively priced coal. While coal-based power sold under long-term PPAs faces much lesser price variability, market-priced gas has large variability and would require the changes to be passed on to the consumers for which regulatory approvals will be needed.[25] So far, Indian power tariffs have been rather stable, and even peak hour pricing has not been made effective across the country. Therefore, for market-determined gas supplies to grow, a market price regime across the energy sector—coal, oil, power, natural gas—would be of much help. Future trends are in the above direction, particularly after the pathbreaking reforms made in petroleum sector that freed prices in 2015–17 (Jain, 2018).

7.8.6.4   Process Choices

Due to technological constraints, energy consumption based on natural gas in 'other industry' categories is not that significant. In cement manufacture, limestone is reduced in kilns by burning it with coal. Heat is a major end-use in many industrial processes. So far, coal has a major share in providing heat to industry, and the situation might only change if, natural gas became cheaper to coal, which presently does not appear to be the case.[26] Similar considerations impacting gas demand—prices and availability—apply more in small-scale industries, too. Should there be a major shift in technology choices towards natural gas (for example in steel making), it would give the much-needed impetus to natural gas.

7.8.7 GAS DEMAND SCENARIOS IN INDUSTRIES IN 2030

Coming to gas demand estimations, one major challenge in industries is that financial viability of natural gas versus other fuels cannot be predicted, and based on assessment of fuel pricing outlook, industry locks itself into technologies. In the past, natural gas of the imported origin has not been competitive especially in comparison to domestic gas, thus resulting in adoption of other fuels (Jain, 2011). This leads us to look at extrapolating natural gas demand from several other indicators. On the basis of the factors noted above and specific factors as being relevant to different major industries, its demand has been estimated below. Table 7.14 gives historical consumption of gas by category. For the previous years, the available data of gas use in Industries is not present for major industries separately. A close look at the data (Figure 7.8) reveals that when averaged, the share of aggregated demand of industries (refineries, petrochemicals and miscellaneous industries) has been around 45% of the total RLNG consumed in the country over the past five years. As Industries are expected to dominate the RLNG market, the same share (45%) may be assumed for future as well and the rest may go to other gas-consuming sectors.

7.8.7.1   Refineries

The data for natural gas consumption in refineries became available as a separate category only after March 2018 (Table 7.14). For the two years (2018–19 and April–July 2019) the individual share of refineries has been nearly half of the total RLNG as consumed in Industry. What follows from this is that on an average as Industry consumes 45% of all RLNG (over 2015–19), the share of Refinery based consumption would be half of this, or 22% of total RLNG consumed in the country.

On price consideration, natural gas is quite competitive as a fuel in comparison to crude oil in oil refineries. On an average, 8% crude oil gets consumed in the refining process. This leads to a normative demand of 53 MMSCMD of natural gas for the existing annual refining throughput of 250 MMT (243 BCM of natural gas). However, only one-third of the above or 18 MMSCMD of gas is currently being consumed in this sector (Figure 7.8), with the rest of the fuel coming from other sources (fuel oil, etc.). Going forward to 2030, a large refinery capacity expansion has already been announced (RRPCL, n.d.).[27] As per IEA (2021), India's own demand for petroleum products in 2030 would push the refining capacity in the Stated Policy Scenario to 6.4 million barrels of oil/day, or more than 320 MMTPA of refining capacity (IEA, 2021; Delloite, 2019). By applying the 8% fuel norm, if all the fuels used in refining were to be natural gas, a demand of 64 MMSCMD (energy equivalent of 8% of 320 MMT of crude) is generated. In a few other studies, a marginally lower refining capacity has been projected.[28] However, as seen in the past, refineries have used natural gas only to the extent of one-third of their actual fuel need, with the balance heating fuel coming from liquid fuels. We may assume that with greater availability of natural gas due to improved infra and greater competitiveness, natural gas might meet at least one-half of the fuel needed in oil refineries in 2030 (32 MMSCMD or so). This demand based on past consumption trends may be taken as the minimum number or the LDS scenario.

From a purely supply perspective, refinery sector has been consuming 22% share of all RLNG. In the light of RLNG supply estimation of 250 MMSCMD in 2030, (Section 5.6), then at 20%–22% share, it would receive nearly 50 MMSCMD of RLNG. This upper limit of supply constraint of 50 MMSCMD may be accepted as the HDS in 2030. It is notable that this is still lower than the normative fuel demand of 64 MMSCMD (in energy equivalence) for refining and liquid fuels will still be consumed.

7.8.7.2   Petrochemicals

In this sector also, on the lines of as to how natural gas demand in refining has been generated, the LDS has been derived from the bottom-up analysis (likely growth of the sector), while the HDS or optimistic scenario is estimated from apportioning the likely supply of RLNG in 2030. To determine the demand on the lower side, the growth in petrochemicals sector has been taken. IEA (2021) had estimated that demand for ethylene, the basic petrochemical for which natural gas is an important feedstock (along with naphtha), is likely to rise by two-third, from 6.6 MTPA in 2020 to 11 MTPA in 2030 (IEA, 2021). The gas consumption in ethylene may also rise in the same ratio, unless its proportion with naphtha changes which is likely. With naphtha prices being higher, a larger share of natural gas might be consumed in petrochemicals alone. As may be seen in Figure 7.8, 9 MMSCMD of gas was consumed in petrochemicals in 2019–20, which comprised 12% of all RLNG (LNG imports were 29 Mtoe or 72 MMSCMD in 2019, Table 5.3). We may assume that the entire additional feedstock will come from natural gas (instead of an increase by two-thirds), thus aggregating to demand of 18 MMSCMD in LDS in 2030.

On the supply side (HDS or optimistic scenario), it needs to be seen as to how much RLNG supply could be expected from the regas terminals in 2030 for this sector. Gas consumed in petrochemicals in the past has been nearly 12% of the total imported gas supply. Taking the same share in the likely RLNG supply of 250 MMSCMD, a consumption of 27 MMSCMD (rounded off) is likely. This is taken as the demand in the HDS (upper limit of supply).

7.8.7.3   Other Industries

This category comprises of assorted industries such as paper, iron and steel, varied manufacturing, automobile, textile, aluminium and others. These units are not large consumers of gas, and only when aggregated, do they add up to be the largest sub-sector in Industries (nearly 40% of natural gas consumed in Industry). It may also be noted that unlike in refineries and petrochemicals sectors, there is no outright competitive advantage for natural gas across 'other' industries. In several of these units, cheap supplies of coal (brick kiln) and biomass (agro-based units) disincentivise the uptake of gas. This category entitled as 'Others' in Table 7.14

is presently receiving some domestic natural gas (particularly under court orders as in the case of Taj Trapezium zone in western UP), and small volumes to local industries near gas fields. Seemingly while gas demand is growing, however, supply of domestic gas to 'other industries' is static. No new natural gas is being allocated to this sector from domestic production. Therefore, the estimation for 2030 for this category is being done only for RLNG with no likelihood of domestic gas being allocated to this sector.

Due to this grouping of industries being so varied, it is very challenging to do a bottom-up analysis so as to generate demand scenario, and the analogy as applied in refinery and petrochemicals sub-sectors to generate LDS may not be applicable for these. For the sake of simplicity, the respective shares of both domestic and imported gas used in 'other' industries being 40% within cumulative gas consumption in Industry during 2018–19, and first half of the subsequent year (Table 7.14), the same share may be assumed for 2030. Now we go about estimating the demand within the 'other industries' by prorating their share within the Industries sub-sector as a whole. Having derived the demand in the major industries at 50 MMSCMD in 2030 (32 MMSCMD in refining and 18 MMSCMD in petrochemicals) by pro-rating 40% for 'other' industries, a demand of 33 MMSCMD is generated in the LDS.

However, from the supply perspective (HDS,) we may use the same analogy as being used for the larger industries—share in total RLNG supply—with one change. This sector has been receiving domestic natural gas supply also, which is not the case for other large Industries. Hence, when estimating the optimistic case of HDS scenario, their share in the future RLNG supply needs to be determined on the basis of all gas consumed by 'other' industry (19 MMSCMD). The share of gas used in this category (Table 7.14) against total RLNG supplied in the country in the past two years (Figure 7.8) has been nearly 25%. When the latter share is applied to the likely total RLNG supply of 250 MMSCMD in 2030, it yields a gas supply of 62 MMSCMD. This is a high number, however, as discussed earlier, and forms the upper limit and may be reckoned as the supply constraint (HDS). Moreover, Industry is already expected to be a major driver of gas demand and is not expected to receive any new allocation of domestic gas.

7.8.8 AGGREGATE NATURAL GAS DEMAND FOR INDUSTRIES

Within the Industrial sector, RLNG demand of the three main sub-sectors— refineries, petrochemicals and 'Others'—has been estimated for 2030. The demand has been estimated at two forecast levels—lower one is based on sectoral demand derived bottom-upwards, and optimistic one by apportioning the total RLNG supply that has been estimated to be available on the basis of regas capacity growth estimations.

In Figure 7.9, the estimated demand of the three industry types (refineries, petrochemicals and others) has been shown. The optimistic side represents the HDS while the lower scenario is LDS specific. The above discussion yields an optimistic demand of 139 MMSCMD and the lower side is 83 MMSCMD in 2030.

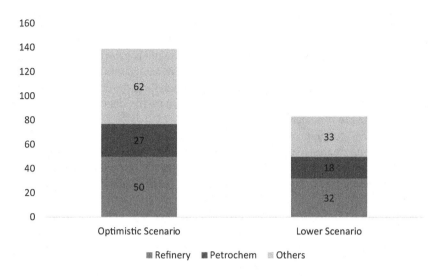

FIGURE 7.9   Estimated RLNG demand of industry sector in 2030 (MMSCMD).

7.9   AGGREGATE DEMAND FOR NATURAL GAS IN 2030

7.9.1   MIXED OUTLOOK FOR DEMAND IN DIFFERENT SECTORS

Obviously enough, gas demand estimations for 2030 are sector-specific and vary a lot across the demand sectors. In the transport and cooking sub-sectors of urban areas (CGD) natural gas could entirely replace liquid fuels, primarily because as compared to liquid fuels, it is cleaner, cheaper and more convenient to use. In the other sub-sectors, while there is a genuine scope for demand to be robust, however, price competitiveness and government policy on clean air will play a bigger role than within these sectors. In case of power generation, future for natural gas looks grim. Hence, any attempt to assess its role in future cannot be a top-down approach, and ought to be a sectoral approach or bottom-upwards.

7.9.2   POOR OUTLOOK IN POWER SECTOR

Expectedly growing demand for power in India could have been a demand booster for natural gas. However, its prospects in the bright electricity scenario of India is rather dim. Underlying factors contributing to this scenario were discussed, drawing largely from the Government's 19th EPS and NEP (published in 2017). Due to a mismatch existing between power demand growth and upcoming capacities of cheaper sources like renewables, it is likely that gas-based power might simply be non-competitive. This is expected to be the case even as PLFs of coal-based capacities fall, given the government's commitment for 175 GW of renewable power in 2022, wherein, the technology costs have also fallen, and going further 500 GW capacity of non-fossil origin is envisaged for 2030. The unutilised capacity in TPPs will be at hand to provide cheap power by raising their PLF, should there be a spurt in demand. The new emission norms can raise the cost of coal-based power of existing TPPs, however, this might also lead to their greater acceptance from an environmental perspective though not agreed upon by experts.

The LCOE of both coal-based power and renewables is lower than natural gas-based power. If, there was to be a large availability of domestic gas priced at a discount to LNG, it may mark a shift in favour of gas. However, the proposed pricing policy for domestic gas, does not assure this kind of a rebate. The discussion on grid integration for balancing the grid in high renewable capacity case, is not likely to boost natural gas demand.

7.9.3 Urea Manufacture Policy as the Main Determinant of Natural Gas Demand

As regards natural gas availability for urea manufacture, a number of gas demand projections for urea manufacturing were published in the period before 2017. At that time, there was limited clarity on the upcoming capacity. After 2017, various measures have been announced to increase domestic urea production by reviving old plants and setting up the new ones. It is thus important to note that setting up domestic urea manufacturing capacity was a policy decision not particularly linked to the economics of imported urea as such, and is instead based on a policy decision to achieve self-sufficiency.

7.9.4 Robust Demand in Industries

The estimation of natural gas demand in Industries is limited by poor availability of segregated data of consumption by source—RLNG and domestic gas. The existing supply of domestic gas is not expected to change much, and new domestic supply may go to the sectors already prioritised by the government such as CGD and urea. The ability of industry to pass on the fuel price changes to the consumer varies, and this makes it quite important to categorise industrial consumers. The industries that comprise the present section are the larger industries such as refineries, petrochemicals and others. As the available data includes consumption of small industrial consumers along with that of minor non-industrial consumers (e.g. tea estates), the present discussion includes assorted industries that are not included in the larger categories (Table 7.14).

A major assumption while estimating natural gas demand in Industries has been that domestic gas may not be available for this set of consumers. Assuming that the marginal price of natural gas may be equal to the price of imported gas, there will be no difference left between domestically produced gas from such fields and RLNG. Therefore, there may be a unified gas market and demand may not be divided between users of cheaper domestic gas and such sectors as can afford expensive imported gas. In order that the analysis is valid even when natural gas comes from domestic fields under the new pricing policy, it is instructive to estimate demand by sheer ability to consume 'market-priced' gas. Industry may be the first

TABLE 7.16

Aggregated gas demand in 2030 in MMSCMD (BCM in parenthesis)

	Domestic Gas		RLNG		TOTAL (Domestic and RLNG)	
	Higher	Lower	Higher	Lower	Higher (HDS)	Lower (LDS)
Industries	15	15	124	68	139 (51)	83 (30)
CGD	108	89	85	65	193 (71)	154 (57)
Urea	17	17	47	39	64 (23)	56 (20)
Power	25	25	98	19	123 (45)	44 (16)
TOTAL	165 (60)	146 (54)	354 (130)	191 (69)	519 (190)	337 (123)

candidate to absorb freely priced gas for which the estimated volumes in this study may be helpful.

7.9.5   CGD to Be the Largest Driver

In Table 7.16, the results of the estimation exercise have been aggregated and tabulated, too. In both the scenarios, LDS and HDS, CGD appears to be the number one in terms of volume of natural gas demand followed closely by Industries. In the LDS, Urea comes at third place and Power is ranked last. However, in the HDS, the third and fourth positions change inter-se. The results are quite in contrast to the present situation in Figure 7.1 where CGD is at present, the last ranked natural gas-consuming sector. Industries (classified as miscellaneous end-uses), are at the second place and have the same outlook for 2030.

7.9.6   Air Quality Concerns a Booster for Natural Gas

While renewables will meet power demand without any carbon emissions, it is the non-electric demand segment where emissions have few choices left other than natural gas. Usually, air quality concerns in urban areas have low tolerance. The demand growth from CGD segment has been discussed above. Similarly, industries may also be driven by air quality regulations. The National Clean Air Programme (NCAP) and the recently constituted Commission for Air Quality in the national capital region (NCR) of Delhi are aimed at addressing air quality and they have been promoting substitution of polluting fuels by natural gas. The coming days may see even tighter regulation, and this will directly benefit the latter.

7.9.7   Aggregate Demand Outlook for 2030

As regards the classification of demand by domestic and imported gas, the cooking/transport demand has been assumed to be met by domestic gas resulting in CGD becoming the largest end-user of this source of gas. The CGD sector has broadly two groups of consumers—one group gets access to an administered preferential price in the form of CNG and PNG, and the second group of commercial/industrial consumers generally use it based on price competitiveness as they rely mostly on market priced RLNG. For the first group, the demand for natural gas assumes continuous supply of lower priced domestic gas, while for the second group, an interplay of prices of different fuels determine its demand. It is assumed that CGD would receive the largest allocation of domestic gas. Since a decision has already been taken to accept RLNG in urea manufacture, and capacity augmentation is already underway, only the present domestic gas supply to this sector is likely to continue. As regards Industries, since they run on entirely commercial lines, one does not envisage any allocation of domestic gas to this sector. Power sector has already been found to have an overcapacity in coal-based capacity thus leaving little demand for higher-priced gas-based power.

It has already been stated in the introductory paragraphs of this chapter that high share of estimated domestic gas allocated to any sector as provided separately in Table 7.16 does not necessarily mean that this demand might vanish if domestic production was short of actual demand. The demand for PNG/CNG would be valid even if, domestic gas supply was not to materialise. In Chapter 5, a likely domestic gas supply of 100 BCM (from natural gas/CBM/coal gasification) has been estimated on the optimistic side for 2030, which is more than the HDS demand for domestic gas at 60 BCM. While the demand for RLNG has been estimated to range between 69 and 130 BCM/year, it is also to be verified as to whether the estimated regas capacity in LNG receiving terminals in 2030 would be sufficient to meet this demand. In the discussions on supply of natural gas in Chapter 5, it has been estimated that RLNG supply would be 91 BCM (60% capacity utilisation of regas capacity of nearly 151 BCM/year). Hence, there would be an adequate regas capacity available to supply even the higher end of range of demand of 130 BCM/year in 2030.

7.9.8 Comparison with Projections by Other Agencies

Here, we take a look at how the estimated demand numbers actually compare with projections of other agencies in Table 7.2. For 2030, projections of only two agencies—PNGRB and IEA—are currently available. The other two agencies—erstwhile Planning Commission and OIES—have projected only until 2022 and 2024, respectively. For 2030, PNGRB has projected a gas demand of 746 MMSCMD, while IEA's projections are in the range of 340–388 MMSCMD, nearly half of what the former has estimated (In the 2015 version of India Energy Outlook, the projections were lower). The scenarios under this study of 337–519 MMSCMD are in between the above two projections, albeit closer to the IEA's projection on the LDS. If, the projections of the other two agencies are extrapolated, it is found that Planning Commission is already wide off the mark. Against its projection of 606 MMSCMD in 2022, in 2019–20 only 175 MMSCMD gas was consumed (7% of the PES) and it cannot rise by three times in the next two years so as to match the 2022 projection. The OIES projection is available for 2024 at 148 MMSCMD at a much lower side to IEA's number for 2025 under its Stated Policies Scenario (259 MMSCMD). It is apparent that both Planning Commission and PNGRB, the two government agencies, have been highly optimistic when compared to the external agencies.

7.9.9   Likely Share of Natural Gas in Commercial PES in 2030

Another critical approach to testing these scenarios might be to approximate the likely growth in natural gas demand from the present time, and then compare it with the past trend to check whether the rate of growth seems reasonable and achievable too. From 175 MMSCMD consumption in 2019–20, the range of projected natural gas demand (337–519 MMSCMD) is approximately between 2 and 3 times of the former value. Going back by an equivalent period of 11 years (2019–30), in 2007–08 India's annual natural gas consumption was 33.4 Mtoe (BP Statistics) or 38.84 BCM (106 MMSCMD). The demand for natural gas demand grew by 1.6 times in 11 years and the new projections envisage a much higher increase. While the share of gas in 2007–08 was 7.5% in PES, it is now lesser at 6.3% (2019–20). If, the growth rate in India's PES is lower than what it has been in the past, at the projected growth rate in gas consumption, the share of natural gas in PES would then only go up from what it is at present. Given that the government has committed itself to natural gas, this is quite feasible. As a part of this study, India's total commercial PES for 2030 has not been estimated. Therefore, we have to rely on demand scenarios of other agencies, which is not a preferred approach though, but it is just being offered for the reader's information. When compared with IEA's India's PES projection for 2030, the above natural gas demand estimates come out to be between 13.8% and 17.4% share under different demand scenarios. The latter high share is in the SDS scenario, wherein total PES is quite low. IEA has projected a total energy demand of 994–1237 Mtoe/year in 2030 under Sustainable Development Scenario (SDS) and India Vision Case (IVC) scenarios (IEA, 2021). It may be seen in Table 7.2 that IEA's own natural gas demand projection for 2030 places the gas share between 9% and 11% of PES. The projections in percentage share under this study are higher than those of IEA, however, it may not be exactly so if, the PES in 2030 were to be higher than what IEA has maintained thus far. IEA projects that in the STEPS Scenario, the share of natural gas might rise to 9% in 2030 and Indian aspiration of achieving yet higher share is not met. But, in an ambitious scenario of higher economic growth as envisaged in the other two scenarios, a higher level of LNG imports to meet higher energy demand may then boost the share of natural gas to 11%–12% (IEA, 2021).

In the absence of statistical models to generate demand scenarios and having taken only historical growth rates and policy levers, the demand projections should be viewed by the policymakers only as likely trends. The results of the study need to be analysed to understand the drivers *behind* the numbers rather than the sheer numbers themselves. In light of such large variations in projections of agencies discussed above, it may be quite appropriate to focus more on the discussion around such factors as impinge on natural gas demand, and analyse the rise in demand within

**BOX 7.1 WILL INDIA'S ENERGY TRANSITION
AGENDA PROMOTE DEMAND FOR NATURAL GAS?**

This chapter draws upon key learnings from the previous ones so as to offer an estimate of the likely demand for natural gas in 2030. Factors that might impinge on demand such as preference for clean energy including regulatory measures on curbing emissions have already been considered. Nevertheless, with India's declaration of clear timelines for net-zero and higher ambition for non-fossil fuel, there may be a knock-on effect on projections already made. India has a large dependence on coal which will have to be 'phased-down' and lesser GHG emitter capability specific fuels inducted. Natural gas may then get a fillip in some areas where it may be a natural choice in place of coal.

Presently, the largest share of coal consumption is in power generation, followed up by industry where steel is the major consumer. In the former, renewable based power is on the ascendancy and could displace coal entirely over time. However, as discussed in the chapter until electricity storage costs come down, coal will continue not only as a source of base-load power but also for peak load demand. Renewables also need to reach significantly high capacity so as to make a noticeable dent on coal-based power, especially as their utilisation factors (between 15% and 21%) are small. India's commitments to ramp-up renewables to 50% of its power generating capacity and also ensure that 500 GW of this capacity is of renewable origin, does not help the cause of gas much. It is thus likely that the existing natural gas-based power generation capacity (some of which is presently stranded) may be harnessed to balance the growing intermittent nature of renewable sources. The demand for natural gas for this capacity has already been included in the High Demand Scenario for 2030. Now coming to steel, the call for net-zero emissions target realisation will put a pressure on this sector to move away from coking coal-based blast furnace route. Hydrogen technology in the DRI process could be a good alternative in the medium term. There are news reports that this technology is being commercially established at some locations in Europe. However, in the specified time frame of this study (2030), it may not impact coal demand. The same may be true for other industrial processes where coal still holds a monopoly. It is notable that even natural gas is a fossil fuel. Any pioneering effort in innovation towards the substitution of coal may be in the direction of non-fossil fuels and not natural gas alone. Therefore, it might be fair to assume that the drive to energy transition in India may not boost natural gas demand, while it might dampen coal demand.

India is currently making rapid strides in the direction of PNG and CNG, especially in urban areas, and the same has been unequivocally acknowledged in this chapter to hold the largest share of natural gas demand in the years to come. This could receive a setback in the transport sector, should EV revolution happen quickly with fast moving cost reductions in lithium-ion batteries and related technology. What follows is that global action against carbon emissions may indirectly impact the Indian energy mix, by advancements in clean energy technology and cost reductions. However, on its own, there may not be any meaningful difference to the swinging fortune of natural gas

sub-sectors over the study period rather than draw conclusions merely on share allocation in overall PES for commercial energy. The current study has attempted to address the above issues.

NOTES

1   While natural gas and crude oil prices are determined freely at global level, on a calorific parity basis, most liquid fuel derivatives from crude oil are now more expensive than natural gas.
2   On calorific parity basis, it has been seen in the past several years, the final price of natural gas (particularly domestically produced) is lower than liquid fuels. This is also because the state VAT and excise duty levies are lower on CNG/PNG.
3   The Government's earlier gas allocation orders for domestic natural gas gave top priority to Urea manufacture.
4   The government has been allocating domestic gas (produced by NOCs and under PSCs) to sectors as per a priority order that has been modified from time to time.
5   Even the courts oversaw pricing of CNG and PNG to ensure that their directive of clean fuels was not thwarted.
6   While PPAC (Ready Reckoner) gives data of CNG sales but not for PNG. On the other hand, the monthly reports of PPAC give total domestic natural gas sale data by sectors. The consumption of PNG per HH connection has been estimated by deducting CNG sale from domestic gas sale in CGD.
7   In this study, average of 11 (actual sales are between 10 and 12 cylinders of 14.2 kg each) LPG cylinder consumption has been approximated with 186 SCM of natural gas.
8   In Delhi, the share of CNG sales is around 60%.
9   The PLF of gas-based plants was 24% in 2018.
10 Out of 175 GW, the solar component is 100 GW, which requires balancing in the evening. The 60 GW component of wind capacity will involve seasonal variation.
11 In 2010–11, India's gas production shot up to 52 BCM, the highest ever and declined thereafter (MoPNG, 2017).
12 P. 21 The actual capacity in 2017 was much lower at 25,329 MW.
13 The projects are being executed on the basis of firm PPAs with central and state government agencies.
14 (CEA, 2018b) P.1. The achievement of 175 GW of renewable capacity by 2021–22 would lead to 36.5% share in total capacity but only 19% in total generation.
15 The Calculator on the website of PRAYAS was used to estimate how much power is generated at different PLFs from different technologies.

16 Jain (2011) A detailed discussion on policy issues in India's urea sector is available in 'Natural Gas in India: Liberalisation and Policy'.

17 In 2015, the government mentioned in a Press Statement that urea demand in 2024–25 is likely to be 38 MT (Business Standard, 2015).

18 This is not to be confused with the higher natural gas demand scenario of the instant research.

19 In this sense, urea production via imported natural gas may not fully meet the aims of self-sufficiency.

20 R-LNG supply to these plants has been contracted with GAIL. See Singh and Chakraborty (2017).

21 PPAC has started publishing data by industry sourced from domestic/imported supplies for the period only after 2015.

22 The price comparison between natural gas and petroleum product has already been discussed in the sub-section on CGD.

23 IEA (2015) The difference in base number of natural gas consumption in 2012–13 between 12th Plan and IEA is due to difference in categorisation of Industry which make them non-comparable.

24 In many States, VAT rates on natural gas are low. Delhi has nil rate while Punjab has 3%.

25 CIL's coal prices are steadier also because they are not market priced but indexed as per consumer/ wholesale price indices and prices were last fixed in early 2018. It supplies 80% of domestic coal.

26 In the case of industries, RLNG is rendered expensive also due to additional costs on gasification, ocean transport and re-gasification compared to piped natural gas.

27 Along with other new capacities, a 60 MMTPA refinery (approximately 1.2 million barrels of oil/day) has been announced on the west coast (RRPCL, n.d.).

28 Delloite (2019) This study undertaken with support of Government of India has projected a much higher (438 MMTPA) refining capacity for 2030. It has also projected a base natural gas demand in refining of 29 MMSCMD and an optimistic demand of 36 MMSCMD in 2030.

8 Way Forward

8.1 SUPPORT NEEDED BY NATURAL GAS

There is a heightened global action against the utilisation of polluting fuels, and closer home, India too, faces challenges of improving air quality and erratic weather patterns. Natural gas is a fossil fuel but emits lesser carbon dioxide upon combustion as compared to oil and coal. India has a high share of coal in its energy mix, and natural gas could therefore help reduce emissions by substituting it. For India, which is a large emitter of carbon in absolute terms, it could help reduce the country's carbon intensity. The share of natural gas in commercial PES has been static at 6% or so for many years. Large reserves of natural gas discovered across the world in the last two decades including discoveries made in India have kindled hopes of its abundant availability. On the pricing front also, natural gas offers a viable option. Earlier, its prices were linked with those of oil with near parity on a calorific basis, and have now got de-linked. In energy equivalence terms, at prevailing prices, natural gas is cheaper than oil but more expensive to use than coal. Therefore, on environmental, availability and economic criteria, natural gas is a preferable option over oil and coal. The Indian Government has declared an ambition for natural gas to achieve a 15% share in commercial PES by 2030. However, similar aspirations held out in the past were not realised. Several studies including the India Hydrocarbons Vision 2025 (prepared by the Indian Government's top planning body, Planning Commission, in 1999), and successive Five-Year Plans offered projections of a high share of natural gas for different time frames. In spite of the ambition and many steps taken towards facilitating this fuel, natural gas has not fared as per expectations and its share at 6.5% in 2019–20 is nearly the same (6.9%) as it was two decades back in 2000. In fact, India has even seen a reversal in natural gas share from a high of 9% in the energy mix in 2010–11 to 6% at present.

Looking to the high ambition of the government and value proposition offered by this fuel for the national economy, this study makes an in-depth analysis of the key drivers of natural gas demand and supply to assess the likelihood of the aspiration to be met in the near future. On the basis of the above, what steps might support a higher uptake of natural gas are being suggested in this chapter.

Energy mix is shaped up by a number of factors that cannot be anticipated with certainty, and its evolution ought to be envisioned under assumed scenarios. Fuel share estimations ought to be seen more as trends—rise or fall, and realisation degree of the same. It is when trends are later found to be widely off the mark that a need arises to seek answers by applying various analytical tools that exist in the academic literature as to why did the estimations go wrong. The story of growth of natural gas in India falls in the category where estimations have gone wrong even within the short term. One way is to study the trends in other countries, and then apply the learning outcomes to the instant case. This approach was followed in this study and trends in evolution of energy mix, and that of natural gas in particular, in other leading energy-consuming countries were examined. The above analysis has been applied prospectively to determine as to what might be the role of natural gas in India in the medium term (2030). Towards this enquiry, it combined quantitative tools with empirical ground-level trends in a bottom-up analysis of India.

This book fills the continuing gap in available studies that looked at natural gas only in parts. So far, poor domestic production and the rationale for imported supplies have received a lion's share of attention. Dampening of demand due to high price of imported natural gas at a premium to domestic production has also been a subject of greater scrutiny. However, these studies do not offer a comprehensive analysis of role of multiple non-price factors such as air quality, energy security, delivery infrastructure (trunk pipelines and LNG terminals) and importantly, regulatory role of the government in promoting a balanced energy mix. Inter-governmental agencies and Industry bodies have urged the policymakers to facilitate growth of natural gas. The lack of a comprehensive enquiry on as how to address the challenges faced by this fuel is still missing, and thus has deprived the policymakers of good quality advice on steps that might help raise its share in India's commercial PES. This book attempts to fill this gap too.

The study is essentially supported on three pillars. The first pillar is an analysis of the 'flexibility' of the Indian energy mix to adopt new fuels in preference over older fuels depending upon a fuel's overall merit, with an aim directed towards achieving a 'balance' across various fuel types. Many scholars have supported the view that a higher diversity in energy supply mix (measured in terms of variety and balance) is a proxy for energy security. The second pillar is a study of past trends in growth of natural gas in India and the world's leading energy-consuming countries, to be able to compare the Indian natural gas story with them, and thereby identify reasons for differences. The findings are likely to guide the future strategy to help realisation of the Indian aspiration for a high natural gas share. The third and final pillar is a bottom-up analysis of the demand and supply side factors, which might shape the share of natural gas in India's energy mix in 2030 under two scenarios that ought to be seen as likely trends and not firm demand estimates. A bottom-up demand estimation of India's main gas-consuming sectors has been made under two key scenarios:

  i. Low Demand Scenario (LDS) and
  ii. High Demand Scenario (HDS)

The above scenarios may be seen in Table 8.1 and it connects with the Indian aspiration of 15% share in 2030.

This chapter is divided into three main sections. Following this opening section, in the second section the main findings of the study that comprise the conclusion have been presented in a summarised manner. The third section discusses in detail the policy recommendations coming out of this study. This is the central piece as the purpose of the entire endeavour is to support the policymakers in meeting their ambition.

8.2   SUMMARY OF FINDINGS

The main objectives of this study are as follows:

- to examine the role of different factors in determining the demand for natural gas;
- to evaluate the natural gas demand potential in the medium term (2030);
- to make recommendations as to what policy measures need to be taken to achieve the above potential.

Six determinants were identified to address the above. They are not specific to any particular objective, but all of them put together will help respond to the above mentioned objectives.

- How has the diversity of energy mix of leading energy-consuming countries including India evolved over the medium term?
- What trends are clearly visible in the energy mix of these countries?
- What factors/consuming sectors are responsible for higher growth in demand for natural gas in major gas-consuming countries?
- What is the price competitiveness of natural gas vis-à-vis competing fuels in different consuming sectors in India?
- What might be the impact of clean energy agenda, particularly renewable energy, on demand for natural gas?
- What might be demand for natural gas under LDS and HDS in 2030?

The first two questions relate mainly to energy mix, which is an outcome of structural factors, and have been answered via an enquiry focussed on natural gas in India. This was considered useful so as to determine whether the Indian energy system has been as rigid or flexible as other countries. In the initial stage of this book, we analysed the degree of flexibility in identified countries to enhance or reduce the share of different fuels in their energy mix, and even induct new fuels depending on changing preferences. A statistical method—Shannon Wiener diversity index (DI)—was applied to seven major energy-consuming countries to examine the above and numerically grade the degree of evolution in their energy mix over 1980–2019. A movement in DI captures the shifts in energy mix towards achieving a balanced energy mix with multiple fuels in near equal shares.

During the period 1980–2019, the energy mix of the world's top seven energy consumers, including India, has undergone significant evolution, which is still an ongoing one. It has been found that some trends of growth/decline in respective shares of different fuels were common albeit the degree of change varied amongst countries. Consequently, the Shannon Wiener DI for each of these countries via measuring the diversity in energy mix has risen at a differing rate. On specific trends in fuel shares, India is the only one in these seven countries to have registered an increase in the group share of fossil fuels. What naturally follows from the above is that share of clean energy group of fuels—new renewables (wind, solar and small hydro), nuclear and hydro—has fallen in India (within clean energy the share of new renewables did grow). The second trend is that while Japan is the only country to have enhanced coal in its energy mix, in India the share has been static (and it is the only one in this category). Thirdly, what is most discernible about India is that its DI rose at the slowest rate over 1980–2019, and the countries that had a lower DI in 1980 other than that of India have performed better with a more rapid growth—Brazil has overtaken India's DI, while China's DI is closing in the difference. Large shares of two fuels (coal and oil) characterise India's energy mix and very low shares of a handful of other fuels resulted in an imbalance amongst the different fuels, and a low DI. Hence, India's energy mix has been rigid with shares of existing fuels being perpetuated, while most of the countries have performed better towards achieving a more evenly spread share of different fuels.

The remaining four questions pertain directly to natural gas and have been discussed chapter four onwards. These relate to the fuel-specific factors that have shaped the share of natural gas in India's energy mix. To start with, a comparative analysis was undertaken of the triggers responsible for the growth of natural gas in the world's leading energy-consuming countries (1980–2019). This was done with a view to understand as to what factors have commonly worked in favour of natural gas and what haven't really worked. In 1980, its share in global energy consumption was 19%, rising to 24% by 2019. Climate change debates became loud only in the decades after 1980, and it can be assumed that different energy sources were largely reflected in that era in the energy mix of countries consistent with an inherent merit in fuels and being much in accordance with national preferences. The common drivers relevant to growth of natural gas in the study countries, were then applied to India to see both the consistency and contradictions on their likely impact on this fuel. The following trends have been identified across the countries and within India:

- Early uptake of natural gas was found to help it achieve higher shares in later years. Conversely, countries with a poor intake continue to have low shares. Erection of natural gas delivery specific infra helped countries to achieve the above objective. In India, too, owing to poor domestic endowment of natural gas, it could only make a small beginning and thus limited gas-related infra could come up. India's natural gas consumption was a mere 1% of commercial PES in 1980, and still remains low at 6.5% even in 2019 (along with China), being the lowest in the seven countries.
- Large domestic natural gas production in countries of study has been correlated with high consumption. And the converse was also found to be true. Low natural gas production in India (3% of total commercial energy supplied in 2019) has resulted in a small share of natural gas in PES. In countries with supply of natural gas by transnational

pipelines, the above noted handicap has been overcome. However, owing to geo-political reasons India does not have overland connectivity with large natural gas producing countries in its immediate neighbourhood.

- When global sectoral consumption of natural gas is analysed, Power and Industry sectors come at first and second place. However, in the large energy-consuming countries studied in this study, Industry and Power are the top two sectors. The Indian situation is also consistent with the other large energy consumers. Going onwards to 2030, Industry is likely to be a major driver of natural gas demand.

- The share of natural gas-based power generation in an overall generation from all sources is not high in major energy-consuming countries. In India, too, a similar situation is observed. Incidentally, the share of natural gas-based generation is even lower than that for other study countries. What follows from above is that high share of natural gas-based power is not an essential factor for a high natural gas share in PES, and for India to achieve a large natural gas share, it is not necessary for natural gas-based generation to assume a high share in overall electricity generation scenario.

- Lately large energy consumers are moving towards clean energy use including substitution of coal by natural gas-based power. Even though India is also trending towards clean energy now, and new renewables are growing robustly, the power sector is not trending towards natural gas which could fast replace the more polluting coal-based generation. The emergence of renewable-based electricity might further reduce the chances of natural gas outreach in India.

Price is a major determinant of demand, and even in the case of natural gas, its role cannot be overlooked. How might natural gas be competitive on price terms with other fuels in future is highly uncertain. There are well-considered expert agencies in this area, both in the inter-governmental and private sectors, that offer price projections. Without attempting to project prices in the instant study, price comparisons have been made between natural gas and competing fuels as per the consuming sector (urea, power, etc.). For this, recent prices of natural gas (both domestic and RLNG) and other fuels have been taken, and arbitrage calculated. The above exercise was undertaken with the assumption that without a broad understanding of competitiveness of natural gas, it may not have been possible to estimate the future demand scenario. Hence, prices have been considered as being one of the crucial factors in generating demand scenarios. Only in case of power generation, natural gas is outbid by other fuels, whereas in most other end-uses where liquid fuel is the competing fuel, barring furnace oil, the price of natural gas (even RLNG) has been found to be competitive. The summary of key findings is provided below:

- In the industrial and commercial sub-sectors of CGD, natural gas is found to be competitive over market-priced LPG and HSD. However, it is more expensive than furnace oil. For cooking, it is cheaper than commercially priced LPG, and also in transport it is cheaper than both petrol and diesel. This analysis has been carried out for a number of vehicle types in terms of cost per vehicle kilometre.

- For urea production, in light of two policy decisions—one of conversion of all naphtha-based urea plants to natural gas feedstock and second, opting for self-sufficiency in urea by domestic production even based on RLNG—the issue of price is not germane. Nevertheless, naphtha-based urea is more expensive.
- In power generation, natural gas is more expensive than most other competing sources—coal, wind and solar. As other sources—nuclear, biomass, hydro and small hydro power—are not expected to be major players in power generation, their prices have not been compared as such.

Broadly speaking, natural gas has been found to be competitive against all forms of liquid hydrocarbons, except for the heavier fractions (e.g. furnace oil). Due to highly polluting nature of furnace oil, it is not a major player in India's energy basket. However, natural gas turns out to be more expensive than coal and renewable sources in power generation.

On an overall basis, the learnings from other major countries indicate that lack of rich natural endowment of natural gas as well as a late start for natural gas in the country's energy basket have resulted in other energy sources acquiring larger footprints. Even geo-political reasons have denied the country an opportunity to obtain its supplies via overland pipelines. But, the sectoral drivers are a good fit for natural gas in India. From a deep understanding of the drivers that worked or did not work towards growth of natural gas in India, a bottom-up demand generation scenario for all the four main consuming sectors—urea production, power generation, CGD, and, Industry and others—has been undertaken and aggregate numbers presented (Table 8.1).

The following sector-specific projections have been generated for the year 2030 under two scenarios—LDS and HDS:

TABLE 8.1
Aggregated Natural Gas Demand in 2030 in MMSCMD (BCM in Parenthesis)

	Domestic Natural Gas		RLNG		Total Natural Gas	
	Higher	Lower	Higher	Lower	Higher (HDS)	Lower (LDS)
Industries	15	15	124	68	139 (51)	83 (30)
CGD	108	89	85	65	193 (71)	154 (57)
Urea	17	17	47	39	64 (23)	56 (20)
Power	25	25	98	19	123 (45)	44 (16)
Total	165 (60)	146 (54)	354 (130)	191 (69)	519 (190)	337 (123)

- For urea production, the LDS envisages no new urea plants coming up beyond the five plants already announced and currently underway for revamp. In this scenario, the urea demand in 2022 is to be fully met by domestic production, but with no plausible increase in urea production after that. The above yields a firm natural gas demand of 20 BCM in 2030. In HDS, which assumes even the urea demand of 2030 would be met by domestic production, it is estimated that the demand would rise to 23 BCM.
- The outlook of natural gas for power generation is thus bleak. If, there was no noticeable growth in existing natural gas-based power generation capacity (and even this being required only for balancing variable renewable power), then the LDS scenario of natural gas demand is of 16 BCM (2030). However, in HDS this rises to 45 BCM in 2030 only by existing capacity being utilised optimally at high PLF.
- Looking to the encouraging commitment received for both PNG and CNG in 9th and 10th CGD bidding rounds in urban areas, a large LDS natural gas demand for CGD sector is of 57 BCM (2030). In the HDS, higher penetration of natural gas in all sub-sectors of urban energy consumption, the estimated demand rises to 71 BCM. This is the most promising sector as urban air quality concerns, and the government's proactive action of contracting rights to erect CGD networks is expected to be a great motivator.
- In the last sector—Industries and others—there is a high degree of uncertainty. A large availability of natural gas, perhaps, from domestic discoveries if, fully supported by regulatory action on emissions, could be the major drivers. This sector is also considered to be the major consumer of RLNG. A projection of 30 BCM and 51 BCM has been estimated in the LDS and HDS for 2030, respectively.

Adding up the above, a likely natural gas demand of 123 BCM and 190 BCM is estimated for 2030 in LDS and HDS scenarios, respectively.

8.3 POLICY RECOMMENDATIONS

Against this specific background of large presence of government companies in energy sector whose actions determine the energy landscape in a big way, the role of a suitable policy framework becomes quite important. Natural gas is a comparatively new fuel for India, and thus needs a helping hand. It has been stated at the outset that the Government has given a call for achieving 15% share of natural gas in India's commercial PES by 2030. The study also revealed that there being a major investment in liquid fuel business both by private and public sector companies, it may be sheer reluctance on their part to promote natural gas. These companies are already meeting the energy demand of such sectors as have to migrate to natural gas, and any delay in their erection of gas-specific infra will impact the latter. While examining the demand and supply side factors for all the four consumption sectors, the role of policy measures was found relevant in regulation, infrastructure, price (subsidy), direct investment by PSUs, emission control, etc. The policy recommendations have been grouped under the following few headings.

8.3.1 ENHANCING DIVERSITY OF ENERGY SUPPLY

The low DI of India's energy supply vis-à-vis other leading energy consumers reflects a closed energy system that has been unable to take advantage of evolving competitiveness in the energy market. The cues that emerge from this study offer a view that India's continuance (even increase) in its dependence on coal (and oil) may have denied it an opportunity of migrating to a more balanced energy mix. The recommendation for the policymaker is to develop a revamped 'Integrated Energy Policy' for India that would allow fuel substitution on the basis of relative merits in respective fuels. The above policy ought to define 'energy security' in a wider term going much beyond self-dependence to include 'diversity' as well. The narrow definition of 'Diversification' by merely advocating more oil import sources from different geographical regions and maintaining/enhancing self-reliance for other fuels, does not provide an insurance against energy insecurity coming from denial of technological and other opportunities that new fuels bring along. India may also need to proactively support utilisation of cleaner fuels such as natural gas, new renewables and nuclear energy that presently have small shares in an overall energy mix. Further it must join the global 'energy transition' at work since 2005, which is favouring clean energy. Only an overarching energy policy can address issues of diversity of fuels.

8.3.2 A COMPREHENSIVE NATURAL GAS POLICY

While the study proposes framing of an Integrated Energy Policy, nevertheless within natural gas, there is a dire need of a comprehensive policy that encompasses selective aspects like exploration, production, pipelines, pricing, RLNG, gas storage and markets, in an integrated manner. This calls for Indian policymakers to devise a policy solely dedicated to natural gas in synchronisation with the integrated policy, so that the factors that are holding natural gas back may be clearly identified and suitably addressed. The above policy framework must comprise of various steps to create gas distribution infrastructure and even allow for initial redundancy (under-utilisation), and higher uptake in due course. This has been the case on a global basis with redundancy in LNG receiving terminals and trunk pipelines. India needs to achieve robust growth in LNG terminals that are working at almost full utilisation, thereby denying additional supply to match the capacity of trunk pipelines. A tight supply situation gives negative cue to possible consumers. On the other hand, the tariff policy does not insulate the owners of trunk pipelines from losses accrued due to under-utilisation in the initial years. In this regard, it may be mentioned that power transmission operators get a matching tariff to cover their entire capex as soon as the project achieves Commercial Operation Date (COD). The instant study has a number of sub-policy recommendations for an integrated gas policy:

- Firm natural gas supply contracts should be encouraged when pipelines are authorised by the regulator, like the ones signed by urea plants undergoing revamp at five different locations. In the initial stage, long-term GSPAs help in growth of gas-related infra. Once the size of gas market grows, then short-term contracts may assume larger volume.
- Industries and commercial consumers within CGD sector may be reluctant to migrate to new fuels mainly due to lack of information and one-time capex that may be required for burning of natural gas. Clean air regulations can drive adoption of natural gas over existing polluting fuels. Regulatory mandates may be in order to provide clean air to the citizens. A closer engagement between the related ministries may thus help.
- Pipeline growth needs to be dovetailed with development of CGD networks. PNGRB's pipeline regulations may adopt such milestones as synchronise with the timelines given in newly awarded CGD licenses. This worry was also underlined by the survey respondents.
- Natural gas utilisation policy may be suitably designed to help usher-in a vibrant gas market rather than dividing it into different sub-markets. The sectoral allocations may be phased out so that when domestic natural gas prices align with RLNG.

8.3.3 Pricing-Related Policy Recommendation

Natural gas prices for the domestic producer have undergone a number of policy changes. Starting from different prices under different Production Sharing Contracts (PSCs) that were signed from time to time when fields were given away, to pricing freedom for new natural gas that might come, the pricing regime has undergone a transformation. Now there is a stable pricing outlook with the mandate to give a near-market price to all new gas. While this ought to meet the expectations of E&P companies, but unless the policy of end consumer pricing for the sectors that use natural gas is reformed, gas producers/suppliers may continue to face uncertainty. The study recommends that pricing policy for urea, power, cooking/transport sub-sectors may be freed of government controls. The producers in these sectors are reluctant to enter into firm natural gas purchase contracts as they do not have the ability to pass on the market price to consumers. For example, in urea, the government needs to insulate urea producer from its subsidy policy that does not reward efficiency in energy consumption norms. As higher natural gas price means higher subsidy, it puts a 'back pressure' on upstream gas price and disincentivises E&P sector. Any subsidy to consumers may be direct in the hands of consumers and not on the fuel price. In light of different ministries controlling pricing of natural gas-based products, one ministry (petroleum or finance ministry) may issue a common policy that assures the natural gas consumer-producers of a long-term policy stability. While LNG prices vary as per price formulae, by and large several competing fuels such as coal, electricity under PPAs including wind/solar have more stable prices on offer due to regulatory oversight. This deprives natural gas an even playing field as there is no pricing confirmation from a regulator that also addresses the consuming sectors. A consumer pricing policy alone could address the above lacunae. The latter may be dovetailed into the sectoral policy. Further, in power sector, looking to the attributes of being clean and amenable to quick-start, the National Electricity Policy (NEP) may make reservations for gas-based power on the same lines as Renewable Purchase Obligations (RPO) for renewables. The power prices for gas-based generation as derived through bidding, could well be blended with the procurement cost of cheaper sources including that from coal (the government has imposed RPO on thermal power producers, too). Freeing energy prices through the revamped Integrated Energy Policy is a must so that the fuels competing with natural gas may not lend any disadvantage to it by way of any distortion. Thus allowing free transmission for gas-based power as has been previously allowed for renewable power would also go a long way. India needs a revamped energy pricing policy, that addresses the aim of providing natural gas a level playing field. Surely the petroleum pricing reforms in diesel, LPG, kerosene need to be taken forward into natural gas-consuming sectors.

8.3.4 RECOMMENDATION OF FURTHER STUDIES TO HELP DRAFT BETTER POLICY

For the reasons discussed above, natural gas will need an inter-related policy. This will in turn require an informed knowledge of various other sectors such as India's industrial economy and India's geology and engineering issues. Such studies would help much and have been grouped under this broad set of recommendations as below.

- Power sector reforms hold the key to natural gas demand. Linked to the above is also the issue of electrification of energy demand—electric mobility, electric cooking, electrification of processes in industry, providing heat through electricity, etc. Electricity based processes have higher efficiency and are less polluting than solid fuel combustion. Hence, there is a well felt need of a study to determine potential demand via higher electrification.
- The study took a conservative assessment of demand for Industries sector as it assumed no allocation of domestic natural gas to it, and linked the demand with availability of LNG. There is uncertainty around the growth of industries that use natural gas in their processes (petrochemicals, DRI, and the like). It would help to study the potential in the above and actively work to dovetail the same with natural gas policy.
- Lastly, there is a pressing need of a sophisticated technical enquiry into the domestic natural gas potential in the Indian sedimentary basins. Since the entry of private sector into E&P in 1998, large tracts of Indian basins have been explored and a National Data Repository (NDR) has also been erected with data available in public domain. However, even now large uncertainty looms around what might be the domestic oil and natural gas true potential. A deep technical study that looks at the seismic and well data, as well as the discoveries made under evaluation may help at least to generate credible natural gas production scenarios.

8.4   TO SUM UP

It is not easy to 'conclude' a discussion on prospects for natural gas in India especially in light of multiple viewpoints on this complex subject. There are any number of industry watchers who have a strong belief that India would be no different than other major energy consuming countries, and natural gas will achieve a significant share. In the last century we saw that it was the legacy of coal that was gradually overtaken by oil, and then natural gas took over. Now, the world is witnessing a renewables' revolution. This has led many commentators to state that natural gas is the bridge fuel to renewables. Another major fossil fuel consumer, China, which is slower than the developed countries on the path of transformation of its energy mix, also seems to be following the above roadmap. There is another set of commentators who argue that in India, we may jump forward to renewables without a major role for natural gas. For the latter to be a bridge fuel, it must first establish itself and then pave way for renewables. In the countries where gas is offered as a bridge fuel, it has already displaced coal and is now the natural candidate for displacement in favour of renewables. For India, it is believed that the technological breakthrough in battery storage, EV, energy efficiency and then, hydrogen, fuel cell may directly find a large market and become a natural partner of renewables. Therefore, natural gas continues to baffle us all.

Has the smoke over natural gas reduced over the last few decades? Much to the credit of Indian policymakers for having made bold policy announcements in the last two decades, the book argues that the answer to the above question is in the affirmative. Multiple steps like the setting up of the PNGRB and announcement of a slew of policy measures in the areas such as gas utilisation, pipelines, pricing and aggressive rounds of offer of CGD networks have facilitated investment immensely. The recent measures to align price of gas coming from different streams is directly responsible for the excitement being witnessed around LNG terminals. The decision on revival of shut urea plants and grant of VGF to trunk pipelines connecting the latter is a strong policy statement too. The repeated commitments by the country's top leadership towards raising the share of natural gas in the country's energy mix has made the investors confident. It is clear from the above that if the future of this fuel appears to be hazy at present, it is not due to want of political committment. But for natural gas to more than double its share by 2030, next-gen reforms via the proposed measures herein are undeniably needed.

It has been indicated in the earlier discussions that 'supply side' matters more. The world might end up with a LNG glut in a couple of years, thanks to large discoveries, and push-back from heightened concerns around its fossil fuel character. This is what the Indian LNG terminal operators and consumers might like. The price competitiveness is already established in several sectors. India is an expanding market and it will be a while before EVs and battery storage start displacing fossil fuels. For the next decade or more, fossil fuels will continue to hold sway in India. There is a strong case for natural gas to be a bridge fuel between coal and clean energy sources. If the 'golden age' for natural gas is not now, then it may never be as the golden hue of sun may very well eclipse it.

BOX 8.1   NATURAL GAS IN INDIA AFTER COP 26

COP 26 stands out as India has joined major economies such as USA, China, Russia, UK and most of the European countries to commit to a net-zero emission target in 2070. This is a momentous announcement as now India will soon conceive a roadmap/transition agenda and present it at appropriate fora in future. Having taken a seat at the high table of those committed to clean energy, it will not be the same for fossil fuels utilisation in India. The National Electricity Policy under discussion for its periodic update is already mulling a 'no new coal thermal plant' possibility for India. Hence, COP 26 has definitely changed the energy discourse in India too. Interestingly, while natural gas is also a fossil fuel, but it has escaped a closer scrutiny at the COP. But, there is already a whisper campaign against it, and the day is not far when it might suffer the same fate as coal suffered at Glasgow. The instant book is about natural gas in India, and while the book recognises relative merits in an enhanced share of natural gas in India's energy mix, but the factored in discussion was concluded in the pre-COP 26 period. The boxes at the end of the chapters have tried to weave in the climate-related announcements of India at Glasgow. In this concluding box, an attempt is being made to summarise an overall impact of the latter as far as the fate of natural gas in India in the 2030 timeframe is concerned.

Globally natural gas grew as a fuel option not so much for being a clean fuel. In many oil fields, natural gas production took place as an 'associated' fuel and had to be put to good use rather than flare-up. Initially, a major driver was its use in replacing oil in power generation, sparing oil for transport end-use (this led to oil indexation in determining the price of natural gas). In India, however, it has received impetus, particularly in the congested urban areas, for being a low emitter of polluting exhausts in cooking and transport sub-sectors. The two-decades old story of court mandated conversion of the Delhi's public transport fleet to CNG to rid the city of poor air quality arising out of fuel emissions has already been mentioned in this book. Therefore, with natural gas having been acknowledged as an answer to challenges of poor air quality, India's bold commitments of climate action at Glasgow are not expected to make a dramatic difference to its story. What needs to be seen is might this fuel receive a new impetus to help meet the intermediate 2030 goals. Also, might any steps towards the 2070 net-zero agenda see affirmative actions in favour of natural gas in the immediate.

In the first four chapters of this book, a strong case for natural gas has emerged. However, the picture changes over in the subsequent chapters. We first discuss the positive story. It has been acknowledged that post-COP 26 India's energy challenges have expanded—not only meeting the energy needs of the country in an affordable and secure manner, but also sustainably. Natural gas meets the sustainability criterion, particularly when compared with coal, as being the dominant fuel in India. It was further argued that it helps promote diversity in the energy mix and economic progress. The discussion around diversity also found that energy security is linked with diversity. Therefore, in the post-COP 26 scenarios, natural gas appears as a strong candidate for an effective promotion in the country's energy mix. To what extent can it be inducted within the timeframe of the instant study of 2030 is a matter of detail. It was also noted that there is a strong role for public sector enterprises, including that of national energy policies in India. As yet, the latter has not spelt out a roadmap towards net-zero emission attainment, and even the 14-year-old Integrated Energy Policy of the country pre-dates the recent national commitment towards a renewed energy transition. India may now draw out the latter, and this may clarify the contribution of natural gas. Therefore, while the first four chapters make a case for the latter, when evaluated against the recent developments, the actual realisation of the potential is largely left to the government's implementation worthy stance.

The following three chapters of the book are not sanguine about natural gas. They dwell on challenges such as lack of price competitiveness and supply concerns too. Natural gas is found competitive only against liquid fuels that eminently makes a case for this fuel in meeting cooking/transport end-uses. In power generation, a weak case exists (renewables are more competitive), while a moderate case was made out in Industries. Indian sedimentary basins have so far not yielded large increments to gas supply, and imported supplies are now being regarded as a serious option. The domestic pricing policies have split the gas market wide open, and domestically produced gas price being at a discount, there is a fractured gas demand denying competitiveness to imported LNG in several demand sectors. In the energy transition agenda, the twin factors of price and supply could still be overcome if there was a premium for clean energy use. India has so far not adopted carbon pricing while it does have a high tax on petroleum products and coal. But the latter are to some extent neutralised by a maze of subsidies, through state budgets, cross subsidy and other such variants. A strong chorus from developing countries for capital transfers to offset losses in the clean energy transition is yet to bear any credible outcomes. Thus, it is quite likely that the national clean energy strategy might include a net positive carbon tax (or carbon price) on coal and oil, that helps make natural gas become competitive, which would logically catalyse more supplies, even as LNG from overseas. A challenge is brought up in the last but one (seventh) chapter. It brings forth natural gas bottom-up demand scenarios to the table and marries them with likely innovations in process technologies. The chances of the latter offering cost-effective clean energy solutions (non-natural gas ones) appear to be high. Fast paced advancements in EV technology, coal gasification and hydrogen-based energy solutions may trip natural gas in the immediate, even before it can play the role of a 'bridge fuel'. In a sum total perspective, even under the energy transition scenario, natural gas appears to be the fuel of choice limited to city gas distribution, and alongside a small role carved out in other demand sector.

References

Abhyankar, N., 2012. Political economy of natural gas market in India. *Stanford Energy J.* URL https://sej.stanford.edu/political-economy-natural-gas-market-india (accessed 2.26.20).

Alam, M.S., Paramati, S.R., Shahbaz, M., Bhattacharya, M., 2017. Natural gas, trade and sustainable growth: Empirical evidence from the top gas consumers of the developing world. *Appl. Econ.* 49, 635–649. https://doi.org/10.1080/00036846.2016.1203064.

Atalla, T., Blazquez, J., Hunt, L.C., Manzano, B., 2017. Prices versus policy: An analysis of the drivers of the primary fossil fuel mix. *Energy Policy* 106, 536–546. https://doi.org/10.1016/j.enpol.2017.03.060.

Aydin, M., 2018. Natural gas consumption and economic growth nexus for top 10 natural gas–consuming countries: A granger causality analysis in the frequency domain. *Energy* 165, 179–186. https://doi.org/10.1016/j.energy.2018.09.149.

Babajide, N., 2018. *Indian Energy Security Status: What Are the Economic and Environmental Implications.* IAEE Energy Forum; Energy Forum 2018. https://www.iaee.org/en/publications/newsletterdl.aspx?id=469.

Batra, R., 2009. *India's Move to Cleaner Fuels.*

Bayramov, A., Marusyk, Y., 2019. Ukraine's unfinished natural gas and electricity reforms: One step forward, two steps back. *Eurasian Geogr. Econ.* 60, 73–96. https://doi.org/10.1080/15387216.2019.1593210.

Bery, S., Ghosh, A., Mathur, R., Basu, S., Ganesan, K., 2017. *Energizing India: Towards a Resilient and Equitable Energy System.* New Delhi: Sage Publishing.

Bhattacharya, A., Bhattacharya, T., 2014. *ASEAN-India Gas Cooperation: Redefining India's "Look East" Policy with Myanmar (No. ERIA-DP-2014-1).*

Biały, R., Janusz, P., Łaciak, M., Olkuski, T., Ruszel, M., Szurlej, A., 2019. The role of LNG supplies in balancing natural gas demand in EU countries. *E3S Web Conf.* 108, 02014. https://doi.org/10.1051/E3SCONF/201910802014.

Bildirici, M.E., Bakirtas, T., 2014. The relationship among oil, natural gas and coal consumption and economic growth in BRICTS (Brazil, Russian, India, China, Turkey and South Africa) countries. *Energy* 65, 134–144. https://doi.org/10.1016/j.energy.2013.12.006.

Bloom, A., Townsend, A., Palchak, D., Novacheck, J., King, J., Barrows, C., Ibanez, E., O'Connell, M., Jordan, G., Roberts, B., Draxl, C., Gruchalla, K., 2016. *Eastern Renewable Generation Integration Study.* Denver, CO: National Renewable Energy Laboratory.

Bogoviz, A. V., Ragulina, Y. V., Lobova, S. V., Alekseev, A.N., 2019. A quantitative analysis of energy security performance by Brazil, Russia, India, China, and South Africa in 1990–2015. *Int. J. Energy Econ. Policy* 9, 244–250. https://doi.org/10.32479/ijeep.7585.

BP, 2019a. *Full Report – BP Statistical Review of World Energy 2019.* BP, London, UK. https://www.bp.com/content/dam/bp/business-sites/en/global/corporate/pdfs/-energy-economics/statistical-review/bp-stats-review-2019-full-report.pdf.

BP, 2019b. *Statistical Review of World Energy – Under-Pinning Data, 1965–2018.* London, UK. https://www.bp.com/en/global/corporate/energy-economics/statistical-review-of-world-energy.html.

BP Statistics, 2020. *Statistical Review of World Energy 2020.* London, UK. https://www.bp.com/content/dam/bp/business-sites/en/global/corporate/pdfs/energy-economics/statistical-review/bp-stats-review-2020-full-report.pdf.

BP Statistics, 2021. *Statistical Review of World Energy 2020*. London, UK. https://www. bp.com/en/global/corporate/energy-economics/statistical-review-of-world-energy. html.

Business Standard, 2015. *Govt Introduces Uniform Gas Price For Urea Plants*.

Business Standard, 2018. *Ind-Ra: Pooled Natural Gas Prices for Urea Manufacturers to Continue to Increase in Short to Medium Term*.

Business Today, 2020. *Reliance-BP to Auction more Natural Gas from KG-D6 Block in February*. PTI.

CEA, 2015. *19th Electric Power Survey Report*. New Delhi: Central Electricity Authority of India.

CEA, 2018a. *National Electricity Plan*. New Delhi: Central Electricity Authority, Ministry of Power, Government of India.

CEA, 2018b. *Committee on Optimal Energy Mix in Power Generation on Medium and Long Term Basis*. New Delhi: Central Electricity Authority, Ministry of Power, Government of India.

Chalvatzis, K.J., Ioannidis, A., 2017. Energy supply security in the EU: Benchmarking diversity and dependence of primary energy. *Appl. Energy* 207, 465–476. https://doi.org/10.1016/j.apenergy.2017.07.010.

Chander, S., 2019. *Rationalization of Prices for Balanced Fertilization*. Indian Journal of Fertilisers 15 (5) Published by Fertiliser Association of India. New Delhi. Pp 486-7 https://www.faidelhi.org/Frank%20notes/IJF-May-19.pdf.

Chow, E., Elkind, J., 2005. Hurricane Katrina and US energy security. *Survival*. 47, 145–160. https://doi.org/10.1080/00396330500433449.

Chyong, C.K., 2019. European natural gas markets: Taking stock and looking forward. *Rev. Ind. Organ*. 55, 89–109. https://doi.org/10.1007/s11151-019-09697-3.

CII-NITI Aayog, 2018. *CII* [Online Document]. New Delhi: Confederation of Indian Industry.

Cohen, G., Joutz, F., Loungani, P., 2011. *Measuring Energy Security: Trends in the Diversification of Oil and Natural Gas Supplies*. https://doi.org/10.1016/j.enpol.2011. 06.034.

Cooke, H., Keppo, I., Wolf, S., 2013. Diversity in theory and practice: A review with application to the evolution of renewable energy generation in the UK. *Energy Policy* 61, 88–95. https://doi.org/10.1016/j.enpol.2013.06.089.

Corbeau, A.-S., Hasan, S., Dsouza, S., 2018. *The Challenges Facing India on its Road to a Gas-Based Economy*, pp. 1–52. https://doi.org/10.30573/KS--2018-DP41.

CPCB, 2018. *Directions under Environment Protection Act*. New Delhi: Central Pollution Control Board, Ministry of Environment, Forest & Climate Change, Government of India.

CRISIL, 2019. *City Gas Distribution and Fertiliser Sector to Drive Gas Demand Government Push for Cleaner Fuel to Fuel the Demand*. Mumbai: CRISIL Infrastructure Advisory.

CSE, 2019. *Lack of Gas, High Cost "Stranded" More than Half of India's Gas-Based Power Plants*. DownToEarth. New Delhi: Centre for Science and Environment.

CSTEP, 2018. *Benefit Cost Analysis of Emission Standards for Coal-based Thermal Power Plants in India*. Bengaluru: Center for Study of Science, Technology, Environment & Policy.

DECC, 2011. *Planning Our Electric Future: A White Paper for Secure, Affordable and Low-Carbon Electricity*. London: Department of Energy & Climate Change of the UK.

Delloite, 2019. *Rapid Feasibility Study related to the Project Zero Budget Natural Farming in Andhra Pradesh*.

DOE, 2013. *Growing Demand for Natural Gas Emergence of the Global LNG Market.* Washington DC: US Department of Energy.

Dong, K., Dong, X., Sun, R., 2019. How did the price and income elasticities of natural gas demand in China evolve from 1999 to 2015? The role of natural gas price reform. *Pet. Sci.* 16, 685–700. https://doi.org/10.1007/s12182-019-0320-z.

DTI, 2006. *UK Energy Sector Indicators* [Online Document]. DECC. URL https://webarchive.nationalarchives.gov.uk/20130103060014/. http:/www.decc.gov.uk/assets/decc/statistics/publications/indicators/1_20100519134637_e_@@_ukesi 2006ks.pdf (accessed 4.18.20). London: Department of Trade & Industry of the UK.

Economic Times, 2015. Fertiliser companies gain as Cabinet approves gas pooling. *The Economic Times.*

Economic Times, 2018. Natural gas, ATF in GST this week? *The Economic Times.*

Economic Times, 2019. Coal India auction: Coal India to increase auction offering by 14% in FY20. *The Economic Times.*

ERG, 2017. *Comparative Analysis of Fuels for Cooking: Life Cycle Environmental Impacts and Economic and Social Considerations.*

ET, 2018a. *CNG Stations: 10,000 CNG Stations to Be Set up in 10 years: Pradhan.*

ET, 2018b. 9th CGD bidding may fetch Rs 70,000 crore investments: Report. *The Economic Times.*

ET, 2020. Govt to stop substitutable coal import; can go for auction of 100 fully explored new blocks: Joshi, Energy News, ET EnergyWorld. *The Economic Times.*

European Commission, 2018. *A Clean Planet for All a European Strategic Long-Term Vision for a Prosperous, Modern, Competitive and Climate Neutral Economy.*

FAI, 2018. New Delhi: The Fertiliser Association of India.

Gillessen, B., Heinrichs, H., Hake, J.F., Allelein, H.J., 2019. Energy security in context of transforming energy systems: A case study for natural gas transport in Germany. In: *Energy Procedia.* Elsevier Ltd, pp. 3339–3345. https://doi.org/10.1016/j.egypro.2019.01.966.

GOI, 2012a. *Report of the Working Group on Power for Twelfth Plan (2012–17).* New Delhi: Ministry of Power, Government of India.

GOI, 2012b. *Report of the Working Group on Fertilizer Industry for the Twelfth Plan.* New Delhi: Department of Fertilizers, Government of India.

GOI, 2017a. *India Fertilizer Scenario.* New Delhi: Department of Fertilisers, Government of India.

GOI, 2017d. *Indian Fertiliser Scenario 2017.* New Delhi: Department of Fertilisers, Government of India.

GOI, 2018a. Coal reserves [Online Document]. *Gov. India, Minist. Coal.* URL https://coal.nic.in/content/coal-reserves (accessed 6.11.20).

GOI, 2018b. *Cooking IESS One Pager.* New Delhi: National Institution for Transforming India, Government of India.

GOI, 2018c. *Report of the Standing Committee on Petroleum and Natural Gas.* New Delhi: Lok Sabha, Parliament of India.

GOI, 2018d. *Fertilizer Policy.* Government of India, Department of Fertilizers, Ministry of Chemicals and Fertilizers [Online Document]. URL http://fert.nic.in/page/fertilizer-policy (accessed 2.28.20).

GOI, 2019a. *Energy Statistics 2019.* New Delhi: Ministry of Statistics & Programme Implementation, Government of India.

GOI, 2019b. *Growth of Electricity Sector in India 1947–2019.* New Delhi: Central Electricity Authority, Ministry of Power, Government of India.

GOI, 2020. Power sector at a glance [Online Document]. *Gov. India, Minist. Power.* URL https://powermin.nic.in/en/content/power-sector-glance-all-india (accessed 6.22.20).

GOI, 2021. *Annual Report 2019–20*. Government of India, Department of Fertilizers, Ministry of Chemicals and Fertilizers [Online Document]. https://fert.nic.in/sites/default/files/2020-09/Annual-Report-2019-20.pdf.

GOI, n.d. *Physical Progress* [Online Document]. Minist. New Renew. Energy. URL https://mnre.gov.in/the-ministry/physical-progress (accessed 6.25.20).

GPCA, 2017. *Fertiliser Report India*.

Green, R., 1991. Reshaping the CEGB. Electricity privatization in the UK. *Util. Policy* 1, 245–254. https://doi.org/10.1016/0957-1787(91)90057-C.

Grubb, M., Butler, L., Twomey, P., 2006. Diversity and security in UK electricity generation: The influence of low-carbon objectives. *Energy Policy* 34, 4050–4062. https://doi.org/10.1016/j.enpol.2005.09.004.

Gulati, A., Banerjee, P., 2019. *Rejuvenating Indian Fertilizer Sector*. https://www.researchgate.net/publication/339616968_Rejuvenating_Indian_Fertilizer_Sector.

Hauser, P., Heidari, S., Weber, C., Möst, D., 2019. Does increasing natural gas demand in the power sector pose a threat of congestion to the German gas grid? A model-coupling approach. *Energies* 12. https://doi.org/10.3390/en12112159.

Heidari, H., Katircioglu, S.T., Saeidpour, L., 2013. Natural gas consumption and economic growth: Are we ready to natural gas price liberalization in Iran? *Energy Policy* 63, 638–645. https://doi.org/10.1016/j.enpol.2013.09.001.

Högselius, P., Kaijser, A., Åberg, A., 2010. *Natural Gas in Cold War Europe: The Making of a Critical Transnational Infrastructure*. London: Palgrave Macmillan.

HT, 2019. Shut industries not using PNG in Delhi-NCR despite availability, orders CPCB – Delhi news. *Hindustan Times*.

Huang, Y.W., Kittner, N., Kammen, D.M., 2019. ASEAN grid flexibility: Preparedness for grid integration of renewable energy. *Energy Policy* 128, 711–726. https://doi.org/10.1016/j.enpol.2019.01.025.

IEA, 1998. *World Energy Outlook 1998*. Paris: International Energy Agency.

IEA, 2015. *WEO-2015 Special Report: India Energy Outlook – Analysis*. IEA. [Online Document].

IEA, 2017a. *World Energy Balances 2017, World Energy Balances*. OECD. https://doi.org/10.1787/world_energy_bal-2017-en.

IEA, 2017b. *World Energy Balances 2017, World Energy Balances*. OECD. https://doi.org/10.1787/world_energy_bal-2017-en.

IEA, 2018a. *World Energy Investment 2018*. Paris: International Energy Agency.

IEA, 2018b. *World Energy Outlook 2018 : Gold Standard of Long-Term Energy Analysis*. Paris: International Energy Agency.

IEA, 2019. *What Is Energy Security?* [Online Document]. URL https://www.iea.org/topics/energysecurity/whatisenergysecurity/ (accessed 6.10.19).

IEA, 2021. https://www.iea.org/reports/india-energy-outlook-2021 [Online Document].

IGU, 2019. *World LNG Report*. Barcelona: International Gas Union.

IRENA, 2018. *Renewable Energy in National Climate Action*. Abu Dhabi: International Renewable Energy Agency.

Jain, A.K., 2011. *Natural Gas in India: Liberalisation and Policy*. Oxford: Oxford University Press.

Jain, A.K., 2017. *Our Rising Energy Imports-What All do They Mean? The Falling Production of Gas, and Static Production of Oil*. New Delhi: National Institution for Transforming India, Government of India.

Jain, A.K., 2018. A fine balance: Lessons from India's experience with petroleum subsidy reforms. *Energy Policy* 119, 242–249. https://doi.org/10.1016/j.enpol.2018.04.050.

Jansen, J.C., Van Arkel, W.G., Boots, M.G., 2004. *Designing Indicators of Long-Term Energy Supply Security*. https://www.researchgate.net/publication/265629320_

Designing_Indicators_of_Long-term_Energy_Supply_Security?enrichId=rgreq-377daadbc655354cffe45eef56b465fa-XXX&enrichSource=Y292ZXJQYWdlOzI2NTYyOTMyMDtBUzo0Mzk4ND3tsdNDQ1MDI1NDQzzODlAMTQ4MTg3ODUwwOTM0MQ%3D%3D&el=1_x_2&_esc=publicationCoverPdf.

Jatinder Cheema, A.R. and N.V., Cyril Amarch, Mangaldas, 2019. *City Gas Distribution: Creating Demand for India's Energy Future – The Balancing Act – Energy and Natural Resources – India.* https://www.mondaq.com/india/oil-gas-electricity/791280/city-gas-distribution-creating-demand-for-india39s-energy-future-the--balancing-act Published on 22 March, 2019.

Jewell, J., Cherp, A., Vinichenko, V., Bauer, N., Kober, T.O.M., McCollum, D., Van Vuuren, D.P., Van Der Zwaan, B.O.B., 2013. Energy security of China, India, the E.U. and the U.S. and long-term scenarios: Results from six IAMs. *Clim. Chang. Econ.* 4. https://doi.org/10.1142/S2010007813400113.

Kalam, A., 2005. *Dr. A.P.J. Abdul Kalam: Former President of India* [Online Document]. URL http://abdulkalam.nic.in/sp161005-2.html (accessed 4.18.20).

Kar, S.K., Gupta, A., 2017. *Natural Gas Markets in India: Opportunities and Challenges, Natural Gas Markets in India: Opportunities and Challenges.* Singapore: Springer. https://doi.org/10.1007/978-981-10-3118-2.

Koyama, K., 2012. Developing an energy security index. In: *Study on the Development of an Energy Security Index and an Assessment of Energy Security for East Asian Countries.* ERIA Research Project Report 2011-13, Jakarta; ERIA, 2012 pp. 7–47. http://www.eria.org/Chapter%202.%20Developing%20and%20Energy%20Security%20Index.

Kruyt, B., van Vuuren, D.P., de Vries, H.J.M., Groenenberg, H., 2009a. Indicators for energy security. *Energy Policy* 37, 2166–2181. https://doi.org/10.1016/j.enpol.2009.02.006.

Kucharski, J.B., Unesaki, H., 2018. An institutional analysis of the Japanese energy transition. *Environ. Innov. Soc. Transit.* 29, 126–143. https://doi.org/10.1016/j.eist.2018.07.004.

Larson, A., 2019. *Natural Gas and Renewable Energy to Continue Leading the Market.* https://www.powermag.com/natural-gas-and-renewable-energy-to-continue-leading-the-market/.

Lauber, V., Mez, L., 2004. Three decades of renewable electricity policies in Germany. *Energy Environ.* 15, 599–623.

Lebelhuber, C., Steinmüller, H., 2019. How and to which extent can the gas sector contribute to a climate-neutral European energy system? A qualitative approach. *Energy. Sustain. Soc.* 9, 23. https://doi.org/10.1186/s13705-019-0207-2.

LiveMint, 2018. *Bidding for City Gas Distribution Contracts Sees Strong Response.*

Lo, L., 2011. Diversity, security, and adaptability in energy systems: A comparative analysis of four countries in Asia, In: *Proceedings of the World Renewable Energy Congress – Sweden, 8–13 May, 2011,* Linköping, Sweden: Linköping University Electronic Press, pp. 2401–2408. https://doi.org/10.3384/ecp110572401.

Lok Sabha, 2017. *Sixteenth Lok Sabha Ministry of Chemicals and Fertilizers (Department Of Fertilizers) Demands for Grants (2017–18).* New Delhi: Lok Sabha, Parliament of India.

Lok Sabha, 2018. *Twenty Third Report of Standing Committee on Petroleum & Natural Gas (2017–18).* New Delhi: Lok Sabha, Parliament of India.

Lok Sabha, 2019. *Forty Second Report: Stressed/Non-Performing Assets in Gas based Power Plants.* New Delhi: Lok Sabha, Parliament of India.

MNRE, 2019. *No Title* [Online Document]. New Delhi: Ministry of New & Renewable Energy, Government of India.

Mondal, M.A.H., Ringler, C., Al-Riffai, P., Eldidi, H., Breisinger, C., Wiebelt, M., 2019. Long-term optimization of Egypt's power sector: Policy implications. *Energy* 166, 1063–1073. https://doi.org/10.1016/j.energy.2018.10.158.

MoPNG, 2006. *Policy for Development of Natural Gas Pipelines and City or Local Natural Gas Distribution Networks*. New Delhi: Ministry of Petroleum & Natural Gas, Government of India.

MoPNG, 2010. *Hydrocarbon Vision 2025*. New Delhi: Ministry of Petroleum & Natural Gas, Government of India.

MoPNG, 2011. *Report of the Working Group on Petroleum & Natural Gas Sector for the XII Plan*. New Delhi: Ministry of Petroleum & Natural Gas, Government of India.

MoPNG, 2016. *Text of speech of Minister of State (I/C) for Petroleum and Natural Gas* [Online Document]. URL https://pib.gov.in/newsite/PrintRelease.aspx?relid=154888 (accessed 2.28.20).

MoPNG, 2017. *Petroleum and Natural Gas Statistics*. New Delhi: Ministry of Petroleum & Natural Gas, Government of India.

MoPNG, 2018a. Shri Dharmendra Pradhan invites investors to participate and make the most of the India growth story [Online Document]. URL http://pib.nic.in/newsite/PrintRelease.aspx?relid=184712 (accessed 6.10.19).

MoPNG, 2018b. *Indian Petroleum & Natural Gas Statistics 2017–18*. New Delhi: Ministry of Petroleum & Natural Gas, Government of India.

MoPNG, 2019. *Gazette of India*. New Delhi: Ministry of Petroleum & Natural Gas, Government of India.

MoPNG, 2021. *Annual Report 2020–21*. Government of India, Ministry of Petroleum & Natural Gas [Online Document]. https://mopng.gov.in/files/TableManagements/MoPNG-Annual-Report-combined.pdf.

MOSPI, 2018. *Energy Statistics 2018 (Twenty Fifth Issue)*. New Delhi: Ministry of Statistics & Programme Implementation, Government of India.

MOSPI, 2021. *Energy Statistics 2021 (Twenty Eighth Issue)*. New Delhi: Ministry of Statistics & Programme Implementation, Government of India.

Mukherjee, S., 2019. *Exploring Low-Carbon Energy Security Path for India: Role of Asia-Pacific Energy Cooperation*.

New Indian Express, 2017. *Supply of Green Energy at Affordable Cost Is a Challenge: Greenstone-The New Indian Express*. 20 Feb 2017.

NITI Aayog, 2016. *Energising India*. New Delhi: National Institution for Transforming India, Government of India.

NITI Aayog, 2018. *Draft National Energy Policy*. New Delhi: National Institution for Transforming India, Government of India.

Paliwal, P., 2017. Natural gas pricing. In: *Natural Gas Markets in India: Opportunities and Challenges*. Singapore: Springer, pp. 75–93. https://doi.org/10.1007/978-981-10-3118-2_5.

Parikh, J., Biswas, C.R.D., Singh, C., Singh, V., 2009. Natural gas requirement by fertilizer sector in India. *Energy* 34, 954–961. https://doi.org/10.1016/j.energy.2009.02.013.

Paul, S., Bhattacharya, R.N., 2004. Causality between energy consumption and economic growth in India: A note on conflicting results. *Energy Econ.* 26, 977–983. https://doi.org/10.1016/j.eneco.2004.07.002.

Petronet, 2020. *Corporate Profile*. Petronet LNG Limited.

PIB, 2001. *87 CNG Stations in Delhi Made Operational – Supply Satisfactory: Shri Ram Naik* [Online Document]. Press Inf. Bur. URL http://pibarchive.nic.in/archive/releases98/lyr2001/roct2001/04102001/r0410200116.html (accessed 6.18.20).

PIB, 2019a. *Government Launches National Clean Air Programme (NCAP)*. New Delhi: Ministry of Environment, Forest & Climate Change, Government of India.

PIB, 2019b. *Contract for Coal Gasification Plant for Urea Project at the Erstwhile Talcher Unit of FCIL in Angul in the State of Odisha Was Awarded Today*. New Delhi: Ministry of Chemicals and Fertilizers, Government of India.

Planning Commission, 2006. *Integrated Energy Policy Report of the Expert Committee.* New Delhi: Planning Commission, Government of India.

PNGRB, 2013. *PNGRB Vision 2030.* New Delhi: Petroleum & Natural Gas Regulatory Board, Government of India.

PNGRB, 2018. *Details of the Successful Bidders under 9th CGD Bidding Round* [Online Document]. URL https://www.pngrb.gov.in/pdf/cgd/bid9/PN14092018.pdf (accessed 2.28.20).

PNGRB, 2019. *Petroleum and Natural Gas Regulatory Board Press Release.* New Delhi: Petroleum & Natural Gas Regulatory Board, Government of India.

PPAC, 2018b. *Ready Reckoner Petroleum Planning & Analysis Cell.* New Delhi: Petroleum Planning & Analysis Cell, Ministry of Petroleum & Natural Gas, Government of India.

PPAC, 2019. *Ready Reckoner: Oil Industry Information at a Glance.* New Delhi: Petroleum Planning & Analysis Cell, Ministry of Petroleum & Natural Gas, Government of India.

PPAC, 2020. *Monthly Report on Natural Gas Production, Availability and Consumption.* New Delhi: Petroleum Planning & Policy Analysis Cell, Ministry of Petroleum & Natural Gas, Government of India.

PPAC, n.d. *Consumption: Petroleum Planning & Analysis Cell* [Online Document]. URL https://www.ppac.gov.in/content/147_1_ConsumptionPetroleum.aspx (accessed 6.21.20).

PPAC, n.d. *Import: Petroleum Planning & Analysis Cell* [Online Document]. URL https://www.ppac.gov.in/content/.aspx 153_1_ImportNAturalgas (accessed 6.22.20b).

Pradhan, D., 2019. Journey towards a gas-based economy: Decarbonizing India for a sustainable future, In: Shreerupa Mitra (ed.), *Energizing India: Fueling a Billion Lives.* New Delhi: Rupa Publications, p. 280.

PRAYAS, n.d. *Simple-Check: Simple Calculators for Electricity Sector Analysis – Prayas (Energy Group)* [Online Document]. URL https://www.prayaspune.org/peg/resources/simple-check-simple-calculators-for-electricity-sector-analysis.html (accessed 6.25.20).

Pye, S., Sabio, N., Strachan, N., 2015. An integrated systematic analysis of uncertainties in UK energy transition pathways. *Energy Policy* 87, 673–684. https://doi.org/10.1016/j.enpol.2014.12.031.

Ranjan, A., Hughes, L., 2014a. Energy security and the diversity of energy flows in an energy system. *Energy* 73, 137–144. https://doi.org/10.1016/J.ENERGY.2014.05.108

RBI, 2019. Renewable energy and electricity price dynamics in India [Online Document]. *RBI Bull.* URL https://m.rbi.org.in/Scripts/BS_ViewBulletin.aspx?Id=18232 (accessed 6.22.20).

Reddy, B.S., 2018. Economic dynamics and technology diffusion in Indian power sector. *Energy Policy* 120, 425–435. https://doi.org/10.1016/j.enpol.2018.05.044.

Reuters, 2018. *India Expects to Double Gas Production by 2022: Officials.* Reuters.

Rioux, B., Galkin, P., Murphy, F., Feijoo, F., Pierru, A., Malov, A., Li, Y., Wu, K., 2019. The economic impact of price controls on China's natural gas supply chain. *Energy Econ.* 80, 394–410. https://doi.org/10.1016/j.eneco.2018.12.026.

Rogers, H. V, 2017. *Asian LNG Demand: Key Drivers and Outlook OIES Paper.* Oxford: Oxford Institute for Energy Studies.

Rogers, H. V., 2016. *Asian LNG Demand: Key Drivers and Outlook.* Oxford: Oxford Institute for Energy Studies.

Rogers, H., 2012. *The Pricing of Internationally Traded Gas the Interaction of LNG and Pipeline Gas Pricing: Does Greater Connectivity equal Globalization?* Oxford: Oxford Institute for Energy Studies.

RRPCL, n.d. *RRPCL – Ratnagiri Refinery and Petrochemicals Limited* [Online Document]. URL https://www.rrpcl.com/ (accessed 2.28.20).

Rybak, A., 2019. Analysis of the Strategy for the Energy Policy of Poland until 2030 implementation effects in the aspect of environmental protection taking into account the energy security of Poland. *IOP Conf. Ser. Earth Environ. Sci.* 261, 12044. https://doi.org/10.1088/1755-1315/261/1/012044.

Sen, A., 2015. *Gas Pricing Reform in India: Implications for the Indian gas landscape: Gas Pricing Reform in India II.* Oxford: Oxford Institute for Energy Studies.

Sen, A., 2017. *India's Gas Market Post-COP21.* Oxford: Oxford Institute for Energy Studies.

Sinaga, O., Saudi, M.H.M., Roespinoedji, D., Razimi, M.S.A., 2019. The dynamic relationship between natural gas and economic growth: Evidence from Indonesia. *Int. J. Energy Econ. Policy* 9, 388–394. https://doi.org/10.32479/ijeep.7748.

Singh, R.K., Chakraborty, D., 2017. *India Plans to Use U.S. LNG to Revive Fertilizer Plants - Bloomberg. Bloomberg.*

Sinha, S. 2018. Modi calls for slashing oil, gas imports by 10% in next 7 years. *Bus. Line.*

Skea, J., Chaudry, M., Wang, X., 2012a. The role of gas infrastructure in promoting UK energy security. *Energy Policy* 43, 202–213. https://doi.org/10.1016/j.enpol.2011.12.057.

Skea, J., Chaudry, M., Wang, X., Skea, J., Chaudry, M., Wang, X., 2012b. Energy policy: The international journal of the political, economic, planning, environmental and social aspects of energy, *Energy Policy.*

Speight, J.G., 2013. *Shale Gas Production Processes, Shale Gas Production Processes.* Elsevier Inc. https://doi.org/10.1016/C2012-0-00596-0.

Srivastava, L., 2009. *India's Integrated Energy Policy.* TERI [Online Document]. URL https://www.teriin.org/opinion/indias-integrated-energy-policy (accessed 4.25.20).

Stern, J., 2012. *The Pricing of Internationally Traded Gas the Pricing of Gas in International Trade – An Historical Survey.* London: Oxford University Press.

Stern, J., 2017. Challenges to the future of gas: Unburnable or unaffordable? https://doi.org/10.26889/9781784670993.

Steven, D., Jones, B.D., O'Brien, E., 2013. *The New Politics of Strategic Resources: Energy and Food Security Challenges in the 21st Century.* Washington DC: Brookings Institution.

Stirling, A., 1994. Diversity and ignorance in electricity supply investment. *Energy Policy* 22, 195–216. https://doi.org/10.1016/0301-4215(94)90159-7.

Stirling, A., 2007. A general framework for analysing diversity in science, technology and society. *J. R. Soc. Interface* 4, 707–19. https://doi.org/10.1098/rsif.2007.0213.

Stirling, A., Waxman, D., 1998. *On the Economics and Analysis of Diversity Electronic Working Papers Series.*

The Hindu, 2019a. Iraq remains top oil supplier to India. *Hindu.*

The Hindu, 2019b. Fifteen of the 20 most polluted cities in the world are in India. *Hindu* [Online Document]. URL https://www.thehindu.com/sci-tech/energy-and-environment/fifteen-of-the-20-most-polluted-cities-in-the-world-are-in-india/article26440603.ece (accessed 2.28.20).

The Indian Express, 2019. How much urea does India really require? | India News, *Indian Exp.*

TOI, 2015. *Govt wants to Replace LPG with PNG in Smart Cities.*

Tongia, R., Seligsohn, D., 2017. Challenges and Recommendations for Meeting the Upcoming 2017 Standards for Air Pollution from Thermal Power Plants in India.

UNCTAD, 2018. Investment and new industrial policies. https://doi.org/10.18356/a1e0466b-en.

UNFCCC, 2018. *India Second Biennial Update Report.* United Nations Framework Convention on Climate Change.

UNFCCC, n.d. *Nationally Determined Contributions (NDCs).* UNFCCC [Online Document]. URL https://unfccc.int/focus/indc_portal/items/8766.php#eq-2 (accessed 6.8.19).

USAID, n.d. *Greening the Grid: Pathways to Integrate 175 Gigawatts of Renewable Energy into India's Electric Grid*, Vol. I: National Study.

Wang, Z., Luo, D., Liu, L., 2018. Natural gas utilization in China: Development trends and prospects. *Energy Rep.* 4, 351–356. https://doi.org/10.1016/j.egyr.2018.05.005.

Wu, T.Y. W., Rai, V., 2017. Quantifying diversity of electricity generation in the U.S. *Electr. J.* 30, 55–66. https://doi.org/10.1016/j.tej.2017.09.001.

Yergin, D., 2006. Ensuring Energy Security. *Foreign Aff.*

Zhang, Q., Li, Z., Wang, G., Li, H., 2016. Study on the impacts of natural gas supply cost on gas flow and infrastructure deployment in China. *Appl. Energy* 162, 1385–1398. https://doi.org/10.1016/j.apenergy.2015.06.058.

Annexure 1
Profile of Experts Who Were Consulted/Responded

1. Academicians 5
2. National/International Energy Institutions 5
3. Oil and Gas Sector (Upstream) 4
4. Power Sector 3
5. Fertilisers Sector 2
6. LNG/CGD Business 11

LEVEL OF RESPONDENTS IN THEIR OWN ORGANISATIONS

1. Heads 5
2. CEOs 7
3. Senior Level 8
4. Middle Level 10

Annexure 2

Questionnaire for Research on Exploring the Role of Natural Gas in India's Energy Future

Name:

Organisation:

(The questionnaire has a general section common for all respondents, and others related to specific domains such as urea and power. Please feel free to skip the section for which you may not have the desired information)

GENERAL

1. On a scale of 1–10 (where 1 is the least and 10 being most likely), please mark the likelihood of share of gas rising to 10% or more by 2030.

   Ans. [ ]

2. Please rank the order (1–4) in which you see the following sectors as drivers of gas demand in the next decade with 1 being the most important driver.

   Ans.

      i. Fertilisers [ ]

     ii. Power [ ]

    iii. CGD [ ]

    iv. Industries [ ]

3. Will price of gas be an obstacle to its growth in comparison to other fuels?

   Ans. YES/NO [ ]

4. Does the large share of coal in India's energy mix enhance energy security?

   Ans. YES/NO [ ]

5. Low Diversity means lesser number of energy sources with large imbalance in their shares. What has been the main reason for India's low diversity? Please rank the following in order of importance (1–4) with 1 being most important.

   Ans.

   i.   Government policy [   ]

   ii. Lack of energy markets [   ]

   iii. Poor resource endowment [   ]

   iv. High prices of competing fuels [   ]

6. Will diversifying India's energy sources enhance energy security?

   Ans.

   i. YES/NO [   ]

   ii. Do not know [   ]

7. What is your outlook on growth in domestic gas production up to 2030? Rank on a scale of 1–10 (1 being highly pessimistic and 10 being highly optimistic).

   Ans. YES/NO [   ]

8. Will the new pricing policy for domestic gas from difficult fields help in promoting vibrant gas market?

   Ans.

   i. YES/NO [   ]

   ii. Not sure [   ]

9. Is there a strong case for gas on environmental grounds?

   Ans. YES/NO [   ]

10. Will the shift to electric vehicles impact demand for CNG?

    Ans.

    i. YES/NO [   ]
    ii. Give reasons _____

11. If India were to migrate to market pricing in energy sector with DBT for subsidies, would gas get impetus?

    Ans.

    i. YES/NO [   ]

    ii. Not sure [   ]

UREA

12. Is the decision to promote domestic urea manufacture instead of imports a policy decision for achieving self-sufficiency or an objective one on multiple merits?

    Ans.

    i. YES/NO [ ]

    ii. Any other reason: _____

13. Will the decision to accept RLNG as feedstock in local manufacture yield cheaper urea in comparison to import?

    Ans.

    i. YES/NO [ ]

    ii. Depends on _____

14. Why is there poor private sector interest in setting up urea manufacturing units (rank 1–4 in order of importance, and 1 being most important)?

    Ans.

    i. Lack of gas [ ]

    ii. Poor financial viability [ ]

    iii. Policy uncertainty [ ]

    iv. Any other _____

15. At what rate might urea (nitrogen) demand continue to rise in future? (Tick one)

    Ans.

    i. Historical rate [ ]

    ii. May moderate [ ]

    iii. Slow down radically [ ]

16. Will gas (and not naphtha) remain the main feedstock for urea manufacture?

    Ans. YES/NO [ ]

POWER

17. What future do you see for gas in power sector? (Tick one)

    Ans.

    i. A major role [ ]

ii. Moderate role [ ]

iii. Negligible role [ ]

18. If your answer above is (iii)—negligible role—then please rank the following possible reasons in order of priority (1–4) with 1 being the most important reason.

Ans.

i. High Price [ ]

ii. Non-availability [ ]

iii. High growth of Renewables [ ]

iv. Large thermal capacity [ ]

19. Will the new thermal sector emission norms mitigate the negativity against coal?

Ans.

i. YES/NO [ ]

ii. Moderately [ ]

20. If domestic gas were to become abundantly available then would gas-based power capacity rise?

Ans. YES/NO [ ]

21. If your answer is YES to previous question, then please tick the possible reasons for same. (Rank 1–4 in order of priority where 1 is the most important reason.)

Ans.

i. It may become price competitive [ ]

ii. To augment supply to meet rising demand [ ]

iii. For it to balance variable RE [ ]

iv. It is environmentally clean [ ]

22. Do you anticipate pricing reforms in power sector by 2030 allowing gas-based power to receive higher price? Rank your expectation on a scale of 1–10. (10 being most likely)

Ans. [ ]

23. With large unutilised capacity/stranded in thermal sector and growing RE, might gas get overlooked and India move to non-gas-based power system by 2030?

Ans.

   i. YES/NO [   ]

  ii. Any other reason _____

CGD

24. Will the large number of contracts signed under IXth (& Xth) CGD bidding round translate into reality on ground in the next one decade? Please rank the likelihood on a score of 1–10 where 10 is highly probable and 1 is highly improbable.

Ans. [   ]

25. If domestic gas at administered price (APM) is not available, given that presently APM gas is going for PNG/CNG, then will the CGD agenda be impacted?

Ans.

   i. YES/NO [   ]

  ii. Give reasons: _____

26. Do you see a role for RLNG in non-PNG/CNG demand sectors within CGD?

   i. YES/NO [   ]

  ii. Please elaborate: _____

27. Will demand for RLNG in the above sectors be dependent on the government policy on polluting fuels/air emissions?

Ans. YES/NO [   ]

28. Is the availability of trunk gas pipelines by 2027 to provide gas to new CGD networks an area of concern?

Ans. YES/NO [   ]

29. Will the large number of household LPG connections especially in urban areas delay adoption of PNG for cooking?

Ans.

   i. YES/NO [   ]

  ii. Any other reason: _____

INDUSTRIES & OTHERS

30. Is adoption of gas in industries merely a function of price?

    Ans. YES/NO ☐

31. If your answer is NO in the previous question, then what are the other possible reasons? Rank 1–3 in order of priority with 3 having the lowest priority.

    Ans.

       i.   Technology ☐

      ii.   Capital investment ☐

     iii. Poor outlook on gas market ☐
     iv. Any other _____

32. Which fuel(s) are most likely to be replaced by gas in industries? Rank 1–3 in order of importance, 3 being least important.

    Ans.

       i.   Coal ☐

      ii.   Liquid fuels ☐
     iii. Others: _____

33. Will natural gas be the preferred fuel in refineries?

    Ans.

       i.   YES/NO ☐
      ii.   If any other option, please specify _____

34. Will industries be the biggest client of RLNG as compared to other sectors?

    Ans.

       i.   YES/NO ☐
      ii.   If NO, then please specify which one _____

35. Is petrochemical likely to be a major driver of gas demand within industries?

    Ans.

       i.   YES/NO ☐
      ii.   If any other option, please specify: _____

Annexure 3
Tabulation of Answers to Questionnaire

GENERAL

Q.1 Likelihood of rise in share of gas to 10% or more by 2030 ranked on a score of 1–10 where 10 is most likely.

(A)

Score	Number of Respondents
1–3	3
4–6	7
7–9	11
10 (Most likely)	4

Q.2 Sectorial drivers of gas demand in the next decade on a score of 1–4 where 1 is the biggest driver of demand.

Sectors	Responses Rank-Wise			
	1 (Biggest Driver)	2	3	4
Fertilizers	6	3	6	10
Power	3	3	5	15
CGD	10	12	4	-
Industries	7	8	12	-

Q.3 Will price of gas be an obstacle to its growth?

Options	Number of Responses
Yes	23
No	2

Q.4 Does the large share of coal enhance India's energy security?

Options	Number of Responses
Yes	16
No	5

Q.5 Reasons behind low diversity of energy system in India (on a scale of 1–4 where 1 is the most important reason).

Reason	Responses Rank-Wise			
	1 (Most Important Reason)	2	3	4
Govt. policy	7	7	4	4
Lack of energy markets	6	1	6	9
Poor resource endowment	6	7	3	6
High prices of competing fuels	3	9	7	3

Q.6 Will diversifying India's energy sources enhance energy security?

Options	Number of Responses
Yes	19
No	1
Do not know	1

Q.7 Outlook on growth in domestic gas production up to 2,030 (Ranked on a scale of 1–10, with 10 being highly optimistic).

Score	Number of Respondents
1–3	6
4–6	10
7–9	5
10 (Highly optimistic)	3

Q.8 Will the new upstream domestic gas pricing policy promote a vibrant gas market?

Options	Number of Responses
Yes	18
No	-
Not sure	3

Q.9 Is there a strong case for gas on environmental grounds?

Options	Number of Responses
Yes	25
No	-

Q.10 Will the shift to EV impact natural gas demand (for CNG)?

Options	No. of Responses	Main Reason
Yes	11	a. EV will rise only after 2025. Until then CNG will dominate.
		b. India might save $50 billion by moving to EV away from liquid fuels.
		c. CNG is in urban areas, and EV will first enter cities only.
No	13	a. Lock-in of existing fuel distribution infra will obstruct EV, and lack of charging infra for EV
		b. There is adequate space for both to grow.
		c. Both CNG and EV are small incomparison to liquid fuels.

Q.11 Would market pricing in energy sector give impetus to gas?

Options	Number of Responses
Yes	12
No	5
Not sure	5

UREA SECTOR

Q.12 Is the recent decision to promote domestic manufacture of urea a policy-led decision for self-sufficiency?

Options	Number of Responses
Yes	18
No	-

Any other:
a. To safeguard from high prices of imported urea.
b. Motivated by self-sufficiency and independent of volatility in international markets.
c. India being a major urea importer, it could move international markets.

Q.13 Will present policy of RLNG-based urea manufacture (revamp of old units) lead to cheaper urea than imported urea?

Options	Number of Responses	Reasons
Yes	6	a. Due to policy of pooling domestic gas with LNG
		b. Pricing will be similar unless imported urea receives equity gas
No	8	a. Imported urea is much cheaper than urea manufactured from RLNG
		b. Depends on prices of importedurea and RLNG

Q.14 Reasons behind poor private sector interest in urea manufacture. Rank
     1–4 where 1 is the most important reason.

Option	Responses Rank-Wise			
	1 (Most Important Reason)	2	3	4
Lack of gas	9	3	4	2
Poor financial viability	1	9	7	1
Policy uncertainty	6	4	1	5
Any other	1	1	1	4

Main reasons in 'any other':
a.
b.
c.

Q.15 Rate at which urea demand might grow in future.

Option	Number of Responses
Historical rate	6
May moderate	13
Slow down radically	-

Q.16 Will gas remain the main feedstock for urea manufacture?

Options	Number of Responses
Yes	20
No	-

POWER SECTION

Q.17 What might be the role of gas in power sector?

Option	Number of Responses
Major Role	-
Moderate role	10
Negligible role	14

Q.18 If the answer above is **'negligible role'**, then ranking of the reasons on a scale of 1–4 where 1 is the most important reason.

Option	Responses Rank-Wise			
	1 (Most Important Reason)	2	3	4
High Price	14	3	-	3
Non-availability	2	4	2	10
High growth of RE	1	4	11	3
Large thermal capacity	3	8	5	2

Q.19 Will the new thermal norms mitigate the negativity against coal?

Options	Number of Responses
Yes	3
No	7
Moderately	12

Q.20 If domestic gas were to become abundantly available, would gas-based power capacity rise?

Options	Number of Responses
Yes	13
No	9

Q.21 If answer is YES to previous question, then the possible reasons for same ranked 1–4 in order of priority where 1 is the most important reason.

Option	Responses Rank-Wise			
	1 (Most Important Reason)	2	3	4
It becomes price competitive	8	3	1	1
For augmenting supply	2	2	6	5
To balance variable RE	2	6	2	4
As it is environmentally clean	2	3	5	4

Q.22 Are pricing reforms in power sector anticipated by 2030 allowing gas-based power to receive higher price? Rank your expectation on a scale of 1–10. With 10 being most likely.

Score	Number of Responses
1–3	4
4–6	9
7–9	8
10 (Most likely)	-

Q.23 With large unutilised capacity of thermal power and growing RE, might gas get overlooked and India move to non-gas-based power system by 2030?

Options	Number of Responses
Yes	6
No	15

Any other:

a.

b.

c.

CGD

Q.24 Will the large number of contracts signed under IXth (& Xth) CGD bidding round translate into reality on ground in the next one decade? Please rank the likelihood on a score of 1–10 where 1 is highly improbable and 10 is highly probable.

Score	Number of Responses
1–3	3
4–6	11
6–9	7
10 (Highly probable)	1

Q.25 If domestic gas is not available at administered price (APM), given that presently APM gas is going for PNG/CNG, then will the CGD agenda be impacted?

Options	Number of Responses	Main Reasons
Yes	12	
No	6	

Q.26 Do you see a role for RLNG in non PNG/CNG demand sectors within CGD?

Options	Number of Responses	Main Reasons
Yes	21	
No	2	

Q.27 Will demand for RLNG in the above sectors be dependent on the government policy on curbing polluting fuels/air emissions?

Options	Number of Responses
Yes	17
No	6

Q.28 Is the availability of trunk gas pipelines by 2027 (target year for IXth CGD bidding rounds) to provide gas to new CGD networks an area of concern?

Options	Number of Responses
Yes	17
No	6

Q.29 Will the large number of household LPG connections (especially in urban areas) delay adoption of PNG for cooking?

Options	Number of Responses
Yes	8
No	12
Any other reason	
a.	
b.	
c.	

INDUSTRIES AND OTHERS

Q.30 Is adoption of gas in industries merely a function of price?

Options	Number of Responses
Yes	10
No	12

Q.31 If the answer is **NO** in the previous question, then what are the other possible reasons? Rank 1–3 in order of priority (3 being the least important).

	1	2	3 (Least Important)
Technology	3	2	2
Capital investment	1	4	3
Poor outlook on gas market	4	1	2

Q.32 Which fuel(s) are most likely to be replaced by gas in industries? Rank 1–3 in order of importance (3 being least important).

	1	2	3 (Least Important)
Coal	5	11	4
Liquid Fuels	13	7	1
Any other:	2	3	14
a. Solar			
b. Pet coke			
c. FO			
d. Bagasse, wood and industrial waste			

Q.33 Will natural gas emerge as the preferred fuel in refineries?

Options	Number of Responses
Yes	19
No	-

Q.34 Will industries be the biggest client of RLNG as compared to other sectors?

Options	Number of Responses
Yes	22
No	1

Q.35 Is petrochemical likely to be a major driver of gas demand within industries?

Options	Number of Responses
Yes	14
No	4
Any other option	a. Fertiliser and CGD
	b. Limited potential for petrochemicals
	c. Not sure

CAVEATS

1. The questions were arranged in the above order with a General section to start with and other questions categorised by consuming sectors.
2. The respondents were encouraged to leave those sections where they did not have information.
3. Many respondents did not fill replies comprehensively to all the boxes within questions. Resultantly even within replies, the numbers often do not add up as per internal scheme.

Index

Printed in the United States
by Baker & Taylor Publisher Services